Reflections of Prague

Reflections
of Prague

Journeys through the 20th century

Ivan Margolius

WILEY

Published in 2006 by   John Wiley & Sons, Ltd, The Atrium, Southern Gate
    Chichester, West Sussex, PO19 8SQ, England
    Phone   (+44) 1243 779777

Copyright © 2006   Ivan Margolius

Email (for orders and customer service enquires): cs-books@wiley.co.uk
Visit our Home Page on www.wiley.co.uk or www.wiley.com

Other Wiley Editorial Offices

John Wiley & Sons, Inc. 111 River Street, Hoboken, NJ 07030, USA

Jossey-Bass, 989 Market Street, San Francisco, CA 94103-1741, USA

Wiley-VCH Verlag GmbH, Pappellaee 3, D-69469 Weinheim, Germany

John Wiley & Sons Australia, Ltd, 33 Park Road, Milton, Queensland, 4064, Australia

John Wiley & Sons (Asia) Pte Ltd, 2 Clementi Loop #02-01, Jin Xing Distripark,
Singapore 129809

John Wiley & Sons Canada Ltd, 22 Worcester Road, Etobicoke, Ontario, Canada, M9W 1L1

Wiley also publishes its books in a variety of electronic formats. Some content that appears
in print may not be available in electronic books.

A catalogue record for this book is available from the British Library

ISBN-13   978-0-470-02219-1 (HB)
ISBN-10   0-470-02219-1 (HB)

Typeset in 10/13pt Photina by MCS Publishing Services Ltd, Salisbury, Wiltshire.
Printed and bound in Great Britain by T.J. International, Padstow, Cornwall.
This book is printed on acid-free paper responsibly manufactured from sustainable forestry
in which at least two trees are planted for each one used for paper production.
10 9 8 7 6 5 4 3 2 1

In memory of
JUDr Rudolf Margolius ●

●

– Vinen jsem za vůni, která voní,
za marnou touhu po otci,
za verše, ano, vím, za lásku, již jsem ztratil,
za stud a za ticho a za zem plnou běd,
za nebe, za Boha, jenž dny mé přísně zkrátil
v mrtví ráj na pohled –

– I am guilty: of redolent scent I felt
of the vain longing for my dad
of verses, yes, I know for love I lost
of shame and silence and world full of woes
of the heaven, of the Lord who severely shortened my days
in paradise of seemingly dead ways –

Jiří Orten (Ohrenstein), *Poslední báseň/Last Poem*, 1941

Contents

●
●

CONTENTS

Acknowledgements •
•

Many grateful thanks for helping with the preparation of this book go to the following: Mandy Bates, Heda Margolius Kovály, Pavel Kovály, Jan Hanuš, Jan Kaplický, Helen Castle, Sally M. Smith, George Waldes, Jan Lukas, Pavel Tigrid, Diana Earle, Eva Ballová, Monika Pavláková, Věra Brťková, Igor Lukeš, Julius Müller, Paul Edwards, Pavel Kohn, Pavel Škeřík, Eva Hayman, Vera Gissing, Jan Kaplan, Radovan Schovánek, František Svátek, Jiří Gruntorád, Jiří Pollák, Sheila Bates, Jan Tulis, Peter Brezina, Otto Klička, Roger Hunt and all at MCS, Kate Santon, and all at Wiley.

Journey with my Lost Father

> We wave a handkerchief
> on parting,
> every day something is ending,
> something beautiful is ending.

Jaroslav Seifert, *Píseň / A Song*, 1929, translated by Ewald Osers

On returning to Prague I imagined I had seen my father. His slim figure, elegantly dressed in a dark single-breasted suit, white shirt and blue tie, appeared in the distance. He paused at Knihy bookshop in Na Příkopě Street to look inside and check his reflection in the shop window. His hair was swept back, the receding hairline exposing his high forehead. Rimless spectacles framed his grey eyes, glinting in the bright morning light. The permanent smile on his lips, which I so loved, was still there. He checked the time on his Omega watch, lit a cigarette and walked on. Pushing through the crowd, I hurried to catch him but he disappeared into the darkness of Prague's many passageways that criss-cross the inner city. I delved into the labyrinth of shadows to search for him.

At the far opening of one of the long tunnel-like arcades, I spotted our car parked at the kerb. Behind the wheel sat *táta*, my father Rudolf. Terrified I would not reach him before he drove away I started to run. I had to get there before it was too late. I ran desperately, my heart pounding, my long steps getting steadily shorter as I continued, my struggle becoming harder the further I went. I shouted as I ran, my adult voice turning into a child's shriek: 'Wait for me, wait for meee.'

There was no need to worry. Rudolf waited patiently, finishing his cigarette. He appeared gloomy and preoccupied, but as soon as he saw me, he cheered up. '*Ahoj, Ivane!* Where is your Mum?'

he asked through the open window and, after I finally opened the passenger door using the handle I could hardly reach and climbed into the car seat next to him, Rudolf added, remembering: 'Oh yes, she said she'd follow us on a train, we'll have to pick her up from Beroun; she has to finish a dust jacket design for publication.'

Enormously relieved that I had found him I sat there, admiringly looking up to him. I was out of breath, unable to speak.

I was nearly five years old.

His jacket was draped over a battered violin case on the rear seat; the brightly enamelled Communist Party badge decorated the peak of the jacket's lapel. He was reading densely typed documents pulled out from his packed leather briefcase and propped up on the steering wheel, making notes in the margins with a gold fountain pen.

When I was older I learned that the papers must have been from the Ministry of Foreign Trade. Two years earlier, in 1949, he had been promoted to Deputy Minister and since then I had seen him only occasionally. He had to travel abroad, attend trade negotiations, Ministry and Party meetings, consult with other departments and write extensive analytical reports and economic statistics long into the night. Rudolf was putting all his knowledge and skill into trying to improve the difficult problem of the country's ailing centralized economy. His time at home was limited to precious moments, which had to be savoured and appreciated. Even there I saw him sitting in his armchair or at his writing desk constantly leafing through books and documents; regretfully, he did not seem to have that much time to play with me.

I recalled how Heda, my mother, and he had argued the night before. They thought that I was asleep, but fragments of their sentences, whose meaning I hardly understood but found fascinating, penetrated the apartment walls into my bedroom.

'Rudlo, you have to leave your job immediately ... I've talked to lots of our old friends and they all say you have to go, whatever happens ... Your position, high up in the Ministry, puts you next in line as the scapegoat when things go wrong,' she pleaded, sounding very worried. 'Haven't our families suffered enough during the war? It's a miracle that we both survived ... And now this. I can't face any more difficulties ...' They must have been sitting in the living room on the red L-shaped sofa, facing each other. Rudolf got up and started pacing the floor. I heard the parquet blocks squeaking under his steps. Often, seeing other children being looked after by elderly family members, I wondered where my other relatives and grandparents were. Heda explained gently that they had all died during the war but never went into any details.

'Kitten, the Party needs me ... You know I tried to resign once but they ordered me to carry on.' Apparently there could not be any respite, the five year plan had to be fulfilled and the Soviets were putting the Czechs under constant pressure. There was no one else there to take his place.

'But, Rudlo, you've heard about the arrests, the disappearances, all the people at the top are vulnerable ... When did you see your friends Eda, Artur and Evžen last? Where have they gone suddenly? Don't you know they've been arrested? Haven't you noticed most of the ones who are disappearing are Jews?'

'That's preposterous, Heda, you worry too much. The Party would not sink to the same level as the Nazis. There must be a totally rational explanation for this ... I haven't gone through the camps for nothing ... To give up on what honestly I believe is right ... If all the decent people leave now, things will get even worse.'

'Micula Bradová, your cousin, phoned this morning.'

'What about? How's she? We should go and see them, I suppose,' said Rudolf, and I heard him stop and strike a match to light his and Heda's cigarettes.

'It's too late,' said Heda. I heard her blow out smoke.

'Why? Kitten, what's happened?' Rudolf was shocked.

Heda carried on, saying that there had been a party in the town of Ústí nad Labem to celebrate the anniversary of the construction company where Micula's husband Rudolf Brada was a director, and that Micula was as worried about Brada's steep rise in the Party ranks as she was about Rudolf. Micula had decided that it was the right moment to end it, and blurted out loudly in front of everyone how the Party had replaced all the important people in Ústí with incompetent ones and now nothing worked and there was a lot of corruption. On account of her 'little' public complaint Brada had been dismissed; it looked as if he was out of danger. 'I should do the same with you,' added Heda. 'Rudlo, please think of your family and Ivan. It's not just us; we're responsible for him and his secure future now. What if they arrest you?'

Rudolf started pacing again. He was silent for some time. Then he begged Heda to believe him, he thought of both of us all the time, all he did was done for our better life. What reason could they have to arrest him? It could not happen to him, only those who made mistakes could possibly be in danger. His affairs were completely watertight. Comrades at the top including Gregor, his superior, knew that he was doing his best, they endorsed and supported him, he got every decision he made approved from above. He worked day and night, what he did was for the good of us, the country and the Party. He reminded Heda of how President Klement Gottwald thanked him when he had returned from London.

The living room went quiet. Rudolf sat down. I assumed that Heda went over, put her arm round his shoulders and had drawn him to her as I heard her tender offer in reconciliation: 'Look Rudlo, let's go to Lišno – or better still to Nouzov and Doctor Škeřík's as there it'll be more private – for a few days before you go away again, and talk this over more ...' I lost concentration then, and fell asleep.

Rudolf gathered his papers, put them in the briefcase and left it on the back seat. Our car was a beige Škoda Tudor 1101 saloon convertible, with a streamlined body and chrome 'smiling' radiator grille, the first post war production design. We called the car 'Ferda' after the ant, Ferda Brabenec – a heroic character in the Czech children's stories by Ondřej Sekora that I enjoyed leafing through at home. Ferda had folding tubular steel front seats which could be converted into comfortable couchettes when the backs were dropped. Rudolf, with my help, kept the car polished whenever he had a spare moment. He had bought Ferda second-hand three years ago. Not many people owned cars in the early 1950s and Rudolf sat in 'him' proudly. I always enjoyed being with Rudolf, sharing in his pleasures.

'All right, settle down and we'll be off to Nouzov. We'll take the slow route through the countryside. It'll be more fun. Let me roll down the roof and then it will be perfect.'

Rudolf got out to open the roof. This was
appreciate a sunny spring day. We were parked in
Staré Město – the Old Town, where dark classical
on all sides colourfully dressed in both red and red-blue-white flags,
and yellow hammer and sickle signs. The larger than life and rather
intimidating portraits of Gottwald and the Greatest Leader Josef
Vissarionovich Stalin, their names having been made clear to me,
cast their watchful eyes on the bustling square below. Similar
scenery was encountered in the rest of the town. Long red fabric
banners stretched the full height of buildings framing Socialist
slogans and pictures of the Communist heroes Marx, Engels and
Lenin. Even shop windows had their goods shrouded in scarlet
drapery and images of our beloved President. The May Day and
Liberation Day celebrations were imminent. Then the proletarian
masses, whose attendance was compulsory, demonstrated peacefully
through the streets carrying placards, waving flags and singing songs
and praises to our Party leaders. Along the Letná Plain the Party
organized the Czechoslovak Army parade, which I liked watching,
displaying shiny Russian tanks that rolled noisily along the streets
leaving clouds of exhaust fumes behind. The tanks were followed
by trucks towing large cannons and anti-aircraft guns, some with
sharp-pointed Katyusha rocket launchers bunched up on the rear
platforms, and the helmeted, khaki-dressed military units marching
with rifles and machine guns drawn in readiness. 'They are here to
remind us of the Red Army's victory over Nazism and who's in
charge,' Heda had whispered to herself while holding my hand
when we stood on the pavement the previous year.

Presently Rudolf returned into the car and we set off. In
my teens Heda described to me how Rudolf loved to travel; it was
always an adventure for him, a man and his machine in affinity
with nature. In July 1931, as an eighteen-year-old, he and some
friends had bought a 1926 Dodge – an old-fashioned car with a
cubic body and spoke wheels – in Cleveland after they had attended
a YMCA conference there. They had explored the east coast of the
United States, taking turns driving, stopping at all the interesting
sites and spending nights in hostels and hotels. The car served them
well and they sold her at a small profit before returning to Europe.

Gottwald and Stalin (Kaplan Productions Archive)

The boys did not report their experiences to their parents; Rudolf's strict mother, Berta, who doted on her only child, was very protective and would have forbidden him this escape into the American wilderness had she known of it. When Rudolf's father, Vítězslav, learned details of their trip he kept boasting about his son's successful exploits to his drinking companions in Prague cafés.

At the next traffic lights Rudolf pulled a cushion from the back for me to sit on to improve my view. The open car gave our journey another dimension, with extra sounds, scents and light. The wheels whispered on the cobblestones, which we called 'cat's heads'. They covered almost all of Prague's streets; even the pavements were carpeted by smaller granite setts laid out in geometric patterns. We came to Na Františku, the Vltava quayside, and I pointed at the large steamboat, also decorated by red banners, battling against the flow of the river. At the Charles Bridge, we drove under the Old Town

Bridge Tower and I tipped my head back to inspect the stonework. Mysterious dark groups of statues guarded the river crossing and sped us on our way. Many had figures expressing threatening gestures, their extended hands pointing fingers at us as we passed. Rudolf slowed down and translated the strange Hebrew lettering of the unusual gilded sign over the statue of Jesus that we passed: 'Holy, Holy, Holy is the Lord of Hosts'. To reach the left bank we passed through the arch between the western bridge towers. We continued through Malá Strana – the Lesser Town quarter crowded with fairy-tale medieval houses with clay-tiled roofs, hugging the steep inclines leading up to the President's extensive Hradčany Castle, looming darkly over this part of Prague from the hillside. To my young imagination this majestic gathering of buildings looked like the unapproachable den of a sorcerer who spread a callous web from it to capture his unwary prey.

I noticed Rudolf's abrupt visible discomfort while checking the rear view mirror. 'What's the matter, táto – dad?' I worried, not knowing the reason for his sudden change of mood, only thinking that my sinister view of the Castle – or perhaps my parents' night-time conversation – might have something to do with it.

He did not answer for a while.

'Oh, nothing, I thought I saw someone I know being driven behind us.' He spoke softly. Within seconds a big black car overtook us with three people squeezed on the rear seat; the guys on the outside had heavy leather coats and a crestfallen figure was squeezed in between.

At Náměstí Sovětských tankistů – Soviet Tank Troops Square – where the first Russian tank to liberate Prague was displayed, we waited for the junction to clear as the people's militia brigade with their polished rifles, black boots and red armbands marched by, practising for the big day. I glimpsed *Rudé právo*, the Communist daily newspaper, and its prominent headlines. The whole paper, each page, was pinned up in glass display cases, usually with readers gathered round.

'What's that about, táto?' I asked.

Rudolf, distracted and deep in thought, reluctantly read to me while we were waiting: 'A united agricultural co-operative achieves 100 per cent in its milk production target. Another blow to our capitalist enemies. Long live the Communist Party of Czechoslovakia. Long live the Party General Secretary Rudolf Slánský.' Apparently there were shortages in all sectors including food supply. Our economy, despite optimistic proclamations, had not yet recovered from post-war gloom and the Communist Coup in 1948 so the papers accentuated any positive news.

People in the queue outside the state-owned Pramen grocery store watched the procession without interest, patiently waiting their turn to scour the half-empty shelves for the basic ingredients of the Czech diet, vepřo-knedlo-zelo – pork, dumplings and sauerkraut – usually washed down with strong Prazdroj or Pilsner Urquell lager. They were like orderly busy bees waiting to taste the magic pot of honey, which was just out of their reach. They looked scared. Their faces were tired, sour and pessimistic. Many, even women, wore boiler suits smelling of industrial oil. Others were dressed in formless blouses or checked shirts, dowdy long skirts or baggy trousers and drab coats. Most women had no make-up and wore old-fashioned flowery headscarves while men covered their heads with patterned wool hats, so different from Heda and Rudolf's endeavours to look elegant and smart. People did not complain, gossip or protest. They did not trust their neighbours or friends; anyone could denounce them for making the slightest negative remark against the regime. Despite Communist propaganda and empty slogans like

WORKERS OF THE WORLD UNITE,
TOGETHER WITH THE SOVIET UNION FOR THE WORLD'S PERMANENT PEACE,
WE ALL DECIDE ABOUT OUR BETTER LIFE,
TOGETHER WITH THE SOVIET UNION WE WILL BE HERE FOR EVER,

everyone looked after their own family and kept their private thoughts to themselves. They might have been Party members and attended Party meetings but that was only done to increase their standing and prospects in society and at work, and help their children to gain university places, not for their belief in the Red

Revolution. The main aim was to have a proven proletarian background going back generations in their Party personnel 'cadre' file. To make sure order was kept, leather-coated men loitered on nearby street corners pretending to be invisible.

We breezed through the Smíchov suburb, heading south-west, the rushing air ruffling our hair. The Škoda's Red Indian emblem on the bonnet pointed to the relaxed mood of the countryside, providing a welcoming release from the uneasy, tense and stifling atmosphere hanging over the city despite the bright day. Rudolf looked more comfortable, some colour returned to his cheeks and I glanced round to check the road behind. Our Škoda was the only car there.

'Looking forward to Nouzov?' Rudolf asked.

'Yeah, it'll be great!' I replied, and tried to picture the settlement of the modern 1930s summer houses lost among the rolling hills on the edge of the vast Křivoklát forest and the exciting adventures our trip would undoubtedly bring.

The last villas of Prague disappeared behind us.

On the open road nothing much happened. I was bored and demanded 'Do your magic, táto!' Rudolf fumbled in his pocket, trying to find a suitable coin. He knew only two tricks: one with a coin, which he skilfully fished out of my ear, and another with a hat, pulling a handkerchief from its obvious emptiness. I did not know who taught him, perhaps his father did and it went back generations. I always laughed a lot, enjoying the performance, and asked to see the tricks at the most inconvenient time – while Rudolf drove the car. Much later, I regretted that he had no chance to teach me so I could pass this particular skill on to my boys.

Beyond the town of Černošice toward Doutnáč Hill, we penetrated the dense mysterious forests of tall pine trees, dotted with sunny clearings and wild meadows with raspberry canes and blankets of strawberry and bilberry plants mixing with the moss. There was hardly any traffic. Rudolf suggested we had a break and steered into a lay-by which had a clearing above it. We climbed up to it and settled on the moss. He stretched out on the ground, lying back with his arms folded under his head, not bothering about dirtying his shirt or trousers, and whistled a tune. He watched the white clouds chasing each other in the sky. I copied him, wondering which cloud he was looking at, possibly the fluffy one shaped like a white elephant or the one like a spaceship. I tried to nibble some strawberries but they were not ripe.

'I've an idea,' Rudolf said suddenly and he went back to the car and brought out the battered violin case. He remained standing, took his tie off, got the violin out and begun tuning it. 'We'll have a little concert.'

I remained lying down while he started the beautiful melody of the *Romance* by Antonín Dvořák. Rudolf became absorbed, recalling the notes in his mind, half-closing his eyes, as the haunting, typically Czech tones of the violin floated through the Bohemian wood. There was silence from the birds and insects as the violin strings reverberated through the trees, their branches full of needles humming in the wind, providing the accompaniment for the missing orchestra. The surrounding dense boughs formed an acoustic canopy, preventing the sound escaping and reinforcing the enchanted setting.

Ivan and Rudolf, 1951

Below us, a dark group of cyclists stopped, mesmerised. They stood like mysterious salt statues with their bikes between their knees, listening. Dvořák was Rudolf's favourite composer; he knew his major compositions by heart, and especially loved the Cello and Violin Concertos and the *Romance*. Rudolf finished the slow melody line to loud applause and 'bravo, bravo' exploded from below. I joined in and Rudolf was startled, he had been too involved to notice his audience. He bowed towards the cyclists to thank them. He was not exactly Josef Suk, the violin virtuoso, but he was competent and the location made all the difference. I so wished to be able to play like that when I grew up.

After a while we went back to the car. Rudolf started the engine and switched the radio on. From the speaker on the dashboard came the violin melody of Dvořák's *Romance*. Rudolf looked at me in amazement. Sweet moments like this lodge in the mind forever. I could trace my love of music to that point in time; it must have been then when I recognized how much music contributed to the experience of life. Music broke all the barriers between people, even in those difficult times.

We drove out of the woods and onto a field road with a still-young wheat crop planted either side. The green hairy heads of wheat, splattered with stains of early red poppies, formed rhythmic waves along the field surface here and there. The road dipped and bent in between the waves and, at times, its visibility was lost.

Antonín Dvořák, *Romance*

11

A brown hare with long ears and a hairy tail darted off among the stalks, disturbed by the noise of the car. Nonchalantly Rudolf leaned over, opened the glove compartment and pulled out a leather holster. He was busy driving and dropped it in my lap. 'Open it for me but don't touch the trigger,' he instructed.

Astonished, I undid the retaining strap and saw a small gleaming semi-automatic pistol. Gingerly I pulled it out, fascinated, with no time to experience fear. This was fantastic, real cops and robbers! It was so heavy, cold and powerful, blue metallic in colour. Rudolf extended his hand while looking at the road and I passed the pistol to him handgrip first, the barrel pointing away from us like a gunslinger passing a weapon to his comrade-in-arms during a battle for life and death. We drove after the hare, which had foolishly followed the edge of the road. Rudolf put his foot down, then, drawing level, aimed and fired the pistol from the open side window: baaannnggg. His hand jerked back, his other hand steadily steering. The smell of spent gunpowder invaded the car and evaporated through the rolled-down roof and windows. The hare carried on as if nothing had happened, disappearing into the heart of the field. Rudolf shrugged, but kept toying with the gun, throwing it up and catching it, frowning, testing its weight in his hand.

Then as if he had second thoughts, he gave the weapon to me trustingly: 'Put it back, please, big boy, and don't forget I love you with all my heart,' and smiled at me, patted my hair playfully and carried on driving toward our destination.

I mumbled in reply 'I love you too, táto,' but I don't think he heard me over the roaring car engine.

With these amusements, Rudolf came to the top of my limited view of the world. On one hand, an intelligent man, impeccably behaved, conducting important state affairs; and the next minute driving a car while performing magic tricks, followed by the beautiful violin and then the gun! I was proud of my father; I admired his ability to have that many special skills. However, our bonding was never completed and the pistol, officially issued to all high-ranking Party members and ministers at that time, could not provide protection against the fate awaiting Rudolf, Heda or me.

We stopped at the Beroun railway station to watch a few steam trains passing through until mother arrived. Heda emerged from her carriage rather pleased with herself. I was always in awe every time I saw her, especially outside the family circle. Her small thin figure, her round face with a strong firm jawbone and made-up red lips, her auburn hair and large lively green eyes radiated her ever-present overabundant energy and beauty. Wherever she was she exuded an aura of charm and sophistication. Her determined resolve, emphasized by her intelligence and insight as well as her great looks, has always drawn circles of male admirers and Rudolf was thrilled to have her by his side. My mother questioned and probed everything, never accepting any given situation. Her 'life's motto' in difficult times, while shaking her clenched fist, was '*My se nedáme!*' – we won't give in. That is why she was such a great survivor.

Heda also had a story to tell. At one of the stops before Beroun, at Karlštejn, with its magnificent castle where the train track meanders along the Berounka river valley, the female train guard had stayed on the platform without leaving the train door open for herself. Having waved the train off she jumped on the step and tried to open the door. It must have stuck and she was left hanging on the handle outside while the train, puffing smoke and soot, gathered speed. She yelled for someone to pull the emergency brake lever. Heda was sitting in third class on the standard varnished slated seat, each slat fixed with shiny brass screws all lined up, watching this drama unfold. She leaped up and pulled the red handle. She told us as we drove to Nouzov that this had been her dream since childhood – to pull a train's emergency brake – and today her dream had been fulfilled.

At Nouzov, we stayed with a good friend of ours, Dr Rudolf Škeřík who had a teenage son, Pavel, and a friendly fox terrier called Ťapka – Paws. Škeřík had owned the well-known Symposium publishing house since before the war and was an avid art collector. My mother designed dust jackets and bindings for him until 1948 when he was forced to close it down, as private business was not encouraged by the Communists. Their summer villa with large windows, French doors and a pitched, overhanging roof was built on a sunny slope with the dark forest behind; it was set apart from the rest of the settlement's houses. The veranda on the south side, the most popular area of the house, created a pleasant transition between the outside and inside and was the most convenient place to spend the day sitting on rattan armchairs and easy sofas. The villa's privacy was its best attraction, a place that provided a peaceful sanctuary in contrast to the tense and oppressive Prague.

Pavel loved Heda and tried to display his youthful infatuation as often as possible. Both Heda and Rudolf tolerated this adolescent behaviour with amusement. The previous summer Pavel had raced off with his village friends to the municipal pond. In a while they were back, laughing like lunatics. Pavel, barefoot and in his wet swimming trunks, brought an armful of white and pink water lilies still dripping with water and deposited them decoratively at Heda's feet where she sat reading on the veranda while Rudolf, in his customary suit next to her, was absorbed in his paperwork. Pavel's comrades were not far behind, lugging a big white sign with red lettering: 'PICKING OF WATER LILIES IN THIS POND IS STRICTLY PROHIBITED. BY THE ORDER OF THE VILLAGE COMMUNE COUNCIL.'

Later Pavel, who had a red Jawa 250 motorcycle, took me on rides round the village sitting on the tank. To give me another surprise he opened the garage to reveal a grey car with a futuristic, streamlined, teardrop body and a fish-like fin on the rear bonnet. 'What's that?' I exclaimed in admiration.

'That's a Tatraplan we just bought second hand from the Cement Works National Enterprise Company in Beroun. Do you want a ride?'

Without waiting for my answer, Pavel climbed in and sat me next to him. In this car we cut the air smoothly on the forest roads and the typical roar of the rear air-cooled two-litre engine dissipated behind us. I was in pure heaven and, without recognizing it, was becoming acquainted with a car that ran like a string of beads connecting the events of my life.

During the long lunches which stretched into the afternoons the adults had heated political discussions. Dr Škeřík was an experienced, sensible and tall man, and his gesticulating hands underlined everything he said. Rudolf, lawyer-like, listened carefully while smoking his pipe and then calmly put forward an opposing argument in defence of his own view. It was his duty to help his country, he insisted, and not run away when problems arose. Anxious, Heda pleaded with Škeřík to help her. He took her side and tried to change Rudolf's mind. Their opinions were too complex for me to understand or remember. I lost interest and joined the local children, Pavel and Ťapka, to walk in the woods and cycle on the roads. We rowed and paddled on the pond, flew a large kite with a dragon face and roasted sausages on the campfire – I enjoyed the spring, beauty and freedom of the countryside rather than worrying about my parents or my toys in our Prague apartment to which we would soon have to return.

Toward the evening we heard snippets of Dvořák's Violin Concerto from a distance; Dr Škeřík must have persuaded Rudolf to play a movement or two.

2　　　　　　Lonely Times

Crush the loneliness in delight, the darkness in a hailstorm
　of splendour
the ones who have fallen rise in their dreams
And I float like a ship on the horizon of time.

Hanuš Bonn, *Beethoven*

The Nouzov outing was the last time I saw Rudolf for anything but a
short period. Thereafter, there were only fleeting moments remaining
before he disappeared from my life; the protective bubble that I once
envisaged enveloping our closely-knit family burst and vanished into
thin air. My small world fell apart and has remained scattered in
pieces to this day.

One day Rudolf was with us, the next he went to the
Ministry never to return. Where had he gone so suddenly without a
word of goodbye or farewell? For a five-year-old, it was difficult to
comprehend.

Many times I asked Heda where Rudolf was but she
persisted in mentioning evasively that he had to leave to work
abroad rather unexpectedly. From then on Heda became constantly
preoccupied with worry and lost her usual sparkle, smile and self-
assurance. She tried with desperation to hold on to her job as a
graphic designer at the Communist Rovnost publishing house. Her
mind was always elsewhere. She did not care about the state of her
clothes, about her hair or her appearance, which was totally out of
character. Usually Rudolf waited for her when they went out; she
took her time to get ready and do her make-up in order to look her
best and Rudolf had to hurry her on impatiently: 'Why do you
bother? I'd love you even if you were covered in moss and lichen!'

Now most of the time she looked helpless and observed
me with questioning eyes, which signified her grave concern about
the future. Suddenly we had less money to live on and our 'Ferda'

disappeared. I could not quite understand the changed circumstances and was overcome for a time with how lonely our existence had become. Without Rudolf around, even though his presence was normally only felt late in the evenings and at night, our spacious third-floor apartment in Veverkova Street in the Letná quarter of Prague seemed empty, quiet and gloomy. Marie Bednářová, my full-time nanny, once needed to look after me while both my parents were at work, could not be paid any longer but Heda persuaded her to stay on and, when needed, occasionally watch over me after she returned from her new employment in the bakery. I noticed that our previous friends, acquaintances, Rudolf's colleagues and neighbours avoided us like the plague and the frequent comings and goings ceased. Only Mrs Musilová, an old family friend, came to look after me or help Heda with the daily chores. The other regular visitor was a distant relation, Karel Poláček, a former farmer from Libušín and a survivor of Auschwitz who took me on Sunday strolls to see dogs being trained in the nearby exercise grounds. I used to love to watch them obeying complicated orders and admired their intelligence.

Previously I had raced madly round the apartment in a tubular steel pedal car I used to have, going at an incredible speed especially down the long entrance hall and scattering my toys in the process. Late at night, when he got home, Rudolf would complain while tripping over the mess I made. Now I even missed those moans. I had a large red velvet teddy bear, bigger than me, which had a squeaky device in his tummy. I wondered what it was that made the strange sound when the bear was tilted. One Sunday afternoon, Heda and Rudolf went out and Marie rested in her room, supposedly looking after me. I hid in my parents' bedroom and performed an operation with a pair of scissors. By the time they came back the room was littered with the straw that had been used to stuff the unfortunate creature. The squeaky cylinder, now cut open, had been made useless by my surgical intervention. Innocently I returned to my room leaving all the debris behind. When my parents discovered the 'operating theatre' Rudolf grumbled loudly about the young rascal living with them, calling me to clear up the stuffing. Heda pacified him – and me – by promising to stitch the bear back together. He never squeaked again.

With Rudolf gone I felt sad and miserable. Often I went to his wardrobe, took the violin case out, opened it and looked at the bow, the piece of dark-yellow rosin and the abandoned instrument, now lying idle without a sound coming out. With the enclosed piece of velvet, I kept the violin polished. I lay on Rudolf's side of the bed, closed my eyes, tried to remember our trip to Nouzov and heard Dvořák again.

Heda, lacking Rudolf's income, decided to sublet my bedroom to her cousin Pavel Kohn, who was the only close family member on her side who had lived through the war. Under the Communist regime's rules, there had to be the right number of occupiers per certain living area, otherwise people were forcibly moved to smaller accommodation and Heda wanted to keep the apartment for as long as she could manage. She was obviously hoping that Rudolf would be back with us soon. Initially Heda and Rudolf had been advised of the place by a couple who lived there and left the country in a hurry after the Communist takeover; such recommendation was the best way to find anything. Prague was, and still is, notoriously short of good apartments.

Pavel was a keen aquarist and kept his aquarium, full of fancy gear, on the chest of drawers in the corner. After several weeks, Heda received the electricity bill and was astonished to find that it was treble its normal amount. She could not think why, especially as without Rudolf she went to bed early and worried about him in the darkness rather than having the apartment in a blaze of light. Only the soft illumination coming from the Tesla Largo radio's large glass dial and the mysterious green light of its Cyclops-like tuning eye accompanied the soft late-night classical music from the loudspeaker, by then thankfully devoid of Communist slogans and propaganda. I loved to listen to this radio; my favourite was the weather forecast before every news bulletin – I liked all the foreign countries, which were out of my reach, being mentioned.

Heda barged into Pavel's room and he admitted, greatly embarrassed, that one of his fish had spawned. He'd installed a 500-watt bulb to keep the water at a constant temperature day and night. Luckily for him, by then the spawn had hatched, delivering the little fish, and he was in the process of dismantling it. Heda was furious, shouting at poor Pavel that we could not afford such extravagance, that humans came first.

Halfway through the spring I had fallen ill with a bad ear infection, did not want to eat anything and felt very miserable. Heda had to carry on working and asked Mrs Musilová whom I called *bába* – grandmother – to look after me, acting as a surrogate relative. She sat me at the kitchen table, wrapped my head in warm compresses tied round with a white kerchief and fed me on milky semolina that I hated. When Heda returned in the evening she had to laugh, as apparently I looked like a miserable white rabbit with big floppy ears made out of the corners of the kerchief on top of my head. I cheered up, seeing Heda smiling again after such a long time, and gobbled up further helpings of cold crusty semolina without protest.

Rudolf in Podsedice, 1934

In the summer, accompanied by Heda for a couple of days, I went by train to the western Bohemian village of Podsedice near the town of Litoměřice where my father loved to go. We went to stay with my young lively thirteen- and seven-year-old cousins Eva and Monika, daughters of Micula and Rudolf Brada, who were visiting their grandmother Vilemína. Vilemína, the elder sister of Berta, my grandmother, was a kind, small, grey-haired woman, with a face deeply marked by time. Now she was widowed, having been married to farmer Josef Frieser, mayor of the village. Micula and her brother Franta were very close to Rudolf who, as a child, used to visit when they lived there. Even when Rudolf went to see them as an adult and travelled by the local train, which puffed at a snail's pace, he could not tear himself from the window and urged the train to go faster with every little tree and telegraph pole so that he could be in the paradise of his childhood, in Podsedice. Now I encouraged our train to reach our desired destination quickly in the same way. Our presence with Vilemína emulated Rudolf's youthful visits in a way and boosted Heda's flagging confidence.

The place was famous for its land rich in Czech garnets, which could be found lying in the dust. They were processed, cleaned and cut by the local craftsmen and sent to jewellers all over the world. In the springtime the air of the village was rich with the scent of flowering fruit trees as it is located in the heart of the orchard district. It had the inevitable pond with ducks wading on its muddy shores and a scattering of vernacular houses surrounding it.

I forgot about gloomy Prague, rampaged joyfully through the fields and hills and collected small garnets in empty jam jars with the girls, helped by an old farmhand called Gustav who told us where to find the bigger stones. Gustav had a hunched back and Heda explained that during the war the Nazis had caught him listening to the BBC and broke his back. We watched Heda helping to gather rapeseed on the local agricultural co-operative farm. She was bagging the seed for others to transport to the processing plant. It was a good and healthy diversion for Heda, who tried to forget her troubles for a while.

Back in Prague, under the changed circumstances and with our reduced family size, I had to attend the Veverkova Street

Commune nursery to allow Heda to continue to go to work. However, for me the nursery became intolerable. It was like being thrown into solitary confinement. Our neighbours' children, who were from fairly well-to-do families, as the local apartments were large and therefore expensive to rent, were normally well-dressed and well-behaved and should have been expected to conduct themselves reasonably, but they were told by their parents not to play or have anything to do with me. They whispered in each other's ears and pointed their little fingers or 'thumbed their noses' at me. Frequently they sent a bigger bullyboy to snatch toys from me if they wanted to play with them, or maybe just to spite me. The nursery teachers did not interfere, appeared not to care and quite clearly sided with my opposition. I seemed to be a nuisance to them too.

I was kept in ignorance. I did not know why I was not liked and in the end accepted the situation as something I had to live with. I pottered on my own in the corner of the nursery room while other kids I knew from my apartment block, and with whom I had played freely before, even being invited to their homes, screamed and made mischief and riot on the opposite side of the room. I turned to the wall, took a piece of paper and a few crayons to create my own world of fantasy, free of evil beings, wrath, combats and forbidding landscapes. All my pictures were bright and sunny with colourful flowers, cars, buildings and people. That private outlook kept me cheerful and on my toes.

One mealtime while I was sitting down and eating my portion of tomato soup, a girl walking behind me with a bowl was deliberately pushed and her hot soup landed on my neck and shoulders. They all laughed and thought that seeing me covered in steaming red liquid was very comical. It was not as hot as it might have been but one of the teachers took me to the health centre; she did not say a word to me the whole time, not even wanting to know how I felt or if I was in pain. On my return the kids acted as if nothing had happened. Luckily, a bit of soothing cream eased the scald and I soon forgot all about it.

Even Vláďa, one of my best soul mates, who lived in the same block on the level above and had once asked me to participate in his games almost every day, had avoided me since Rudolf's disappearance. Previously I'd often had lunch with his family. Many a time we were sent together to the 'At the Spa' pub on the corner to get a jug of draught Prazdroj lager for Vláďa's father and sipped it secretly on the way back, walking up the stairs rather than taking a lift to make the journey as long as possible. We went together for walks to the local park on Letná Plain, running on the grass and hiding behind the trees, only stopping now and then to observe the magnificent view of the river, bridges and the city below. Our parents took turns in strolling with us to our favourite sweetshop on Třída Obránců míru – Defenders of Peace Avenue; this was the most glamorous outlet of all the other drab national enterprise shops that displayed uniformly made substandard luxury goods. Here they served delicious cream and chocolate cakes that we could choose from the shop window and then savour inside with a cup of hot cocoa. And now all the past was forgotten. Vláďa stuck his tongue out at me and turned his back.

I closed myself to outside influences and ignored the way I was shunned. By then I did not care one way or the other, I was determined to ride out this crisis on my own. In early November 1952, Heda discovered my lonely predicament and, on account of the happy experience of our summer holiday, decided to send me to Bratislava to spend some time with the Brada family, who had been obliged to move there after Micula's self-engineered manoeuvre to save her husband. I looked forward to an escape from Prague but worried about leaving my mother behind, alone.

Just before I left Heda arranged for a photographer to come to take a picture of me. I dressed in my best outfit, a T-shirt under a home-knitted sweater and patched-up trousers. The man sat me in a high-backed chair holding a small teddy bear; I was embarrassed, not knowing how to respond. Heda, who was looking on sadly, explained that the picture was intended for Rudolf; he wanted to appreciate how I had grown in his absence.

By then I had not seen my father for a very long time, not for eleven months.

The Safety of Bratislava

3

Life is only a chance
Once down, up then
Life flows like a flood
And sea is the end.

Jiří Voskovec and Jan Werich, *Život je jen náhoda/Life is Only a Chance*, 1933

In the early 1950s Bratislava, the capital of Slovakia, the eastern part of Czechoslovakia, was a long way by train from Prague. It entailed a journey of over 250 miles on board an express steam train. There were only two or three departures a day and, despite reserving seats, the carriages became overcrowded. Once all the compartments were full, passengers and their luggage packed into the corridors. By the time the express left the main Prague Railway Station not even a tiny space could be found, but the atmosphere was jolly. Lots of excited chatter and even a few songs were heard coming from the carriages. I watched the passing countryside, already sparsely dusted by snow, with interest, noticing the small villages and towns and children skiing and tobogganing down the barely covered slopes. The telephone and electricity-line poles were running by in staccato rhythm.

I adored the winter, the fresh air, the clean, crisp white blanket of snow; skiing and sledging were my favourite sports and the wintry scene outside reminded me of how the previous year Rudolf had taken me one cold Sunday afternoon to race down the hill at Letná Plain round the corner from our apartment. It was not a very suitable place because there was a concrete retaining wall at the bottom of the slope. I walked up while Rudolf chased me in the snow, lobbing snowballs. At the top, Rudolf aligned the wooden sledge, sat me at the front and pushed us downhill. He braked quite hard with the heels of his boots and we cruised down quite comfortably. 'A bit faster next time, táto!' I encouraged him and ran up the hill ahead while he pulled the sledge. We settled down again; this time Rudolf let go confidently, and we flew. Half way down we went over a bump, Rudolf slid off and the sledge continued with only me at the front.

I had a premonition that something big was going to happen and I would get hurt not just there and then but permanently, that I would be left with an irreplaceable loss. In that fraction of time I had the unmistakeable conviction that I was hurtling unstoppably toward a disaster.

It was a good job I wore a thick woolly hat with a big bobble on the top. By the time the frantic Rudolf reached the bottom I was lying unconscious by the concrete wall. He took me in his arms and, beside himself, carried me home, put me in bed and called the doctor. As I said, it was lucky I had that hat and, after a while, I woke up. To my satisfaction Rudolf was there and to his relief I had only a headache by which to remember the momentous day. 'Táto, I think we went a bit too fast last time. Let's go sledging again,' I demanded as soon as I woke up; at least he smiled before shaking his head.

Perhaps we shall go sledging next year, I thought. I watched the fellow passengers, mainly workers, farmers and members of the Youth Organization of the Communist Party travelling to join voluntary brigades in factories and agricultural cooperatives, unwrapping their parcels, opening their bags, taking out vast quantities of sausages, salami, schnitzels and rye bread, and washing the food down with lager from bottles or with tea or coffee from thermos flasks. Despite the food shortages people seemed to feed themselves plenty.

My aunt Micula had come to fetch me and accompany me on the journey. She was ordinarily a vivacious, strong-willed, decisive woman with shiny dark hair, blue-grey eyes and a cheerful expression but now sat next to me rather absentmindedly, looking dejected. At that time my mother was too ill to travel with me. Heda was exhausted, in pain, nearing a nervous breakdown. For a reason she would not explain she wanted to stay in Prague alone. I supposed she had to go to work and wanted to be there for Rudolf when he came back from abroad.

Soon I had a full stomach, having helped myself to the food and drink prepared for the trip from my rucksack and I needed to test the train toilets located at the end of each carriage, but how to get there in such a crowded train? People were even standing in the compartments. Micula appeared helpless and did not know what to do. I insisted that I had to go; the journey was to last another two hours. Then a bright young man standing by the compartment door took me in his arms and urged the people in the carriage corridor to raise their hands. He lifted me up onto the human conveyor belt and I was passed horizontally over the passengers' heads, brushing the underside of the curved metal roof, all the way along the corridor to the toilet. What a great journey! Everyone laughed, smiled and joked. It was like having a ride at a funfair. Years later I wondered if they would have behaved in the same way had they known who my father was.

Brada, Eva and Monika welcomed us at Bratislava station. Rudolf Brada was chubby, balding and clever and always in a good mood. As soon as he saw tired Micula and me, he had to cheer us up and chuckled, remembering how last Christmas, when I had visited with Heda for several days, I'd had a sip of red wine and danced around like a maniac, went to sleep within minutes and nearly missed all the evening festivities. Luckily they waited for me, and after reciting poems under the Christmas tree the presents could be opened. Heda played with my building bricks, Micula and Vilemína threw my football around, the cousins painted with my watercolours and Uncle Rudolf put my railway set together while I sat on a chair 'reading' a book.

Back in Bratislava, as the taxi we hired cruised through the city streets, my uncle pointed out the famous sights along the way to remind me of the dominant square castle sitting firmly above the Danube and the tall St Martin's Cathedral tower. We travelled to the suburb of Nivy where the Bradas lived in a modern, rather severe apartment block.

Before long I forgot the dreary time I'd been having in the Veverkova nursery and was swept away by the easygoing atmosphere, the good hearty food and comfortable accommodation. My bed, with a soft duvet, was like sleeping on a cloud. The large apartment was well furnished with solid dark mahogany dressers, tables topped with richly embroidered tablecloths, fabric-upholstered chairs and colourful carpets lying on the floors. It was great to be back with the girls, who chattered and smiled all the time, kept me entertained, invited more of their young friends and neighbours and adopted me as their brother and a leader of our little gang. We played hide and seek inside the apartment, screeching and running wildly from room to room, and hopscotch, skipping and ball games on the pavement outside. In the evenings uncle showed us silent film cartoons he had borrowed, projecting them on the white wall of the living room.

Toward the end of November this carefree idyll was broken with two earth-shattering events.

The kitchen was the hub of the Bratislava apartment. I loved it, as it always smelled wonderful, with mouth-watering freshly baked cakes or biscuits covered with nuts, home-made jam, crushed poppy seed, vanilla and powdery icing sugar together with the aroma of freshly ground coffee beans. In contrast to Heda, who never had enough time in Prague, the women of this family – and Uncle Rudolf, who loved cooking – were keen to prepare and make their own food and impress with its homely taste. Uncle stood in the kitchen with a white apron waiting for auntie to roll the dough and cut the biscuits out with cutters of various forms and shapes, then he pasted the topping and arranged them on a baking tray and Vilemína shoved them into the hot oven. I was allowed to sneak in and grab a nibble from the tray once it cooled down any time I felt peckish.

One morning the kitchen lay uncommonly idle without any wholesomeness in the air. Vilemína and Micula sat tensely at the table listening to the radio when I heard both of them cry out. I stopped playing with the cousins, pricked up my ears and heard the unpleasant booming of a Czech official-sounding voice. I was scared, went there and pushed the door open. Looking up from underneath the level of the high table, into the gloomy light of the kitchen, I observed a huddled gathering of two silent silhouettes with their heads bowed, holding each other's hands tightly. Startled, they turned their frightened distraught faces toward me and I saw their tearful, dark eyes.

'I thought someone had just died,' I pronounced, afraid and with my heart in my mouth. I wanted to know everything there and then but in their profound distress they did not know what to do with me and pushed me, bewildered, out of the kitchen and shut the door.

A black cloud of foreboding descended over me; and it never ever lifted.

Several days after the kitchen episode Micula and Vilemína, unusually both looking very tired, drawn and unable to leave the apartment, insisted that at least we, the children, should attend a Catholic mass and pray. I could not understand why. I had done nothing like this before, especially enter a church, but I was a guest of the Bradas and had to conform. The maternal side of my aunt's family was Jewish but had converted to Christianity when Vilemína married and escaped the Nazi deportations. Under the influence of Vilemína, who stayed with her daughter in Bratislava during the winter months, the Brada family were devoted churchgoers. A crucifix hung on the wall in each room and Vilemína looked up at it piously every time she went in. My parents, on their return from the war and as a consequence of all the suffering inflicted on the Jews, decided to fully integrate with the contemporary, predominantly secular, Communist society and cast off any religious beliefs they might have had or been led to during their childhood and youth. They never talked about religion at home and did not want me to feel that I was in any way different from others. Such was my ignorance that I did not even realize that I was Jewish until much later in my life.

Eva, Monika and I rode downtown on a trolleybus, its electric motor smoothly and quietly running on the asphalted city roads. The walk from the trolleybus stop up to St Martin's Cathedral required a tiring climb up a number of stone steps. The Cathedral was an impressive and powerful building and it filled the whole of my view as we approached the heavy entrance door. We tried to open the door with what little strength we had. All of us were grabbing at the handle, pushing it hard, but when we managed it, the nave was so packed that we could not get in and the door slowly shut again due to the pressure of the people inside.

We heard the organ playing from high up in the gallery and smelled the incense that escaped through the door, rising in the form of smoke from the burner, the thurible, carried by the priest pushing with all his might through the throng of the crowd to get to the altar. 'Another angel came and stood before the altar, having a golden censer: and there was given to him much incense that he should offer of the prayers of all saints, upon the golden altar, which is before the throne of God. And the smoke of the incense of the prayers of the saints ascended up before God from the hand of the angel ... ' Many people in heavy winter coats, fingering their squashed hats in their hands, had turned up for the service, which to me was unprecedented. Slovaks are predominantly Roman Catholics and their religion and belief in God's salvation came before their devotion to Communism. Their attendance at church services took priority over presence at Party meetings. Czechs unjustifiably looked down on Slovaks as second rate and Slovaks retaliated by ignoring the politics dictated to them from faraway Prague. Slovaks are independently minded people. Can you imagine, especially nowadays, not being able to get into the house of God because of overcrowding? We tried to listen outside, snatching the service through the thick walls. The stained-glass windows let out a subdued murmur of voices and organ music but there was no participation on our part. Disappointed, we turned back home. Our mission was not fulfilled and we felt guilty.

Much later, I realized that this was a very special day. It was the last Sunday of November 1952.

Afterwards I looked back through my recollections and memories and realized that Heda and Rudolf became my icons, collectively representing the human achievements and suffering of the troubled 20th century. My parents endured all the difficulties of the best and worst times of their era.

It was especially Rudolf whose life seemed to be arranged on a fated path. His destiny seemed to be similar to that of some of the characters in Graham Greene's novels, where an ordinary person finds himself caught up in events larger than his own life. Rudolf's existence was moulded by predetermined occurrences, and the unstoppable whirlwind of political events sucked him into unavoidable destruction.

In 1990, on my return to Prague after a twenty-four-year absence, I decided to find my father. My life would not be fulfilled or worth continuing until I discovered Rudolf again. I had to make a difficult journey back through the last hundred years to assemble the full story.

4

Rudolf

●

●
My life unrolled swiftly.
It was too short
for my vast longings,
which had no bounds.
Before I knew it
my life's end was drawing near.

Jaroslav Seifert, *Autobiografie/Autobiography*, 1979, translated
by Ewald Osers

At the outset of the 20th century Prague was a complex,
cosmopolitan city embracing people of varied backgrounds, skills,
religions and nationalities: Czechs, Germans and Austrians. The city,
next in importance to Vienna and Budapest, the main centres of the
Austro-Hungarian Empire, was the cultural and geographical heart
of the Czech lands and had about half a million inhabitants. The
ruling Austrian aristocracy and German bourgeoisie possessed most
of the wealth and the Czechs, who vastly outnumbered them, formed
the middle and lower classes. At that time about four per cent of
the population of Prague were Jews, and about half of them spoke
German and attended German speaking schools and universities.
However, the Prague Germans were losing their dominant cultural
position with the rise in Czech nationalism. The Czechs always took
pride in their own traditions, their country and their language
and strove for their own cultural emancipation, and the intriguing
Prague milieu provided a backdrop for the competing ethnic, social,
cultural and political trends of the time.

For over a thousand years, Jews lived through turbulent
times as well as in relative harmony with the indigenous population
of Bohemia and the other minorities. They reached Central Europe
both from the east, from Russia escaping the pogroms, and from the
west, from Spain and Portugal after the 1492–97 expulsion decreed

by King Ferdinand and Queen Isabella. Subsequently, in the late 15th and 16th centuries, over a hundred thousand homeless people wandered Europe in desperation trying to find a safe place to settle. From our family records, it transpires that the Blochs – on my mother's side – were Sephardi Jews from Spain, and the Margolius ancestors were Ashkenazi Jews from Eastern Europe.

Predominantly, Jews inhabited the towns and involved themselves in local trade. However, several important decrees and events had an enormous influence on their existence and place of residence. There was the great Prague massacre of 18 April 1389 when over three thousand Jews were burned in their houses and many fled the city. In the 15th and 16th centuries Jews were forced out from the Bohemian towns to live in the countryside. In September 1726, during the reign of the Habsburg Emperor Charles VI, the 'familiant' law was established in order to reduce the number of Jews resident in Czech lands. This law, which lasted until May 1849, stipulated that only the first-born son of the family was allowed to marry and stay in the country; if younger male siblings wanted to start a family they had to leave and live abroad. After Empress Maria Theresa's December 1744 order of renewed expulsion of Jews from cities, they dispersed into the countryside again, forming small communities in villages and settlements and learning country trades: agriculture and associated businesses. Despite that four years later they were allowed to return to the urban areas to bolster the cities' economies which had declined due to their absence, many stayed and enjoyed rural life.

The indictment of Leopold Hilsner, a Jew unjustly accused of the 'ritual' murder of a Catholic girl, Anežka Hrůzová, near the village of Polná in southeast Bohemia in the spring of 1899, stirred anti-Semitic feelings and beliefs in Bohemia and Austria. The accusation involved Czech politicians and intellectuals including Professor Tomáš Garrick Masaryk, who fought against public opinion to help to suppress these sentiments and free Hilsner, originally sentenced to death, after eleven years in custody. Masaryk's attitude mirrored the situation of the period; as a child, he was afraid of Jews: 'I believed that they used Christian blood, so I would rather go several streets out of my way than pass a house where a Jew lived ... Once we had a school excursion and while we were romping and getting into mischief one of our Jewish school-fellows, Leopold Prislisauer, slipped away from us into the yard. I followed him; he had gone behind an open gate and was kneeling with his face to the wall, praying. I was ashamed that a Jew should be praying while we were playing about. From then, all my life I have tried to be careful not to be unjust to Jews ... When did I overcome in myself the anti-Semitism of the common people? Well really, in my feeling, perhaps never; only in my reason ...'

The Hilsner case, similar to the Dreyfus Affair of 1894 in France, underlined the European rise in antipathy against the Jews at that time which culminated in the holocaust of the Second World War.

Rudolf was born to Vítězslav (Siegfried) and Berta Margolius in the leafy Vinohrady quarter of Prague, in 26 Nerudova, now Polská Street, in a large neo-classical house that faced the green park of Riegrovy sady on Sunday, 31 August 1913. This was a date, 31.8.13, which was both mysterious and intriguingly symmetrical, and a palindrome. People born on dates like this are believed to have a self-assertive disposition, favouring a life of responsibility and, in particular, work in connection with finance. In addition, it indicates someone whose views cannot be talked down, and who will not defer to the opinion of others. For Rudolf himself the numbers three, thirteen and thirty-one were special. These numbers governed his whole life and being to his last breath. All important events – and even small, insignificant happenings – occurred either on the third, thirteenth or thirty-first days, months, years or on multiples of these numbers – as if he were programmed at birth by a superior force. At the end of his life, he became conscious of this phenomenon and driving influence in his life but was powerless to change the course of his fate, which was strongly running through this cycle. He believed in its inescapable force.

Rudolf's grandfather, Šalomoun Margolius, born in 1846, was an easygoing man. Nothing was more important than his comfort. He was married to Karolína Pražáková and over the years, they had six sons: Alois, Gustav, Vítězslav, Emil, Rudolf and Eduard.

Šalomoun managed a small farm in Meziklasí in central Bohemia. Then the family moved to an even smaller place nearby called Píšť, where Šalomoun took over a minuscule tavern. The tavern had only two rooms and the children had to wait for the last drinker to leave before they could spread their thin mattresses in the bar. Every time a new baby arrived it was gladly accepted into the world, but Šalomoun was not in a hurry to register the birth. Days, weeks and months passed and despite Karolína's daily nagging, he couldn't be bothered to walk to the synagogue in the nearby town, Dolní Kralovice. By the time he gathered courage to wander out of the house the family had forgotten on which day the baby had been born and by then another son had arrived anyway. When Šalomoun eventually made it to the synagogue he tried to remember two birthdays: 'Oh, Vítězslav was born after that big storm we had last year, Emil came to us during the recent harvest.' So all Šalomoun's children had their birthdays invented. The family had only one pair of children's shoes and so only one child out of six could go to school every day. As Šalomoun never bothered to go praying he did not demand it from his children either; they only kept the main Jewish holidays. After Šalomoun's death in 1924, Alois, the oldest son, inherited the Píšť pub. Emil and Rudolf Margolius lived in Litoměřice and had a liquor and wine factory. Gustav Margolius, together with his friend Rudolf Pacovský, had a similar establishment on Argentinská Street in Prague.

My father's mother, Berta, came from the village of Pnětluky in western Bohemia. Her parents, Jindřich and Emilie Löwy, had five children and Berta was the second-born. They owned a modest house. Jindřich was a garnet merchant; the stones he handled were supplied from nearby Podsedice. Berta had an attractive figure, sparkling eyes, long brown hair and sensuously curved lips. She was very bright, well brought up and had many admirers in local society. In her late teens she became closely acquainted with an Austro-Hungarian Army officer. It was a great love and they yearned to get married. In those days, every officer who wanted to marry had to pay a large bond to the authorities but neither the officer nor Berta's parents had the financial means to arrange this and the marriage came to nothing. Berta became very unhappy and this changed her. She grew

Berta Löwyová

to be outwardly disagreeable and unpleasant although she never meant to be perceived like that.

Soon Vítězslav appeared. He was a burly, well-built man with receding hair, grey eyes and an agreeable, carefree, joyful nature underlined by stubborn perseverance and determination. Like many other men in those days, he had a brush-like moustache covering his upper lip. He was a keen sportsman, played tennis and swam in all weathers. He was mad about Berta but, uninterested, she chased him away. He brought her presents, flowers and jewellery. She always ran off and hid in the barn. 'Miss Berta, you've such wonderful hair!' he called to her through the closed gate.

'It's only a wig!' she replied.

'That beautiful long neck of yours is ready for this string of shiny pearls!'

'It's all bumpy with warts and pimples!'

'Your little nose makes my heart beat faster!'

'It's as sharp as a bird's beak,' Berta responded from a distance.

'The lovely smooth skin of your hands!'

'I scrubbed the floor in the house; it's as rough as the field's stubble!'

'The elegant shape of your ears is so adorable!' carried on Vítězslav.

'They're as big and floppy as an elephant's!' replied Berta, unimpressed.

'And your beautiful white teeth, I love them!'

'I wear dentures,' she called after him, exasperated, and exposed her teeth in a grimace.

Vítězslav muttered under his breath: 'You little minx, I'll get you, don't worry,' and the long, day-to-day squabbles continued. However, Vítězslav did not give up and eventually, in 1912, they married in Litoměřice not far from Pnětluky and later moved to Nerudova Street in Prague. Affectionately, they used Friedl and Bertl as their pet names, to entwine them in rhyme.

A year after Rudolf's birth, Vítězslav was mobilised, becoming a soldier of the Austro-Hungarian Army and joining in the First World War. Luckily, because of his age – he was thirty-five – he was kept in a reserve regiment in Litoměřice that was sent behind the lines to Eger in Hungary but was not engaged in any fighting. In order to escape the food shortages in Prague during Vítězslav's army service Berta travelled with Rudolf to her parents in Pnětluky or went to stay with her sister Vilemína in Podsedice on a number of occasions. There provisions were in abundance and the atmosphere was relaxed. Vítězslav journeyed there or to Prague whenever he could. After the war they moved to Lužická, also in Vinohrady, a pleasant tree-lined street resembling a typical Parisian avenue.

Vítězslav, together with his younger brother Eduard, was in a thriving partnership in the Prague luxury textile agency for J. C. Klaubert & Söhne. Klauberts had a large textile mill with a dyeing and finishing works manufacturing high-quality woollen, half-woollen, half-silk and cotton goods in the prosperous Sudetenland

Margolius Brothers Agency, Rybná Street, Prague, 1930s

town of Aš – Asch. Bratří Margoliusové – Margolius Brothers – as
the agency was called, had its office in the Old Town at Rybná Street
and later at Masná Street opposite the primary school attended by
Franz Kafka in the 1890s. It took them years of resolute dedication
to build the business into a profitable enterprise. Berta took charge of
the Klaubert agency and controlled its staff; she was second-in-
command after the brothers. She placed hard work and strict
discipline first and that was the main reason that the business
prospered. The Margolius brothers themselves were more relaxed
and preferred to spend their time in cafés gossiping with friends,
rather than at their writing desks completing invoices and packing
wooden boxes with woollen scarves, kerchiefs and fabric to be sent
all over the world.

   Berta, by then more rounded in stature and complementing Vítězslav's looks, did not tolerate inadequacies lightly
and demanded respect, obedience and proper behaviour not only
from others in her charge – such as the domestic staff who were
terrified of her – but also from her only son. She loved Rudolf dearly
though she could not refrain from scolding him often, even when he
was an adult. 'Rudlo, sit straight, don't slouch; eat properly, don't

gulp; hold the knife by the end not too close to the blade; go and change your shirt, the collar's dirty; polish your shoes and the soles, they're dusty; tidy up your things, it's all a mess here . . . ' Because of this strict daily routine Rudolf was impeccably behaved.

It was Saturday, 21 December 1918. Vítězslav lifted a pair of folding steps, set them on his shoulder and took the five-year-old Rudolf's hand. 'Today is a special day, come on, let's go out. I hope you're dressed warmly, it's cold outside. Here, let's put this on your coat,' and he pinned a small two-tailed lion in silver on Rudolf's lapel.

They walked a long way down a broad street then called Jungmann Avenue, later Marshall Foch Avenue, Schwerin Strasse, Stalin Avenue and now Vinohradská (Prague street names have kept changing, depending on the political climate and who ruled the country), Vítězslav swapping the steps from left to right. Light snow fell from the overcast sky. Many people joined them, the crowd getting thicker and noisier as they neared Wenceslas Square.

'Rudlo, hold my hand tight so you won't get lost,' Vítězslav ordered.

It was past noon. New Czechoslovak flags hung from windows and the Czech two-tailed lions had already replaced the signs of the double-headed eagle of the Austro-Hungarian monarchy on the corners of the buildings. Another man thrust a small red and white flag into Rudolf's free hand. They reached the top of the square and could not get any further in the throng. Vítězslav set up the steps and hoisted Rudolf on top: 'This way you'll have the best view in Prague!'

They heard a triumphant train whistle from the Franz Josef Station, soon to be renamed after the American President Woodrow Wilson, and the roar of a cannonade. The band of the newly formed Czechoslovak Army struck up a tune from their position underneath the statue of St Wenceslas. The crowds were stirring in anticipation.

'Oh, I can see him now,' shouted the excited Vítězslav. 'Look, Rudlo, and he's being driven in a Czech-made car, how appropriate!' and pointed to the right.

Masaryk's arrival in Prague, 21 December 1918

Despite the cold weather, an open Laurin & Klement phaeton surrounded by marching Czech legionnaires slowly drove along Emperor and King Charles Avenue toward them. Through the fluttering of little flags greeting the procession, the raised bunches of winter flowers and shouts of 'welcome home,' Rudolf saw an old dignified man, with white hair, moustache and beard and wearing a tall hat, sitting in the back of the car and acknowledging the enthusiastic welcome with a broad smile.

'Who's that, táto?' Rudolf asked Vítězslav without looking down.

'It's our new President Masaryk, of our independent Czechoslovak Republic, eight weeks old. He's just arrived from a four-year exile, living abroad, where he negotiated the establishment of our new state with the world powers. Remember this day, a new age has arrived for all of us, we triumphed over the old Habsburg Austro-Hungarian Monarchy, we're all equal, and we're free.'

Rudolf did not understand but he waved; Masaryk noticed him sticking above the people's heads, and waved back, twinkling his bespectacled eyes at Rudolf. Rudolf coloured red and suddenly felt proud without quite knowing why.

As Masaryk arrived in Prague, he confided to the welcoming committee: 'Excuse me if I do not speak much. I really do not know what I am to say to you. For four years I have not been so deeply moved as now.' He refused to enter the state carriage drawn by a team of white horses waiting for him; he did not want to emulate his Habsburg predecessors and asked for an ordinary car.

'What were my feelings as the people of Prague gave me so splendid a reception, and as I drove through the streets in a democratic motor car instead of the gilded carriage that would have been too reminiscent of times that were past? Was I glad, was I joyous? Seeing the rejoicing, the wealth of costumes, colours, banners, decorations and flowers, answering the warmth of the greetings, what were my thoughts? The heavy work awaiting me, the work of building up our restored state decently and well, constantly weighed on my mind,' wrote Masaryk afterwards. He set himself a vision: 'Democracy is not to reign over people but an effort to secure justice. And justice is mathematics of humanity.'

In the story *Description of a Struggle*, Franz Kafka wrote about the Baroque Marian Column erected in the centre of Staroměstské náměstí – Old Town Square – on 20 September 1650 to celebrate the Treaty of Westphalia, the end of the Thirty Years' War and the defeat of Prague's Swedish invaders. 'Today there's a southwest wind blowing. The spire of the Town Hall is moving in little circles. All the windowpanes are rattling, and the lamp posts are bending like bamboos. The Virgin Mary's cloak is coiling around her pillar and the wind is tugging at it. Does no one notice this?'

The sculptor Jan Jiří Bendl designed the Column with the Virgin Mary standing on top. However, the 20th-century, independence-seeking Czechs mistakenly believed that the Column was set up to humiliate them, a memory of Czech defeats since the loss of their nationhood at the Battle of White Mountain in 1620 at the hands of the Austrians; they saw it as a symbol of Habsburg domination. The Column was ceremonially destroyed after the proclamation of Czechoslovak independence on 28 October 1918 at the instigation of the Czech anarchist František Sauer. He led a crowd returning from an anti-Habsburg demonstration on the evening of 3 November. A rope was wrapped around the Column

The toppling of the Virgin Mary's Column, November 1918

and, despite the protests of the Prague Council officials and an elderly woman who knelt praying in the location of the predicted fall, the Column was successfully toppled.

The heart of Europe was freed from the rule of the obsolete Habsburg monarchy and transformed into a vibrant, modern, dynamic state with a highly developed and advanced industrial base, embracing peoples of many nationalities. It became one of the leading democracies of the world in the inter-war period. It took the four devastating years of the First World War, a conflict between the Central Powers of Germany and Austria-Hungary and the Allies, to achieve this success.

Heda

5

'And so they've killed our Ferdinand,' said the charwoman to Mr Švejk.

Jaroslav Hašek, *The Good Soldier Švejk*, 1921

Ervín Bloch, Heda's father-to-be, was the Waldes Otello Koh-i-noor Company factory manager and financial director. He worked there from 1908, when he was twenty-two years old. Ervín always dressed in well-tailored suits, had a small head with short hair in a crew-cut fashion and a neat moustache; his intelligent, piercing brown eyes between a prominent nose followed the world around him carefully. He was hardworking, efficient and well-liked for his direct, no-nonsense approach. Although born in the Bohemian countryside, he was a city-dweller at heart and a resident of Prague. Ervín was not an intellectual but was interested in arts and literature, collected first editions and enjoyed the company of Jewish writers and artists whom he met in cafés, clubs and at his home.

In 1903 businessman Jindřich Waldes founded the Waldes Company in Prague. It manufactured pins, needles and other sewing devices. As its main product this innovative company made a specially patented concealed fastener device which became essential for those modern women who sought a light, flowing form of dress which liberated them from the 19th century's burdensome and fastidious clothing. The fastener's manufacture was complicated. This tiny object of two halves was made of a pair of circular metal pieces worked over several times. It incorporated a small spring and needed sophisticated machines to insert it and to lock the two halves together. It was a fortuitous invention. The Waldes factories, with their modern automatic manufacturing processes, were located in Prague-Vršovice and other major cities in Europe and America.

Ervín was popular in the Waldes factory; for his birthday, the staff even composed a rhyme:

'Our Director Ervín Bloch
Often rumbles like a broken clock
But no one is fooled by this noise
Because we love his heart's voice.'

On 19 August 1914 Ervín, recently mobilized into the 10th Company of the k.u.k. 91st Infantry Regiment, carried a rifle in his hands and cautiously proceeded forward through the pine forest. Dry needles were catching on his private soldier's uniform, sometimes coming through the fabric and pricking his hot skin under the army tunic. At his right, out of the corner of his eye, he saw Václav Maček who was also from Ostředek, the same village that he was born in near Benešov in Bohemia. He noticed that Václav was also following his movements; it was easier to fight in this foreign land, on the Mountain of Cer, if you had a friend at your side, someone you knew and trusted. They had played together as boys, had stolen apples from the orchards of farmer Pecha, climbed fences to gather strawberries in the neighbours' gardens, roamed local forests collecting mushrooms, caught red crayfish from the cool streams and chased girls round the village square.

The lines of the infantry formation were advancing uphill, the trees obscuring the view. More sun was coming into their eyes as they neared the top, making their outlook difficult. It was too late; the flash of Serbian Army fire and the booming of gunpowder stopped them in their progress. Ervín grabbed his lifeless left arm which was bleeding heavily. Before he lost consciousness, he saw that Václav was missing from the line of soldiers continuing their assault of the hill. He did not know what really happened until the next day. By then he had been transported miles south, deep into Serbia.

What Ervín saw was a bearded face of a Serbian official with shining eyes, closely observing him. 'Serbia won the great battle yesterday. We pursued your units, they retreated in disarray across the River Drina and you're left behind wounded. Now you're captured. What's your religion, soldier?' asked the friendly face.

'I'm Jewish,' mumbled Ervín, 'why?'

'Prove it.'

He was puzzled about what to do but then he recited: 'Sh'ma Yisrael Adonai Elohaynu Adonai Echad,' – Hear, Israel, the Lord is our God, the Lord is One – the only Jewish prayer he knew.

The bearded face disappeared and Ervín closed his eyes, having lost any feeling in his arm. After some minutes another face, this time one with a moustache, appeared.

'Who're you?' asked Ervín.

'I'm a Jewish doctor, don't worry, you'll recover soon, I'll look after you. Let's go.' The doctor bid the stretcher-bearers follow him inside the First Military Reserve Hospital in Skopje.

When Ervín woke up the next day he took in his surroundings more soberly and went to explore. He noticed with pleasure that Václav was located in the adjacent wardroom, also smelling of soap and disinfectants. He shuffled over to his bed, supporting his injured arm while he did so. Ervín and Václav did everything together. 'Even the same shrapnel got both of us,' said Ervín. 'How are you?'

Václav had a wound in his right leg and luckily, the fragment missed the bone. 'Not too bad, I'll live. Who's your doctor? Mine is Schindler, a Catholic.'

Václav had also been asked his religion before they took him in and treated him. He had also said a prayer and luckily remembered an appropriate one: 'O God, Who knowest us to be set in the midst of such great perils, that, by reason of the weakness of our nature, we cannot stand upright, grant us such health of mind and body, that those evils which we suffer for our sins we may overcome through Thine assistance. Through Christ our Lord.'

'Amen,' finished Ervín and explained that his doctor was called Kohn; he had needed to prove himself too and had found it really difficult. Ervín's father Vilém was not very religious; he went to the synagogue perhaps twice a year. He walked to Benešov playing his mouth organ all the way and Ervín rarely went with him. The Blochs celebrated Passover and fasted on Yom Kippur. At Passover Ervín arranged for a delivery van from the Waldes factory to drive to Ostředek loaded with matzoth and, in return, the villagers sent the van back filled with the large walnuts that thrived there. Ervín confirmed that he was more a Czech than a Jew. Somehow, surprisingly, with all the bedlam, guns, blood and sweat, human civilisation still survived. Even as prisoners of war they were looked after with the utmost respect and treated by medical staff of the same faith to satisfy their personal beliefs and needs. Ervín felt proud that this true feeling for others, for individuals, for foreigners of any persuasion, had not been lost to them even so far away from their home, in this unsettled country where many religions converged and clashed.

Until October 1915 Ervín and Václav were in the prisoner-of-war camp in Idadija when the Central Powers captured Belgrade and defeated Serbia. After Serbia's defeat they were repatriated. In April 1916, in Vukovar, Ervín contracted typhoid; the epidemic involved a large number of Austro-Hungarian troops. After recovering he, together with Václav who had also been ill, was sent to Brück an der Leitha in Austria to join the Ersatz Battalion where all the new recruits and formerly ill or wounded soldiers were concentrated. Ervín's arm was almost paralysed – he could hardly move it – and Václav stooped, as his thigh muscles remained permanently damaged. In May 1916 they were discharged due to their injuries. It had been nearly two years since they were at home and it was up to them to get back to Bohemia. They walked with many others, sleeping under the open skies, in abandoned barns or on edges of woods, begging for food. The journey eventually took them to their native Ostředek. The village lies in a pleasant valley, has about sixty houses and a small Baroque castle in a rampant garden, a brewery and a church.

Vilém Bloch, a modest, heavily bearded man of simple tastes, the village general goods store and tavern owner, greeted them with a tune on his mouth organ, while Ervín's mother Kateřina, a small woman with a gentle appearance, looked delighted that her son was safely back home. They crowded into the bar, sitting on the long benches by the beer-stained tables, while customers from the store across the corridor, with children at their feet, filled the bar doorway to watch. The buzzing flies disturbed the sweet smell of hops

permanently hanging over the drinking den. Vilém placed a tankard
of beer on a white, well-used porcelain table coaster for each drinker
from a big tray he balanced skilfully on one hand. He marked the
coasters' rough edges with lines using a soft pencil, normally kept
behind his ear, to designate the number already drunk; as is the
Czech custom the money for the total consumed was paid on leaving.
The local punters lifted their frothy half-litres, all loudly greeting
the return of the village's popular sons in unison, and singing
accompanied by the mouth organ reverberated in the pub late into
the night.

Despite this welcome Ervín did not stay long and hurried
on to the village of Suchdol near Prague to see his beloved fiancée
Marta Diamantová; now that Ervín was back their wedding was to
be held at the beginning of July. Marta was dazzling, with a round
face, full lips and plenty of brown hair, but most fascinating were
her wide light-grey eyes that had always drawn admiring looks.
Ervín missed her. And his fellow directors at Waldes Koh-i-noor
were also waiting for him anxiously; Ervín had an excellent
reputation at Waldes.

After enjoying himself with Marta's embraces – and all
her fussing about his arm – he went to his apartment in Chodská
Street in Vinohrady to hide in his library of over ten thousand books
and find out all the news – when had he read a book last? He sank
into the comfortable armchair and picked at the stack of papers
accumulated while he was away, except now he could only use his
right arm. His left one was more or less useless except for light work
without any strain; life would change after all. He would be busy
catching up at work with Waldes, in his private life, increasing his
collection of first editions and, after the wedding, starting a family.

In the winter of 1916, Ervín sent a note to his friend Max
Brod whom he had not seen since being recruited in July 1914. They
met sporadically in cafés and restaurants and usually Brod's other
friends were present; their favourite meeting places were the Café
Louvre in Národní or Café Arco in Hybernská. The next day he got
a message to meet in the late afternoon in the romantic Vikárka
tavern located in the shadow of St Vitus Cathedral. The tavern
windows overlooked the deep Jelení příkop – Deer Moat – and

Prague Castle's 15th-century impressively tall northern fortifications reinforced with three towers: the White Tower, Daliborka and Mihulka Gunpowder Tower. Further along the same defensive wall stretched Zlatá ulička – Golden Lane, the Lane of the Alchemists, an ancient blind alley comprising a row of tiny houses. Brod was visiting Franz Kafka who had moved there recently.

Kafka's house was too small to entertain or sleep in and Franz walked to town at midnight when he finished writing. His sister Ottla, who rented the house, allowed him to stay there over the winter months. Here Kafka found the peaceful atmosphere and surroundings he needed for his writing, away from the disturbing bustle of his parents' apartment and his own flat 'At The Golden Pike' house in Dlouhá where the whole structure of the building resonated with the noise of lift machinery. To have a house for himself was something special. Kafka wrote to Felice Braun, his fiancée: 'To step out of the door of one's home straight into the snow of the quiet lane. All of it twenty crowns per month, supplied with all the necessities by my sister … everything in order and beautiful.'

They sat in Vikárka and had tea to warm them up while snow fell outside. Kafka mentioned Felice and his uncertainty about

Golden Lane, Prague Castle

46

the intended marriage. Ervín, who was two years younger than Kafka and had only married six months ago, was extolling his union, revealing that Marta was pregnant with their first child. Kafka, though shy, appeared envious of Ervín's untroubled confidence in his relationship. On their way home Kafka invited them to number 22, down a steep staircase to the basement to see the wonderful view from his low-level cellar window of the Royal Garden, the Belvedere and the Prague suburbs beyond, following the snowstorm that had come through the Deer Moat not long before.

The previous year Kafka had published his *Metamorphosis* story and, despite initial unhappiness, seemed satisfied with the outcome. Brod asked Kafka to show it to Ervín who had not yet seen it and Kafka reluctantly passed a copy to him, the first printed version that appeared in *Die Weissen Blätter*, the October 1915 issue of the Leipzig monthly magazine to which Brod had also been contributing. 'Die Verwandlung', the amazing fate of Gregor Samsa, intrigued Ervín: 'What has happened to me, he thought. It was no dream ... ' and he wanted to read it and have it in his book collection. They left Kafka to his writing and descended the Old Castle Steps toward the Mánes Bridge over the river. Ervín bid Brod goodbye and on the way home, by chance, he found the relevant copy of *Die Weissen Blätter* at Orbis second-hand bookshop in Jungmann Avenue in the Nové Město – New Town.

In the latter part of November 1918, Ervín, always anxious to keep in touch with his friends, arranged to meet Brod in the Montmartre Night Club located in the 'At Three Wild Men' house in Řetězová Street in the Old Town. He had met writers Kafka, Franz Werfel and Felix Weltsch there before the war. Jaroslav Hašek, the author of *The Good Soldier Švejk*, and Josef Lada, its illustrator, were also frequent drinkers there.

When Ervín turned up after eight o'clock he spotted Brod, Weltsch and Kafka at a table almost hidden in the exuberant interior. The newly refurbished Club was divided into three separate areas, Heaven, Hell and Paradise, and was decorated with a curious mixture of Cubist, Futurist and Constructivist motifs. Ceilings embellished with ribs divided into diamond-shaped forms, walls faced with sweeping swirls of stucco underlined by colourful painting, triangulated cornices and dado rails gave the interior a mysterious, cathedral-like setting. The style followed the Cubist movement in architecture, which occurred uniquely in Bohemia from 1910. Czech architects inspired by Cubist paintings brought over from France built several interesting villas, a department store and apartment blocks in the Vyšehrad area and the Old Town.

The Montmartre Club was the first time a public interior had been attacked with such verve. Ervín, an admirer of Modernism, felt passionate about this experimentation in three-dimensional space design but, on greeting his friends, he noted that Brod was not at all enthused about the novel form of art, preferring a more conventional interpretation. Kafka looked tired and pale, having just recovered from the Spanish flu that was spreading through Prague and, although he was interested in their small talk, his mind

Emil Halmon, Cubist fountain, Mánes Bridge, 1911

seemed to be elsewhere. Presently he was to travel to Želízy, north of Prague, to recuperate from his illness.

The new transformation of the Montmartre intrigued Ervín; seeing everything from so many angles simultaneously gave his perception an extra stimulus. The Montmartre Club almost seemed a parody of the style that became not only a way of creating but also a way of living in Bohemia at the time.

Kafka, as a writer, was among the first to become inspired by this multifaceted artistic trend which was reflected in his writing. His stories did not reveal explicitly what they were about. His fiction contained so many meanings and points of view that the primary significance was dissolved in the multiplicity of possibilities: 'But simply to get me away from the place they sent me out on useless errands. And they took care not to send me too far away, so that I had some hopes of being able to get back in time if I hurried. And there was I running as fast as I could, shouting the message through the half-open door of the office I was sent to, nearly breathless so that they could hardly make me out, and back again at top speed, and yet the student was here before me, he hadn't so far to come, of course ... '

Six years later Ervín's friends met together, but under more unexpected and sober circumstances – at Kafka's funeral. On 11 June 1924, at 4.00 o'clock in the afternoon, after Hebrew prayers at the New Jewish Cemetery Ceremonial Hall in Žižkov, Kafka's simple, pall-covered casket was brought out on a cart and hauled through the cemetery grounds, which were shaded by trees overgrown with ivy, to the open grave – plot number 33, in row 14, in block 21. Ervín liked the bleak, serene Jewish service without candles, flowers or music. He followed in the procession behind the casket, joining Kafka's parents Hermann and Julie, his sisters Ottla, Elli and Valli. Brod supported Dora Diamantová, the last female friend of Kafka – surely she must be a distant relative of Marta, he thought. About a hundred other mourners joined the procession. On the way, Ervín overheard how Dora told Brod of Kafka' last moments, lifting his head and smelling a bunch of flowers she brought him.

Brod made a speech. Dora cried out when the coffin was lowered and fainted but no one moved to help her. The Kaddish was recited, raising the profound hope of redemption although there is no reference, no word even, about death in the prayer and its theme is rather the celebration of the greatness of God: 'May His great name be blessed forever and to all eternity ... May there be abundant peace from heaven, and life, for us ... ' It stresses the passing of the beloved person's soul as a 'gathering in' by the one who provided it in the first place. Kafka defined the activity of a writer: 'Writing as a form of prayer,' and believed 'Even if no redemption comes, I still want to be worthy of it every moment.'

It started raining as each mourner threw three shovels of earth on the casket, the rumbling noise running through the otherwise peaceful cemetery, and the grave filled up with soil. Hermann Kafka turned to leave along the path next to the enclosing cemetery wall and the others followed to wash their hands, as is the custom before leaving the grounds. 'But with Franz Kafka – and I would almost say only with him in the entire circle of literary modernism – there is no change of colour, no change of prospect, no shifting of the scenery. Here is truth and nothing but the truth,' wrote Brod in the obituary published in the *Prager Tagblatt* on 24 June, 1924.

As Ervín stood at the head of Kafka's grave, he raised his eyes to the tombstone backing onto it and saw the name of Šalomoun Margolius, who had died four months earlier, not realising his future personal connection with that family name. Kafka's beautiful Cubist crystal headstone is positioned 'head to head' with the Margolius family tomb, which is located in row 13. It is highly ironic that a man who envisaged humankind's haunted existence in the 20th century lies so close to the family tomb of a man who fulfilled the fate which Kafka predicted so precisely in his literary works. 'You are under arrest, certainly, but that need not hinder you from going about your business. You will not be hampered in carrying on the ordinary course of your life,' Josef K. was told in Kafka's *The Trial*, written in Prague in 1914. A more appropriate and concise description of life under a totalitarian regime could not be found. And in the winter of 1914, while writing *The Trial*, Kafka stayed

Kafka and Margolius family tombs, New Jewish Cemetery

for several months with his sister Elli at 48 Nerudova Street, a few doors away from the apartment where young Rudolf and his parents lived. Kafka liked to walk in the shadows under the trees in the neighbouring Riegrovy sady park.

When Ervín Bloch married Marta in the summer of 1916, they lived in his spacious, old-fashioned but comfortable Chodská apartment. They were well off and had all they needed. Ervín could not drive a car because of his injured arm but used his driver, Rudolf Torant from the Waldes Company, who took them wherever was necessary, even to visit Ervín's parents in Ostředek. Ervín supported various charitable organizations for the old, ill and young. Every day he walked almost two miles to work to the Waldes factory in Vršovice to keep fit despite being a company director and having a car at his disposal. When he saw an old woman pulling a cart up Francouzská Street, he did not hesitate to take off his smart coat and jacket, roll up his sleeves and help her to push the cart up the steep incline.

Marta was a homely person who liked to be a hostess and used her social skills to meet people; many came to have a chance to admire her looks and charm. Marta and Ervín organized discussion meetings in their apartment where they entertained friends who included artists, painters and writers. At Christmas, they had a decorated tree for the sake of their Christian friends and the Waldes clients who came to see them. Marta gave money to poor Czech girl students to support them and enable them to finish their studies. Often they came to lunch. There were always strangers at the table having a meal with the family.

Ervín and Marta's son Jiří was born in May 1917 and Heda arrived two years later.

Heda was a pretty and happy child, and made many friends in her neighbourhood though she was teased by fellow pupils in her Vinohrady primary school. They ran wild in the park around the school which stretched all the way to Foch Avenue and were told by their parents not to go that far and be so close to the dangerously traffic-laden route. Heda was encouraged by her friends to play hide and seek in the bushes and scramble over the muddy municipal flowerbeds. She was also urged to climb over fences and was laughed at when she became stuck on the top with her clothing caught by the sharp wires. 'Nothing in the world pains me more, but your feline eyes, they make me sore,' sang Václav Voska, the future theatre and film star, Heda's fellow pupil. In this way he later proclaimed his first love, but he behaved in a rather cowardly way in all the games they played, mocking Heda more and then running off.

Heda was a rascal, a practical joker and a truant at school. She came to lessons reluctantly, consistently late and tried to get out as many times as she could. She faked coughing in class and persuaded others to copy her, creating an 'epidemic'. The startled teacher let off the whole class for the rest of the day. Later, when Heda married, she met the teacher – who could not stop laughing remembering her escapades – in the street, and on top of all that he now had to call her, as was the custom, *milostivá paní* (madam).

Rudolf: Into Adulthood 6

To be, or not to be, or to live, or not to live,
that was never a question for me.

Jan Werich, *Být, či nebýt/To Be or Not to Be*, 1955

In the late afternoon of 28 October 1928 Vítězslav and Rudolf sat in the Slávia café by its large window overlooking the Prague Castle panorama. This famous setting of the solid mass of Castle buildings and St Vitus Cathedral crowns the top of the Hradčany Hill. In contrast to the horizontal Castle, the Cathedral pokes its sharp towers vertically towards the sky. This pleasing prospect, propped up by the stunning steep gardens descending towards the Lesser Town, evolved over more than a thousand years and shows many varied architectural styles. The pure white twin spires of the Church of St George and the surprising, exuberant, three-tier, Baroque-shaped copper cupola placed on top of the Gothic south tower of the Cathedral complete this distinctive landmark.

'Have a Sacher cake with your apple juice, Rudlo,' his father offered. 'I'll have one with my Turkish coffee, though I shouldn't, I really need some exercise.' He patted his middle which was increasing in girth as he got older and called Bohuslav Brázda, the proprietor, to give his order.

'You're fifteen and more than a grown man according to Jewish custom, so I want to talk to you about politics for a while. You remember Masaryk and the day we greeted him in Prague?'

Rudolf nodded.

Vítězslav explained that Masaryk gave support to the majority of the Czechoslovak political parties but that he was most closely involved with the Social Democrats. He gave the Party his political and intellectual backing especially at times when the strengthening of its extreme left had weakened it. Masaryk participated in the development of the Social Democratic Party

53

Hradčany, 28 October 1928 (Rudolf Margolius)

programme and stabilized its centre position. Vítězslav was a Social Democratic Party member. Their Party stood for the freedom of the press, unimpeded political gatherings, independence from state justice departments, state compensation for all unjustly arrested or imprisoned persons, selection of jurors on equal grounds and, most of all, for the abolition of capital punishment.

'What's capital punishment, táto?' asked Rudolf, puzzled though interested in the discussion they had. He was grateful that his father took him into confidence about his deep personal beliefs.

'Yes ... this is a subject which greatly interests me. When a man or woman is found guilty of a crime they may have committed, such as murder or treason, and if it's considered by judges severe enough and they are sentenced to death, they may be executed. I hope I won't put you off your cake, Rudlo. It should be coming any minute,' observed Vítězslav; Rudolf kept looking at him wide-eyed, with an open mouth. 'What's wrong is that innocent human beings have been sent to their deaths many times because they've been accused of something they never did. A mistake, incompetence, a prejudice may have led the investigators to the wrong man or woman. The state and its officers should not take it upon themselves to appropriate people's life this way. I've in my pocket here a famous speech to the jury made by Victor Hugo, the French writer who wrote *Les Miserables* and *Notre-Dame de Paris*, at the trial of his son, a journalist, in 1851. I'll read you bits of it. "If there is culprit here, it is not my son, it is myself. I, who for these last twenty-five years have opposed capital punishment, have contended for the inviolability of human life, have committed this crime, for which my son is now arraigned ... In all that my son has written on the subject of capital punishment, and for writing and publishing, for which he is now before you on trial, in all that he has written, he has merely proclaimed the sentiments with which, from his infancy, I have inspired him ... The right of the journalist is as sacred, as necessary, as the right of the legislator. A man, a convict, a sentenced wretch, is dragged, on a certain morning, to one of our public squares. There he finds the scaffold! He shudders, he struggles, he refuses to die. He is young, yet only twenty-nine. I know what you will say: 'He is a murderer!' Two officers seize him. His hands, his feet, are tied. He throws off the two officers. A frightful struggle ensues. His feet, bound as they are, become entangled in the ladder ... The struggle is prolonged. Horror seizes the crowd ... The victim clings to the scaffold and shrieks for pardon. His clothes are torn, his shoulders bloody, still he resists. At length, after three-quarters of an hour of this monstrous effort, of this spectacle without a name, of this agony, agony for the assembled spectators as well as for the condemned man, after this age of anguish, they take the poor wretch back to his prison. The people breathe again. The people, naturally merciful, hope that the man will be spared. But no, the guillotine, though vanquished, remains standing. And at night, the officers, reinforced, drag forth the wretch again, so bound that he is but an inert weight, pleading, howling for life, calling upon God, calling upon his father and mother, for like a very child had this man become in the prospect of death, they drag him forth to execution. He is hoisted on to the scaffold, and his head falls! And then through every conscience runs a shudder." '

'What happened to his son? What did he do?' asked Rudolf, moved by the speech.

'Hugo's son was called Charles and he was on trial charged with disrespect to the laws, in that he criticized the sentence and execution of a person who had been accused. Charles was found guilty, despite his father's defence, and sentenced to six months in prison and a fine of five hundred francs,' answered Vítězslav. 'Our President Masaryk's also greatly troubled by capital punishment,' he went on. 'He said to the writer Karel Čapek recently: 'A difficult question for me was that of capital punishment. There have been many days when I have had to sign a death warrant, and nights when I have had to think it over; I have marked them on my calendar with a black cross. I have followed carefully to see whether capital punishment has an effect on crime; I have studied the statistics of crime, and especially of murder, all my life, but I do not see that the death penalty has had a deterrent effect on evildoers; at the moment of committing a murder the murderer does not think of the penalty but of the success of his deed. The most definitive effect is on the rest of the citizens, especially on their way of thinking. My argument for the death penalty is not that it is a deterrent, but that there is in it a moral expiation: to take a man's life is such a frightful wrong that it can only be expiated by an equally heavy ransom. I believe and hope that it will be abolished with the consent of all, as people become more moral and civilized.' On the other hand, Bismarck,' continued Vítězslav, 'the German Chancellor, the great opponent of social democracy, supported the death penalty a few years after Hugo stating that 'death was the gateway of life', that to one who believes in everlasting life death opens the gate of eternal prosperity, and to one who does not believe in eternal life death brings peace, sleep and oblivion.'

Vítězslav confirmed that many countries had already abolished capital punishment: Portugal, the Netherlands, some cantons of Switzerland, Belgium and Italy. However, despite these arguments there were still countries, regimes and people who, with open brutality, demanded to persevere with this barbarity – including Czechoslovakia. The ones who were in favour were, in the first place, those individuals who had seized power in government and could not maintain it other than by suppression, terror, blood or violence. As Hugo, the father, did for his son, Vítězslav would do the same for Rudolf too, although Hugo was not successful in rescuing Charles. 'God forbid, but if anything like this ever happened to you, your mother and I would rather kill ourselves than endure this injustice of man to man,' he added gravely. 'Ah, here are the cakes. Thank you. Rudlo, tuck in,' Vítězslav ordered before Rudolf had a chance to protest about his implied intention.

'I'm sure it won't come to that,' he reassured his father firmly.

'Have you brought your Zeiss Ikon, the one you got for your birthday last year? You like taking photos, don't you? There are many special illuminations for the tenth anniversary of the foundation of the Republic this evening, so we'll take some pictures. If you handle it well I'll buy you a Leica soon, I heard about a new camera that's very easy to use and takes very sharp pictures. Look at that beauty outside, there's nothing like this anywhere in the world,' and Vítězslav proudly pointed with his spoon at the floodlit Castle and Cathedral over the river and the darkening heavens above.

The next summer Vítězslav decided to organize a special trip for Rudolf and himself. As a member of the Hagibor Sports Club, he borrowed a Canadian canoe from the Czechoslovak Touring Club for a two-week trip down the Vltava river. They packed their rucksacks and camping gear, said goodbye to Berta and took a train with the canoe carried in the postal wagon. They went to Vyšší Brod in the Šumava Mountains in southern Bohemia. Rudolf was looking forward to the journey on the river and all the scouting adventures it would bring. He had read Karl May's stories about the Red Indians avidly and this was the way he would be able to emulate some of their exploits.

Even at Vyšší Brod, some distance from the Vltava's source, the water was running fast and was not regulated by weirs; the famous dangerous Čertovy proudy – Devil's Rapids – were just above the town. They launched the canoe in the calmer water below, having wheeled it from the railway station on a small trailer. Rudolf sat in the front. Vítězslav took charge, steering at the rear with the baggage stored in the middle bay. On the first day they went over

Týn Church and the Powder Tower, 28 October 1928 (Rudolf Margolius)

some foamy rapids, around big stone boulders and through an open weir sluice, getting wet from the rushing river. By the evening, when they put up their tent on the riverbank and Rudolf volunteered to cook a tin of meat and potatoes on the campfire, they were dead tired.

The mornings were glorious, with mist rising from the river and the wet grass covered in dew. Rudolf boiled water for coffee and cut thick slices of rye bread for breakfast. Soon they carried on and the only noise heard was the water being sliced by powerful paddle strokes and then dripping back from their thin edges. They saw ducks diving and rabbits running on the banks. Sitting in the low craft was being as close to nature as you could ever be, and Vítězslav and Rudolf were enchanted. At every turn of the river there was a surprise: majestic castles on the rocky hills, old stone bridges arching the water, thick forests crowding the banks, steep weirs where they had to carry the canoe to get round to the lower level and be able to continue. In some stretches the magic of the countryside required total respect and they sat without moving, carried along by the slow flow. In the evenings they swam and caught a fish or two and roasted them on sticks over a fire.

On their way down the river, they had a fright when a water mill with a dangerous inlet situated above a weir appeared after one turn. The strong stream kept pulling their canoe into the channel towards the mill wheel, which could have crushed them and their fragile craft into smithereens. Vítězslav paddled backwards furiously as they were pulled nearer and managed to bring the canoe to an overhanging tree branch. Rudolf grabbed it and they inched themselves toward the bank. They celebrated by stopping for lunch at a riverside hotel, sitting on the terrace, enjoying a glass of beer and a properly prepared meal. By the time they reached the outskirts of Prague they were weather-beaten seasoned travellers and Rudolf confessed to his father that this was the best holiday he had ever had. Vítězslav hugged him and stated that, despite their hotel stop, Rudolf's primitive, campfire-smoke-infused concoctions tasted much better than anything he had eaten before, 'even what Berta can muster, but don't tell her'.

7
●
●
Heda: Life´s Endings and Beginnings

That longing to walk on and never pause
anywhere, only at the source!
And move again as a wave of wheat
Through the landscape of soul, bewitched.

Josef Hora, *Máchovské variance/Mácha Variations*, 1945

On Sunday, 4 May 1930, Emil Diamant, Heda's seventy-year-old maternal grandfather, went to play mariáš, a popular Czech card game, with fellow firemen in the Municipal House on Republic Square. Emil Diamant was a retired general-goods store owner and a voluntary fireman station officer in Suchdol. Many a time he proudly strutted around the village sporting his smart uniform and polished helmet, twirling his large handlebar moustache. Hedvika, Marta and Karel, his children, used to sing at him in unison:

'Firemen are on the move,
Pulling water cannon along the route,
Our old man lounges about,
While his firemen sweat a great amount.'

After Emil's wife Emilie died of Spanish flu in 1921 he moved from Suchdol to live with his eldest daughter Hedvika, her husband Josef Kafka and Máňa and Míša, their children, in the Prague quarter of Karlín. He hardly ever went out about the town. However, that Sunday he decided to visit his other granddaughter, Heda, the child of his daughter Marta, who was lying in bed with a heavy temperature. He tried to cheer her up and shook hands with his grandson Jiří.

Ervín warmly greeted Emil, his father-in-law, and asked him what he planned for the rest of the day. When Emil mentioned

Municipal House

the Municipal House, Ervín told him that he despised its fastidious Art Nouveau design and hardly ever went there. However, he liked to tell a story about its architect Antonín Balšánek who, during the digging of its two-storey-deep foundations located adjacent to the late Gothic Powder Tower, one of the most important Prague buildings and national treasures, carried a Browning in his pocket to shoot himself with should the Tower collapse. Balšánek could not have lived through such a disgrace. Emil liked the tale and promised himself to pass it on to his firemen friends.

Having visited all his close relatives that day Emil rode the tram to Republic Square. He was looking forward to a good card game with his comrades and a big tankard of cool Pilsner lager. He found his friends in the basement bar huddled round a copper-top table. They made a space for him and ordered a round of lager from the barman.

Standa pulled a pack of colourful cards from his pocket. These were the Central European playing cards – zelené (greens, leaves), červené (reds, hearts), žaludy (acorns) and koule (orbs, bells) – the equivalents of spades, hearts, clubs and diamonds. Standa started with his jokes while mixing the pack trying a German accent: '*Kaiserlich und königlich* minister of transport issues a regulation – during train collisions the most vulnerable carriage is the last one and therefore we stipulate that this carriage is never connected to the rolling stock.'

Emil began chuckling.

Standa continued with another one while dealing the cards: 'A man comes to see a priest carrying a dead dog. "My dog, my best friend, a member of our family died. Can you please bury him?" he asks. "I cannot do that but there is a religious sect living at the other end of the town and they'll do it for you." "Will they do it if I offer them ten thousand crowns?" "Oh, why didn't you say that your dog was a Catholic in the first place?"' They all laughed, including Emil, drank their beer and Standa went on. 'You'll like this one, Emil. A Jewish husband and wife were having dinner at an expensive restaurant when this young woman came over to their table and gave the husband a kiss, then said she would see him later and walked away. "Who's that?" asked the wife. "Oh, she's my mistress," replied her husband. "Well, that's the last straw, I want a divorce," shouted the wife. "I can understand that," explained the husband, "but remember if we get divorced it'll mean no more shopping trips to Vienna, no more seaside holidays in Grado, no more days spent in the best hotel in Carlsbad, but the decision is yours." Then a mutual friend entered the restaurant with a young woman on his arm. "Who's that woman with Aaron?" asked the wife. "That's his mistress," said the husband. "Ours is prettier," replied the wife.' More explosions of merriment.

Cards were dealt among the four players and the atmosphere was electric. 'Leaves!' Pepík declared the colour of the trumps and unthinkingly pulled the green ace.

'What a stupid move, Pepík, a trump ace you can only kill with a fist like mine!' Emil exclaimed and swung his arm, laughing, fuelled by the beer and the jokes, and continued to laugh even while slipping from his stool under the table. At the same moment, his smile froze on his face and nothing would ever change this happy expression again. Subsequently this event became the Bloch, Margolius and Diamant families' legend of a 'joyful' carefree death that none of them, except Vilém Bloch and Alois Margolius who died in 1935, were able to aspire to at the end of their lives.

Jindřich Waldes, Ervín's employer, was a passionate art collector. He established the Waldes Museum in Prague to show his sewing products, and this also displayed some of his art collection which included paintings from all the major Czech painters but primarily František Kupka's work, the first artist to create abstract compositions. In April 1919, although they had met before, Waldes and Kupka became closely acquainted and stayed very good friends until 1938; Waldes supported Kupka financially by buying his work. Kupka lived in Puteaux near Paris. They visited each other either in Prague or when Waldes travelled to the States or within Europe to inspect his Koh-i-noor factories; he would stop for a few days with Kupka. Ervín, as business director of the company, looked after the company finances as well as Waldes's private affairs. Every time Waldes bought a painting, Ervín had to arrange for the payment which was delivered in person to the artist.

Ervín used to complain that Waldes kept spending the factory profits on his painters rather than improving conditions in his workshops and investing in the future production and welfare of his workforce, although these were already exceptional. For example, there was a suggestion box in the factory and any worker with ideas for innovation was rewarded; in one case the whole family received a free fortnight in a Paris hotel.

Through Ervín's financial dealings with Kupka, they became better acquainted with each other and the painter came to visit the Blochs several times. Ervín boasted about Heda's drawings – she always enjoyed this activity – and Kupka taught her. 'You have to move your arm from the shoulder,' he used to say, and showed her how to do it.

At one visit, Ervín passed money to Kupka from Waldes for a painting he had bought. The painter gave Ervín a volume he'd had bound to his own design, the first edition of the well-known Czech writer J. S. Machar's *Stará prósa* (Old Prose), published in

František Kupka's bookbinding design

1902 with a dedication from the writer to Kupka, for Ervín's library of first editions. By coincidence, this is the one and only book that survived from Ervín's extensive book collection, with the help of Mrs Musilová who concealed it for the duration of the war. The Gestapo confiscated the rest.

By the time Heda was seventeen her parents were sending her abroad during the high-school summer holidays. Marta loved Paris and accompanied Ervín on trips there. They spoke French as well as Czech at home and wanted Heda to improve her knowledge of the language and learn about life and culture in foreign countries.

In 1936 Heda travelled to France to stay with the French family of a Lycée professor of the language in Guethary, a small village on the Atlantic coast near Biarritz. Heda's visit lasted until 18 July when she was sent home to Prague as the French family worried about her safety; white puffs of smoke had become visible on the slopes of the Pyrenees from the seaside village. The Spanish

Civil War had started and those were cannons firing in the distance. There was great concern and commotion on the French side, although Heda was too young to appreciate the significance of this event. The liberal Red Spain, representing democratic Republican principles, tried to fight off the Black rebellion of Franco's Nationalists and conservative forces. The Soviet Union aided the Republicans and Germany supplied arms to Franco, both unscrupulously using the war to test their new tanks and aircraft. The fighting in Spain foreshadowed the Second World War and the instigation of bombing campaigns of towns and cities. The Communist International founded by Lenin in 1919, whose aim was the overthrow of the international bourgeoisie, organized volunteers from many countries, known as the International Brigades. Many prominent idealistic intellectuals and left-wing working-class men escaping the post-Depression period entered Republican service; nonetheless they lost after three years of gruesome war. There were 1,500 volunteers from Czechoslovakia, and subsequently in the 1950s the survivors suffered persecution in their own country for their brave war effort and experience of life in the West.

In 1937, another family of a French language professor accommodated Heda, together with German and Danish girls, this time in La Rochelle and she had the opportunity to explore the wild Ile de Ré, off the Poitou coast, full of abandoned gardens with trees overflowing with fruit. There was no labour available to pick it. A Persian blue-eyed kitten slept with Heda, accompanied her on her walks and to the beach and became accustomed to her. The owners thought the kitten would not survive without her and gave it to Heda to take home. The kitten enjoyed sleeping on her shoulder. She worried about taking the animal on the long journey and across the borders, and phoned Ervín and asked what to do; he did not encourage her to bring the cat but thought that she should not have any problems. Heda found a metal perforated box to make the move more comfortable.

In the train, the kitten slept happily on Heda's shoulder. When the train arrived at the German-Czech border Heda put her into the box and placed it on the luggage shelf in the compartment; the kitten seemed to be satisfied and fell asleep. Customs officers searched through the compartments checking people's baggage and Heda sat anxiously awaiting what would happen. In her compartment, an officer saw her box first and demanded to see the contents. Heda opened the box dutifully and the little kitten jumped into the officer's hands. He was so charmed by the animal that he played with her the whole time his inspection was supposed to be taking place. He heard the whistle of the impatient driver, hurriedly put the kitten back in the box and left the train. The rest of the passengers were delighted that they had been able to smuggle goods through customs without paying any duty and a procession of them came to the compartment enquiring about when the lovely young lady was going to travel again with another kitten so they could join the same train.

The next morning, after Heda's arrival in Prague, she could not find her feline friend. Eventually she opened the wardrobe and found the kitten asleep, balanced on the shoulder of her French coat. The same kitten − Heda called her Baculinka (Toddle-cat) − grew into a wonderful cat and, despite being French-born, life in Prague seemed to suit her well.

In 1939 the Blochs moved to a much smaller apartment in Pankrác, a long way from their flat in Vinohrady. Heda could not take the cat with her as there was no space, and with a heavy heart gave her to the neighbour to look after. Several days after their move, she heard a loud mewing under her window. Incredibly the cat, entirely on her own, had by instinct got half way across Prague to a place she had never been to before, just to find Heda again. It was a miracle and Heda vowed never to give up her pet again, although when the Nazi deportation orders arrived, she had no choice but to send the cat to her now widowed grandmother Kateřina in Ostředek.

Two years earlier the Blochs had upgraded their outdated accommodation in Chodská to an apartment in the Constructivist Firemen Association Building in Blanická Street, also in Vinohrady. Ervín had chosen it because he admired its strong modernistic design, but Heda was not happy with the change. Ervín tried to persuade her that it would be better there: 'When you run to your school in Slezská, as you usually do because you're always late, you won't have to slow down on the corners − from here it's straight on!'

Between the Wars 8

The breath of song in the clouds.

Hanuš Bonn, *Čekání/Waiting*

On Christmas Day in 1933, having eaten the traditional goose and dumplings for lunch and gone through the presents that the members of the family had given each other the night before, Vítězslav suggested taking Rudolf for a walk through Prague. Vítězslav was in a good mood. Although the economic situation was difficult this was the first year they had made a reasonable profit in the Klaubert agency and their lives had become more comfortable. Berta could send some money to her sister Vilemína, they could go on holidays abroad and afford to buy a car – a black, angular, air-cooled-engine Tatra 54 – which they shared with Vítězslav's brother and partner Eduard. Their country was prospering because of a stable democratic environment and the hard work, ingenuity and dedication of the people.

Vítězslav and Rudolf needed some fresh air and exercise after all that celebratory food, including the carp on Christmas Eve, and the inactivity of the festive break. Outside they saw Christmas trees in apartment windows; they did not have one but joined in the Christian celebrations otherwise. They walked up Lužická Street and Rudolf locked arms with his father to stop him slipping on the icy pavements. They took tram number 2 from Vinohrady Water Works, decided to alight at the National Theatre and walked across the Legions Bridge to the Lesser Town, looking at the Castle and the river with pieces of ice floating down.

Vítězslav told Rudolf: 'Yesterday I read something in the *Lidové noviny* and wanted to show you the most important place in Prague, in fact in the universe; probably the biggest Czech contribution to the outside world.' Having reached Vítězná Avenue at the foot of the Petřín Hill, they turned into Šeříková and entered a

Prague at Christmas (Václav Jírů)

narrow cobbled street. Rudolf noticed its name on an enamelled plaque on the corner: Říční.

There were acacia and chestnut trees along the pavements, now bare in the winter, and old houses of classical architecture lining either side. At first glance there was nothing extraordinary to make this different from the many other Prague streets in the quarter. There was even a small Gothic church of St John the Baptist 'At the Laundry', its name presumably emphasising the river location, which added yet another form to the varied city panorama. Further up stood a semi-detached three-storey apartment building with windows to the street as well as to the side and rear, and with access galleries – pavlače – in the yard.

Vítězslav continued when they reached the house number 11: 'Here a word was born which forever changed the world. It was the year 1920. The brothers Karel and Josef Čapek and Josef's wife Jarmila occupied the first floor apartment. Karel, the younger one, was a writer and journalist, Josef painted and wrote, and they worked and lived together. Josef had a good-sized study on the corner overlooking the street and the yard; Karel's was a narrow room to its side which accommodated a comfortable sofa where he did his thinking and sleeping. It looked on to the yard and the pavlače. Karel had an idea for a play about artificial people and he walked over to his brother's study where Josef furiously painted on a canvas propped on its easel, holding an extra paintbrush in his mouth. Karel told Josef that he wanted to write a play.

' "What kind?" Josef asked. Karel explained the basis of the plot.

' "Then write it," mumbled Josef indifferently and kept painting.

'Karel was looking for the right word, what should these "labourers" be called? Josef did not seem much interested but he mumbled over the brush: "Why don't you call them robots?" and carried on painting as if nothing had happened. So in this house, for the very first time, a word was mentioned which forms part of the common vocabulary of every language in the world, and it's based on the Czech word for hard work – robota.'

'How did you hear this, dad?' asked Rudolf.

'As I said,' replied Vítězslav, 'yesterday in the paper Karel Čapek admitted the truth in a letter – that it was his brother Josef who invented the word robot; many assumed it was Karel when he published his play *RUR Rossum's Universal Robots* later the same year. They all moved away and live not far from us in Vinohrady. Apparently, Čapek had the idea for the artificial beings not through the famous Prague automaton, the Golem, supposedly created by Rabbi Yehuda Löw ben Becalel at the end of the 16th century, but while riding on an overcrowded Prague tram. Suddenly it struck him how modern conditions made people uncaring about the usual comforts of life. They stood squashed in the tram, not like sheep but like machines. He started to think about people not as individuals but as machines, and during the journey he reflected on an expression which would indicate a being able to work but not think. Come on, let's get warm in the Slávia, our favourite spot, and then we should

69

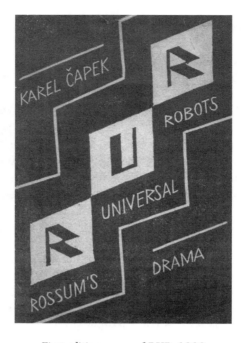

First edition cover of *RUR*, 1920

sample Berta's cakes at home, she must not be lonely on this special day!'

Rudolf had known Heda since her childhood. They lived about thirty metres apart in Prague and Rudolf's high school was in Slovenská Street, just round the corner from Chodská. On 13 June 1932, for the first time, on his return from school with his matriculation certificate, Rudolf noticed the thirteen-year-old Heda running to the shop to buy a bag of marbles. Rudolf walked toward her, looked at her in surprise and smiled. Heda ran on and glanced back. The young man stood on the corner of Lužická and Chodská and kept staring at her, transfixed. In the evening, Rudolf saw Máňa Kafková, by chance Heda's maternal cousin, who was then his girlfriend, and told her: 'Today I met such a pretty girl. I shall wait for her and marry her.'

After six months, Heda was invited by Máňa for tea. There were about ten other young people there, including Rudolf. Immediately he went over to Heda and reminded her of their first meeting. From that day they met quite often in the street while going to school or roaming round Prague in the late afternoon. Rudolf was six years older than Heda and, because she saw him often, she regarded him more as her brother than her future partner. In his spare time, he took her to lectures in the Klementinum or exhibitions in the Prague Municipal Library on Mariánské náměstí, or to skate at the stadium on the Štvanický Island in the middle of the Vltava. They sat in the Mánes Gallery Café, Rudolf's favourite place, to enjoy the river setting. In 1928 this site was cleared and a white Functionalist building housing a restaurant, café, clubroom and exhibition gallery for the artistic group Mánes was erected here. The architecture rather romantically followed the notion of the mill buildings bridging the river channel from the Rieger Embankment to the Slovanský Island. The gallery is open to the busy quayside while the restaurant is turned towards the river and the green island.

Frequently Rudolf and Heda went to the Barrandov Terraces restaurant and gardens south of the centre of Prague. This spectacular setting, named after the French geologist Joachim Barrande who explored there, is on top of the limestone rocks high above the Vltava river. If you wanted to be somebody in Prague you had to appear on the Terraces, with its backdrop of the proud, white-rendered building, and mingle with the famous who rested there while filming in the nearby Barrandov studios. In the evening, they had a meal at the medieval U Mecenáše restaurant in the arcade opposite the 18th-century Baroque St Nicholas Church in the Lesser Town. Another place that drew them was the Petřín Hill and the Nebozízek restaurant which offered stunning views of Prague. Rudolf had a friend who was an organist and who played in the Church of St. James the Elder (Sv. Jakub Starší) in Malá Štupartská Street in the Old Town. Both Heda and Rudolf came and climbed the steps up to the magnificent organ of 8,277 pipes to sit there and enjoy hearing him practising recitals; St. James boasts the best acoustics in Prague.

The powerful, heavy Čechie-Böhmerland motorcycle vibrated between his legs as Franta Frieser, Rudolf's cousin, brother of Micula, his best family friend, sped along the country road from Litoměřice to Podsedice. It was almost midnight on Sunday, 31 May 1936. The bike, manufactured by Albín Hugo Liebisch in Šluknov-Kunratice, was one of the most advanced designs with a long tubular steel frame and amazing cast light-alloy wheels. Spring was in full bloom and the night air was heavy in expectation of the new day. The ribbon of road, enhanced in the headlight, skirted the fields hugging the rolling hills, dipping and diving in exhilarating ascents and descents. On the bends, Franta's knee almost touched the road surface as he swept smoothly round, his hair flattened against his young face. The machine was getting warmer and the high hum of the 600 c.c. engine settled into a comforting rhythm. Franta was returning from the May Dance celebrations held in the Litoměřice town hall. The local girls he had danced with preoccupied his mind and the beer he had drunk did not help his concentration. Far ahead, a slow old taxicab taking four merry drinkers home was moving in the same direction. Hidden by a sharp bend, this car was approaching the brow of a hill almost stopping under the weight and because of the steep climb. Franta came round the bend from behind, far too fast to see the obstacle in front of him. It was too late to take evasive action. The motorcycle crashed into the back of the taxi and Franta catapulted over it.

In Prague on the Monday morning, Rudolf had his interim examinations for his doctorate in law. He was expected to do very well and obtain the best marks. He had swotted continuously for more than a week, closing the curtains in his room to avoid being distracted. The phone rang in the apartment and the news came through of Franta's death. Rudolf, who was just leaving, became greatly disturbed, repeatedly hitting a door-jamb with his clenched fist and scraping his knuckles until they bled. His exam result was not as expected and he failed to achieve *cum laude*. He graduated a year later on Saturday, 13 March 1937. For several months afterwards, until October, he worked as an attorney's clerk with Dr Guth in the town of Žamberk in northern Bohemia.

If Heda had any problems at home because of her poor school results, Rudolf helped to smooth the way with her parents. After a few years Rudolf left Máňa and in the meantime Heda stopped seeing her friend Pavel Tigrid. Heda passed her matriculation and Rudolf began to date her seriously. Occasionally he would throw the idea of marriage into the conversation. Heda protested that she was too young, that he was almost like a brother to her, that she had other admirers and her intended course of study – medicine – was due to start soon. The year was 1938. The uncertain political climate loomed over them. Ervín did not think that studying medicine was appropriate under the circumstances and decided that for the time being Heda should become a pharmacist. She realized the difficult situation but still resisted Rudolf's offer of marriage. Even at high school, before her exams, Heda already sensed the changed times. Her mathematics teacher, who was rather old and seemingly out of touch, asked her what she wanted to study. Heda replied that medicine was her favourite. The old woman straightened out briskly and said: 'Yes, the Jews always take the best places and nothing of consequence is left for us Czechs!' Heda was appalled and reported the incident to the headmaster who rebuked the teacher and ordered her to apologize.

Heda and Rudolf went to dance at the highly modernist Hotel Juliš on Wenceslas Square, in the ballroom located in the basement. The orchestra played the sentimental song *Sweetheart, Do You Remember the Day* ... when Rudolf stopped in the middle of the dance and said: 'Look, marriage is a serious thing and you're too young to decide such important matters so I've decided for both of us. We'll get married next year in March and I won't accept no for an answer!'

Heda burst out laughing and said 'All right, I agree!' She knew she could never find a better man and they carried on dancing, but more lightly and joyfully.

Like Ervín, who was of the Brod and Kafka generation and was a member of those writers' circle of friends, Rudolf had become a friend of the next generation of the most talented artists, particularly the Jewish poet Hanuš Bonn. Rudolf knew Bonn well as they studied law together at the Charles University. Rudolf and Heda met Bonn and other Jewish poets such as Jiří Orten (Ohrenstein) in cheap Prague cafés where they liked to congregate. Rudolf loved poetry and his poet friends tested their writings on him and Heda, anxious to hear their opinion. While they sat at a round table drinking Turkish coffee Hanuš Bonn started with his new poem 'Waiting':

And that I suppose is the time
That fragile slip astray
The breath of song in the clouds
And sailing away

And that I suppose is the earth
That heavy sigh
Ripening in pain
In tenderness of quiet death

And that I suppose is me
That source lost
That is cursed in the draught of time
From the earth it spurts with thirst
In silver voice of chime.

Orten gulped some coffee first before reciting his piece:

A train arrived and we set off on our voyage
Over many a river and bridge
Through trepidations smartly forward
Far away from a mysterious orchard,
From love, from worships
With kisses warm on our lips.

Then Bonn offered in counter-attack:

We are like a river
we always flow
on a wishful wave
that breaks in the depths
by that for ever the same

defiant unrest
of river banks we ask
where are we
where do we flow?

Rudolf clapped, excited and encouraging them: 'Well done you two! We want more, keep on writing.'

Both Bonn and Orten were tragic figures affected by the deepening political crisis in Czechoslovakia. During the Protectorate, Bonn worked at the Jewish Religious Council compiling lists of the Jewish population on the orders of the occupation forces. These lists were used to send Jews to ghettos and extermination camps. When Bonn was told the reason for the registers, he refused to carry on and was deported to Mauthausen concentration camp, located on the left bank of the Danube east of Linz, in October 1941. He died a few days later, apparently while trying to escape. Bonn was twenty-eight years old. Orten was run over by a German military ambulance car in Prague in the same year, at the age of twenty-two.

Rudolf and Heda, as well as enjoying poetry, loved going to the theatre and especially to the best-known Czech comedians Jan Werich's and Jiří Voskovec's shows at the Osvobozené divadlo – Liberated Theatre – located in the basement of the Art Nouveau U Nováků Palace Building in Vodičkova Street. Their dramas, accompanied by the newly composed music, were witty, colourful and entertaining, and laced with sharp political satire aimed mainly at Germany's expansionist plans.

Voskovec and Werich worked with the modern and theatre music composer and songwriter Jaroslav Ježek. Ježek was a genius but could hardly see, having been born with bad eyesight; after an unsuccessful operation at an early age he had lost the sight in one of his eyes and his parents had understandably refused to have the remaining one operated on, though it was also clouding with cataracts. After another illness, his hearing was affected. Additionally, unbeknown to him, he was also born with one retarded kidney and the remaining one was not functioning properly. Perhaps because of all these shortcomings his musical sense flourished to compensate, as is sometimes the case. Voskovec, Werich and Ježek

Voskovec, Werich and Ježek

composed their musical plays and their songs became classic modern pieces sung and admired throughout the Czech lands, such as 'The Dark Blue World' from 1929:

There is darkness
All round me
Darkness I cannot see
A deep darkness I cannot see.
I can only see that
I do not see anything else.
When I concede that I see
I should be able to see more.

There, where has gone my
Up to now perfect sight,

Covers it all
An intense blue light.
A dark blue light.

I alone do not know
Where to go, when and how.
And that I have on my head
A dark blue hat,
What illusion is that.

I am not in want,
So what to do,
As I like to have a bite.
So what to do,
That despite not in want,
The tummy's tight.

Five Sundays seven hours three months and a year
Melancholically I observed the sphere.
The dark blue earth sphere.

During the war, while living in exile in New York, Werich played a record of Ježek's songs on the local radio. Benny Goodman, whom Ježek respected but never met, heard the songs from the next-door studio. He poked his head in and asked, amazed, 'What is it?'

'That's one of my friend's compositions,' answered Werich.
'That's an excellent piece of music, who's your friend?'
'He died already. He was a Czech and his name was Ježek.'
'But he wrote it here, didn't he?' asked Goodman.
'No, not at all, he wrote it in Prague, before the war.'
'That's amazing,' replied the astonished Goodman.

9 An Impotent Army

There was a great nocturne
And in that darkness was a key
On whom falls the turn
Has to go off to sea

František Halas, *Mobilizace/Mobilization*, 1938

From 1 October 1937 until 25 March 1939 Rudolf was in the Czechoslovak Army's compulsory service and, by the time he was discharged, he had climbed from the rank of private to third lieutenant in reserve. He was enlisted initially in the 28th Infantry Regiment of Miroslav Tyrš and Jindřich Fügner (founders of the Czechoslovak Sokol movement) based in the Prague suburb of Vršovice, and later he was transferred to the 5th Infantry Regiment of Tomáš Garrick Masaryk. Rudolf was in the 10th Platoon of supporting weapons – heavy machine guns and mortars. The regiment had its headquarters in the barracks on Republic Square in Prague.

Sergeant Major Ervín Rouček led the platoon made up of the recruited privates; these were university graduates whose military service had been deferred due to their studies. Rouček was an ordinary professional soldier with a basic education. He was very strict, a typical bossy sergeant, who shouted and screamed orders, required utmost obedience and made the new recruits' life a misery. Rudolf's best friend Jan Hanuš, a composer, was in the 9th Platoon and both Heda and Anna, Jan's girlfriend, waited outside the barracks for their men when they had permission to leave. When they came out they were ashamed to take their caps off – their heads had been shaved.

Heda's high school organized an annual autumn ball. Rudolf invited his soldier friends and Rouček tagged along. 'Possibly from loneliness because nobody could be a friend with such a swine,' Rudolf observed. Unfortunately, Heda's charm captivated Rouček

Jan Hanuš and Rudolf Margolius at Kvíček, 1938

and he insisted on dancing with her all evening. Every time Rudolf tried to butt in and take over Rouček ordered him back to the table. Rudolf set up a plan. He and his fellow soldiers, including Jan, surrounded the dancing couple; they all stood to attention saluting and Rudolf shouted in the military voice he had learned: 'Private Margolius reporting for duty to relieve Sergeant Major Rouček of his current assignment!' Rouček froze, saluted and reluctantly let Heda go. To save his face Heda said in a high voice that she was too tired to dance any more and they all went to sit down. Every one round them laughed including Marta, Heda's mother, who was watching from the ballroom gallery.

Then they all sat at the table, got quite merry and the young privates poured out their grievances. It turned out that Rouček was nervous because of their superior background and education, and admitted that he deliberately used his military skills to get better of them. Rouček promised not to be such a 'bastard' only if Heda would come to the pictures with him. They agreed to see a new comedy film with Lída Baarová, a well-known Czech actress, in the leading role and arranged a date. Rudolf waited outside the cinema and afterwards all three went to have a drink in the nearby café. From then on Rouček mellowed and became more lenient with his soldiers.

On 23 September 1938 Czechoslovakia was mobilised and people took up arms to defend their country from threatened German aggression – against the wishes of her powerful but reluctant allies. The Sudetenland Crisis was caused by the German minority's determination to become part of the Third Reich and endangered the survival of the Czechoslovak Republic. The terms of the Locarno Treaty, signed on 16 October 1925, lent Czechoslovakia French aid and assistance if attacked by Germany. However, the contemporary French point of view was expressed by the eminent French jurist Joseph Barthelémy in an article in *Le Temps*: 'Is it necessary that three million Frenchmen, all the youth of our universities, of our schools, of our factories, of our country as a whole, should be sacrificed with the object of maintaining three million Germans under the domination of the Czechs?'

The British attitude was similar. 'How horrible, fantastic, incredible it is that we should be digging trenches and trying on gas masks here because of a quarrel in a far-away country between people of whom we know nothing ... However much we may sympathise with a small nation confronted by a big and powerful neighbour, we cannot in all circumstances undertake to involve the whole British Empire in war simply on her account. If we have to fight out it must be on larger issues than that,' was British Prime Minister Neville Chamberlain's reaction to the conflict in the heart of Europe; it was broadcast on the radio on 27 September. At the time, however, Britain was also preparing for war. The Navy was mobilised, gas masks were being issued to civilians and air-raid trenches were being dug in public parks.

In Czechoslovakia, it was a very cold autumn. Rudolf and Jan's platoons were sent to the small village of Kvíček near the town called Slaný in northwest Bohemia. The hills around Slaný were protected against any possible tank attack towards Prague from the direction of Germany with kilometres of spools of barbed wire wound around the 'Czech Hedgehogs', special tank barriers, each made out of heavy steel sections weighing 270 kg.

On Friday, 30 September at 12.30 a.m. the Munich Agreement was signed by Hitler, Mussolini, Daladier and Chamberlain without any Czechoslovak government presence. When Germany then started to occupy the Sudetenland it was considered unnecessary to keep the barriers, as the route to Prague could not be practically defended. The platoons were ordered to remove them. Both Jan and Rudolf worked for days in groups of four dismantling the reels of barbed wire and the barriers, carrying them from the fields to the nearest road, and then transporting them by lorries to the Slaný railway station. It was −20 °C and they were kept going on hot tea, bacon and bread. They considered it the heaviest work they had ever done and from a moral point saw no benefit of this to the curtailed remnant of Czechoslovakia; it made the country even more vulnerable, defenceless and open to aggression from all sides. Later they learned that the barriers were confiscated by the Wehrmacht, moved firstly to defend the German−French border and then to battlefields in France to protect German trenches and the coastline.

Vítězslav, Berta and Heda came to see Rudolf while he served at Kvíček. Vítězslav was particularly concerned about the political situation and what the fate of truncated Czechoslovakia and her people would be. They talked on the train but Berta tried to ignore Heda. She did not approve of her; in her eyes, Heda was too young and, Berta thought, much too clever for Rudolf. Heda did not allow Berta to dominate her as was Berta's custom when dealing with people around her, and she resented that. When they met Rudolf, the young people strolled ahead holding hands and Berta ambled behind with Vítězslav, continuingly pestering Rudolf and making sure that he was still in her charge. Rudolf and Heda wanted to walk off and kiss and cuddle − they didn't know if they would see each other again − but Rudolf could only squeeze Heda's hand secretly and look at her sideways, smiling.

On his return from Munich, Edouard Daladier, the French Premier, was greeted with cheers and flowers when he landed in Paris. He was astounded. 'Bloody fools,' he muttered. Chamberlain leaned out of a window at 10 Downing Street and said to the crowd below: 'I believe it is peace in our time ... Go home and sleep quietly in your beds.'

On 30 September the distressed Czechoslovak President Edvard Beneš, via his Minister of Foreign Affairs, sent telegrams to his embassies in London and Paris: 'Remind the government and their general staff that by the Munich Agreement they have forced us to surrender our border fortifications undamaged and equipped. Remind them that by their decision they have helped further to arm Hitler against themselves, for in the fortifications we are to surrender by 10 October there are two thousand million crowns' worth of cannons, machine-guns and ammunition.'

It was Beneš who instigated the construction of those fortifications, fully equipped bunkers along the Czechoslovak borders and more in another line closer to Prague. He correctly predicted the danger to the country developing from the German side and had the Czech defence line modelled on French defences.

Many Czech people, including Rudolf, were marked for life by the humiliating takeover of the Sudetenland and the subsequent occupation of their country without a single bullet being fired. Rudolf felt betrayed and greatly troubled by his inability to fight for his native land despite being a fully trained soldier of the modern and well-equipped Czechoslovak Army, and actually being in the service at the time. The whole nation wanted to defend the country by all available means. The Munich betrayal had the inevitable effect of Czechoslovak politicians turning eastwards to the Soviet Union for the future support and safeguarding of the Republic. This turnaround brought far-reaching consequences to the political structure of post-war Europe, contrary to the aim of the British and French; at the time of Munich they thought that Nazi Germany would be a deterrent to the expansion of Soviet influence.

Chances of Survival 10

●

●

Only in the fateful custom he around glances
and notices a snip of time,
which secretly turns and comes back and into grey
   colour changes.

Jiří Orten, *Hořká/Bitter*

Heda and Rudolf were engaged on 13 March, 1939. The next day, late at night, the Czechoslovak President Hácha was brutally treated by Hitler in Berlin, forcing him to agree to the German occupation. In fact, Hácha fainted and needed urgent medical attention. Bohemia and Moravia trembled with uncertainty about the future while Slovakia separated, becoming an independent Fascist state. On 15 March, five-and-a-half months after the Munich Conference, Hitler's German Army marched triumphantly into Prague while her incredulous citizens watched from the pavements, broke down and wept, waved their fists and shouted abuse at the troops. The Führer visited Prague on the same day, arriving after the curfew imposed by the occupying forces. SS units secured Hradčany Castle while Hitler observed the conquered city from its upper windows with satisfaction.

It was a disastrous occasion for the Republic, abandoned by its allies. The Czechs protested against the occupation on a number of occasions, fighting with German civilians and SS guards while German police opened fire on demonstrators. Czech universities were closed and workers and industry were mobilised to boost the Reich's war effort. Although there was no fighting on Czech territory until the end of the war, the Czechs were terrorized by the SS and the Gestapo at every opportunity. The German occupation removed the Czech rule of law and substituted a totalitarian system based on Nazi ideology. The Protectorate of Bohemia and Moravia – Protektorat Böhmen und Mähren – became a police state run by the

Wehrmacht in Prague (Kaplan Productions Archive)

SS. The Nazis planned to Germanize the racially suitable Czechs and exterminate the remainder.

Heda and Rudolf married less than a month later on 3 April 1939 in the Vinohrady synagogue. By then it was impossible for them to accomplish their intended honeymoon trip to Great Britain. While others planned their escapes from the dangerous heart of Europe, their happy marriage – where Heda and Rudolf saw only each other and were oblivious to all external events – made them prisoners within the Protectorate. When they realized their perilous situation it was too late. Heda and Rudolf applied for passports to emigrate to Palestine. They received their documents only to have them confiscated a few days later. They had missed their chance.

With the occupation came many changes. From 26 March the direction of traffic altered throughout the Protectorate from driving on the left hand side to driving on the right, based on

Adolf Hitler at Prague Castle (Kaplan Productions Archive)

the German custom. All traffic signs, street, city quarters and town names were now bilingual.

As early as 17 March 1939, only two days after the occupation, Jewish doctors were forbidden to practise; then followed lawyers and other professions, and officials in the government services. In August 1939 the Prague police posted a proclamation forbidding Jews to visit cafés, restaurants, libraries, theatres, hotels, public baths or be treated in hospitals. In January 1940 Jews were forbidden to carry on any business in the territory of the Protectorate. Jewish companies were taken over by German trustees; Jewish bank accounts were restricted and were not allowed to earn interest. A month later, all Jews were issued new identity cards marked with a large red capital 'J'. In September 1940 Jews were allowed to use only the end platform of the last wagon of a Prague tram or train, and only if it was not full. Two years later, they could not travel on

Rudolf and Heda at their wedding

public transport at all. Jewish children were banned from Czech schools and private lessons were forbidden; Jews had to report regularly to the local police stations. They could only shop or go to the banks between 3.00 and 5.00 p.m. Their membership of clubs and societies was revoked. Their telephones and wireless sets were taken away. Jews were not allowed to leave their area of residence or travel out of towns for extended periods. They were excluded from public, religious, cultural and economic life. A 'ghetto without walls' was created to intimidate and terrorize the Jewish population.

From 19 September 1941 all Jews had to wear a yellow Star of David – the Judenstern with 'Jude' written inside – on their garments when outside their place of residence. Heda and Rudolf were advised: 'You have to stitch down the corners of the star and wear it on the left side, directly on your heart, not any higher or lower.'

Soon after the Nazi occupation the Blochs, together with Heda and Rudolf, moved from Blanická Street – now Schlozerstrasse – in Vinohrady, the smart part of Prague, to an apartment building

Judenstern

with a coin-operated lift in Zlatokorunská Street – renamed Goldenkronerstrasse – in the less salubrious Prague suburb of Pankrác. They all felt severely the burden of the occupation and the restrictions made on Jews, which vastly influenced their way of life. Previously, they had been equal to their fellow citizens and now they were the second-rate, the outcasts. The degradation caused by wearing the star in public, being stared at by all the passers-by and sneered at by German patrols who harassed and interrogated them and checked their identity cards at every opportunity, was unbearable.

At the prescribed time for Jews to shop Marta went to queue to buy bread and tinned soup: Jews were only allowed a restricted choice of items. She stood at the end patiently. After a long while she moved forward. The SS guard walked past, saw her yellow star, pulled her out of the line and ordered her to stand at the end again. The Czechs in the same queue took no notice and ignored her largely out of fear for themselves; if they showed any signs of sympathy the Germans could also pick on them. Fifteen minutes later the SS came again and Marta had to move back. By the time she reached the grocery door the owner was shutting the store and she walked home empty-handed. Heda, Rudolf and the Blochs starved rather than be further humiliated.

Both Ervín and Vítězslav wondered what affect it would have had if Masaryk and the other European leaders had persevered with their aim of a strong federation framework within the old Austro-Hungarian territory. They speculated that with support and guidance of the Western Allied Powers, until the federation found the strength to cope on its own, it would have been more likely that the rise of the Third Reich would have stalled.

On 3 September 1939, two days after Hitler invaded Poland, Britain and France declared war on Germany and Europe became embroiled in the Second World War. With the help of the Soviet Union under the Nazi–Soviet pact Poland had been overrun; the SS rampaged through Polish territory implementing forced resettlements and decimating the population by murder. This tactic served as a warning to the Czechs that if they fought against the German occupation they would share Poland's fate. Within a year the Third Reich had captured most of the European Continent. Germany attacked the Soviet Union in June 1941 and the war truly became worldwide after the Japanese bombing of Pearl Harbor in December 1941. German victories encouraged the SS and the Gestapo to intimidate the population in the occupied countries, especially the 'Enemy of Humanity' – the Jews – and other 'racially inferior' minorities.

Half way through September 1941, Adolf Hitler and SS Reichsführer Heinrich Himmler met to discuss the Jewish question. On 18 September Himmler wrote to Arthur Greiser, the SS Gruppenführer of Varta district of Poland based in Poznań: 'The Führer wishes to clean and free the Reich and the Protectorate from the west to the east of all the Jews. Therefore this year I will transport them out of the Reich and the Protectorate initially to the east, to the territories that were taken over two years ago by the new Reich and from there they will be moved further east next spring.'

Himmler requested Greiser to accept 60,000 Jews into the Łódź Ghetto.

A week later Hitler assured Josef Goebbels that Berlin, Vienna and Prague would become the first cities in the new Reich to be clean of Jews. A meeting was held between SS Obergruppenführer Reichsprotektor Reinhard Heydrich, SS Gruppenführer Karl Hermann Frank, his deputy in charge of the Protectorate, and others on 17 October 1941 at 4 p.m. in Prague. It was about future plans within the Protectorate, and the notes of the meeting confirmed the intended action:

> 'At first 5,000 Jews will be evacuated from Prague to Litzmannstadt, this will be announced briefly in the press expressing the efficiency of the Reich's plans ... Further evacuation point will be Theresienstadt in which 50,000 Jews will be temporarily housed and then they will be moved further east. After the evacuation of Jews from Theresienstadt, the town will be repopulated by Germans and made into a German Life Centre ... As regards these plans none of them must ever enter the public domain, even the tiniest details. All present at this session are emphatically informed about the strict confidentiality of this discussion.'

The infamous Wannsee Conference on the Final Solution to which Heydrich sent invitations on 29 November 1941 was postponed, due to the Pearl Harbor attack, from the original date of 9 December to 20 January 1942, although the wheels of destruction had been put in motion months before.

Heydrich, the hated head of the Protectorate, had ostentatious plans for Prague, which he wanted to transform into one of the leading cities of the Third Reich, the gateway to an SS-controlled empire in the east. He decided to change the city into a centre of German art and culture and planned to rebuild Prague using Berlin as the model, linking the former Czech capital to the rest of Germany with autobahns. When he arrived in Prague he went to a concert of German music in the Rudolfinum Hall standing on the right-hand riverbank, which was renamed the German House of Culture – Das Deutsche Kulturhaus. This neo-Renaissance building was designed as a concert hall and gallery. On leaving, he noticed that on the roof were sculptures of famous musicians, painters and sculptors. Among them stood a statue of Felix Mendelssohn-Bartholody. The composer came from a Jewish family though he had converted to the Christian faith, and Heydrich ordered the statue to be removed.

The Czechs had a difficult time during the German occupation and especially after Heydrich's assassination by the British-trained Czech and Slovak agents Jan Kubiš and Jozef Gabčík in May 1942. Following this there were constant threats of random searches, arrests and brutal revenge killings, with even the entire massacre and deportation of the population of the villages Lidice and Ležáky taking place.

The Brada family lived in the town of Seč on the river Chrudimka where Rudolf Brada, as an engineer, worked on the construction of a dam. Brada, a former officer in the Czechoslovak Army, together with his friend Rudolf Syrovátka, was a member of the Czech underground resistance movement whose units hid in the hills above the town. One day a Wehrmacht tank platoon entered the town and all the women and children were ordered to line up along the road while the tanks rolled through. The soldiers demanded information on the partisans and their hideouts. The five-year-old Eva Bradová stood with her mother at the edge of the pavement but none of the women offered to betray their men. A soldier grabbed a girl standing next to Eva, a neighbour she used to play with, and threw her under the passing tank. To this day Eva remembers the sound of the girl's skull being crushed by the heavy metal tracks.

From October 1941 until April 1945 in the Protectorate of Bohemia and Moravia planned deportations of Czech Jews were organised to the Łódź (Litzmannstadt) and Terezín (Theresienstadt) ghettos, or directly to the extermination camps sited in the occupied Russian, Polish and Baltic States territories. In the Protectorate the Jewish population numbered 88,000 people; out of this total 48,000 Jews lived in Prague. After the war and over 130 transports, 10,000 returned. From the five deportations to Łódź of 5,002 people, only 276 came back.

In commemoration of the Czech Jewish victims, 77,297 names are on the walls of the Pinkas Synagogue in Prague. From 1954, every morning for the next five years, two academic painters, Jiří John and Václav Boštík, drew twenty lines of names on the white-washed walls of the synagogue. In the afternoon they went back to work on their own canvases.

Many radical Czech and Jewish intellectuals, artists and writers perceived the mortal danger of the German occupation and tried to flee abroad to save themselves and their families from the Nazi atrocities. The decision to leave and its timing became a matter of life or death.

On Tuesday evening, 14 March 1939, Max Brod and his wife arrived at the Wilson Railway Station in Prague and boarded a waiting express train to Stockholm. Ervín Bloch came to the station with Heda to say goodbye to his friend. Brod's other acquaintances were there to wave him off. Most of them were planning to leave in the coming weeks, urged on by their German friends, who with hindsight must have known about the upcoming tragedy.

On the same train that the Brods boarded were 160 Jewish families with their children. The train left after unexplained delays at eleven o'clock at night. After five hours, the express stopped in Ostrava on the Czech–Polish border and German soldiers with swastika armbands were already standing in the station. The passengers, observing the soldiers, did not realise the seriousness of the situation. Czech customs officers moved through the compartments and within minutes the express carried on; an hour later it was in Cracow. That same morning Bohemia and Moravia was occupied. Max Brod later remembered how close his escape was. What struck him especially was the unmoving figure of the German soldier on guard standing to attention at Ostrava Railway Station. He looked like a sculpture of a Roman legionnaire, young, energetic, athletic, with a handsome face and body. This sight had not produced any fear or foreboding in Brod; beauty in any form greatly charmed him and several times similar feelings led him astray, nearly to his ruin. That very same morning the Gestapo broke into the editorial offices of *Selbstwehr* magazine in Prague where Brod worked and demanded: 'Where's Max Brod?'

'He left last night.'

'So he ran off, too!'

The occupation was a surprise to most of the Czech population as Hitler kept on screaming that he would not have a single Czech in the Reich. It should have been suspicious to the observant that no custom houses or sentry offices were ever built on the German side of the post-Munich borders despite them being erected on the Czech side.

On 15 March 1939, in the morning, Pavel Tigrid and Josef Schwartz, very good friends of Heda and Rudolf, listened to their wireless; they lived together in one apartment then, and heard the news of Hitler's annexation of Bohemia and Moravia. In the mid-1930s they had got together performing in the amateur Young Theatre Collective which used a stage and auditorium in the basement of the new Self-Employed Clerical Workers Association building on Na Zbořenci in Prague, near Charles Square. There they produced literature evenings as well as drama in front of 300-strong audiences. Tigrid also brought Heda and she helped in designing and painting of theatrical scenery.

Tigrid and Schwartz rushed to the Clerical Workers House and started burning all the important paperwork. Two Gestapo men arrived and detained them until the evening. Then both were fearful about returning home; they were Jewish and had radical political views, making them an obvious target for the occupation forces. There and then, they decided to emigrate. Tigrid found out that they needed a number of travel documents including an exit permit. They went to the Wehrmacht office, already set up in Prague, where a German officer requested their birth certificates. Tigrid, who was baptised, could carry on into the next room to receive his permit. Schwartz stood in front of the army officer who looked at him and asked: 'A Jew?' Schwartz shrugged his shoulders, and got '*Heraus!*' as a reply. He was staggering around to get out of the office when he heard the officer say to someone on the phone that he was on his way. Respectfully Schwartz let him out first and then turned and entered the next office instead of following. There he asked the others waiting to let him go first as he was in a hurry to catch a train. The other official issued the permit, being under the impression that Schwartz was properly cleared. Surprisingly there were no problems with the issue of a passport or the leave permit from the Czechoslovak Army. Luckily, the British did not require visas to enter the United Kingdom until the end of March. Tigrid and Schwartz had the mad idea of emigrating with a motorcycle and bought a Jawa 175 with borrowed money.

In Germany they slept in a Leipzig hotel with a warning sign: *Nur für Arier!* In Oldenzaal in the Netherlands, they were shown in front of the British immigration officer who demanded affidavits that they would be financially secure in their new country. Tigrid had a paper saying that his 'firm' had put up financial security for him at an Amsterdam bank; he could carry on. However, Schwartz just had a letter specifying a business trip as the purpose of his visit to the UK. He decided to tell the truth, that he was Jewish and a politically involved student, and that if he were sent back that would be the end of him. The immigration officer exclaimed 'Why didn't you say so straight away? You are a political refugee! Welcome to the United Kingdom,' and rubber-stamped his passport. Schwartz sailed on a ferry from the Hook of Holland, while Tigrid, on the Jawa, went to Amsterdam to collect his money. Two days later, still before visas were officially required, they met in London. The motorcycle had been useful after all.

Dr Rudolf Štursa, nephew of the well-known Czech sculptor Jan Štursa, drove with his friend František Mautner, a Jew, to Dobříš Castle outside Prague, built after the manner of Versailles and laid in an English park, for a day's outing exactly a year before the occupation, on 15 March 1938. Both Štursa and Mautner were Rudolf's friends. On the car radio they heard how the Austrian border customhouses had been turned into youth hostels and the Viennese were welcoming Hitler after the Anschluss. 'This country is being transformed into the newest bastion of the German nation. I know the old east march of the German people will fulfil its new task,' Hitler shouted from the loudspeaker. Mautner asked Štursa what he would do in his place if a similar political situation were to develop involving Czechoslovakia. As Mautner spoke good English Štursa advised him to get a visa from the British Embassy to any of their overseas colonies and, just in case, to be baptised. Štursa remembered his good friend Jan Vochoč, a member of the Old Catholic Church, and promised to arrange a visit.

Vochoč welcomed them to his apartment and was pleased that his faith would have a new member. Vochoč wanted Mautner to read the New Testament and come back in a week's time but Štursa said that Mautner had to leave the next day. Vochoč put on his priest's robe, took a small bottle of holy water from the pocket and read out the baptism ceremony. Vochoč asked Štursa to read from the Testament. He sprinkled Mautner from the bottle three times but at the last sprinkling the bottle fell out of his hand into his fish tank and he had to push his sleeve up to retrieve it.

This mishap did not make him nervous and he shook Mautner's hand, accepting him into his Church. Afterwards Vochoč filled in the baptism certificate in gothic handwriting and wished Mautner all the best for the future. Having obtained his visa Mautner travelled out of Czechoslovakia to New Zealand, the last one to make this journey perfectly legally on proper documentation.

Later Vochoč baptised other Jews in a similar ceremony. Then some wanted the certificate but did not want to go through with the baptism. Štursa recalled an acquaintance of his, a printer called Eduard Fleissig who had a shop in Palackého Street, now Gürtlergasse. He asked him to print a thousand certificates, copies of Vochoč's original. At the J. B. Pichl rubber stamp shop in Celetná (Zeltnergasse) Štursa had a stamp made to use at the bottom of the certificate. Viktor Mautner supplied a pile of old invoices with duty stamps that were attached to the old-fashioned birth certificates, and Štursa carefully steamed these off to use them again on his own certificates. Štursa gave any Jews who came to him a choice: whoever wanted to be properly baptised would get the original certificate from Vochoč, and those who did not want to go through with it for religious reasons would get Štursa's falsified one. After that, the Jews went to the foreign embassies to obtain their exit visas. It was much easier and quicker to obtain one with a baptism certificate as Jews were excluded from many countries by immigration policies. After having more printed, Štursa issued over 1,500 certificates. Oskar Schindler from Svitavy was not the only saviour of Jews on Czech territory; Štursa survived the war, living in Prague till the 1990s.

Mautner was a Communist sympathiser and his 'red' enthusiasm possibly originated from his revolt against his materialistic parents; his father Viktor had a very successful umbrella factory and shop on Peterské Square (Petersplatz) in Prague. For his journey to New Zealand Mautner took with him a gramophone record of the Communist 'Internationale' disguised with a camouflaging label of the very popular song 'Le plus beau tango du monde'. If the customs officer had decided to play it on the gramophone, then instead of Henri Alibert and René Sarvil's lyrics describing the experience of the most beautiful tango in the world, he would have fallen off his chair with:

Servile masses, arise! Arise!
And spurn the dust to win the prize.
So comrades, come rally.
And the last fight let us face.
The Internationale
Unites the human race ...

In New Zealand Mautner entered the army and changed his name to Kennedy. This was done under army orders: if by any chance he was captured, a soldier with a Jewish name had an additional liability. After the war he returned to Prague covered in medals and used to brag about his career, pointing at his glittering chest: 'This one I got for being scared in Africa, this one for shitting myself in Italy and this one for running off in Germany.'

His Communist sympathies left him and he used to argue with Rudolf while they laundered my nappies, trying to persuade him to emigrate to beautiful but boring New Zealand. 'If there were a larger Czech group it would be more fun,' he begged.

Rudolf, on the contrary, became a stubborn idealist, decided his mission was to save humankind from evil, and was not interested. Regretfully it was too late when he realized that his political idealism had blinkered his vision of a world that could not be overturned from iniquity into a utopian society without getting hands dirty in the process. Not then and not even now, sixty years later.

During the Munich Crisis and the threat of war in Europe, Jindřich Waldes – who was Jewish and very wealthy – sent his family to the USA for safety but he, being patriotic, decided to stay in Prague and run the business. In September 1940 Waldes was arrested by the Gestapo and placed in Pankrác Prison. Ervín found a woman who had an apartment overlooking the prison yard and asked her to keep a lookout and report any news of Waldes to him.

On 22 October 1940 Waldes was taken to Jena concentration camp and then to Buchenwald. In the meantime, in the difficult circumstances of the Protectorate, Ervín was negotiating an appropriate sum of money in surety for Waldes so that he could be set free. The Germans wanted the vast sum of 8 million crowns. In the end Ervín got the money together, with the help of the Waldes family and from all the other branches of the company, and delivered it to the German authorities. Waldes was taken onto a ship bound for New York but became ill under suspicious circumstances and died when the ship reached Havana.

Both Ervín and Rudolf were similar in nature, behaviour and interests. They believed that their life was mapped out for them, that they were allocated a task and there was no reason to fight that what was given – exactly as Gustav Janouch interpreted Kafka's words: 'One cannot escape oneself. That is fate. The only possibility is to look on and forget that a game is being played with us.' If they were needed to remain in Bohemia and if it was necessary for the good and comfort of others, then so be it.

Ervín decided to stay on behalf of his family, despite hearing of the open oppression of the Jews in Germany and occupied Austria, his employer's, Jindřich Waldes's, offer to manage the 'Waldes y Cia' branch in Barcelona, and his sisters and friends urging him to leave. Ervín, even while listening to Hitler's provocative speeches on the radio, used to say: 'I won't run away and be afraid of an insignificant Obergefreiter, of a midget in a dirty raincoat.' He always stood to attention when the Czechoslovak anthem was played; he was a patriot and supporter of his country. Ervín's mother, Kateřina, who was eighty and lived in Ostředek, would not travel and from Ervín's point of view could not be left behind. Rudolf, who was to finish military service on 25 March 1939 when the Czechoslovak Army was in the process of being disbanded, was not free to flee, either, before the Germans marched into Czechoslovakia.

For a year from April 1939 Rudolf worked at Waldes in the sales department on Ervín's recommendation. Heda began training in a pharmacy in Pankrác to learn the trade. As soon as she arrived, her new employer disappeared into the basement store, presumably injecting himself with drugs, while leaving the inexperienced Heda in charge, unable to improve her knowledge. She could only give aspirin to people who came asking for medicine, as she did not know any better. One persistent customer came every day complaining: 'My mother is still unable to get up and do anything useful. She lies helpless in bed, moaning all day. Please give me something that would really cure her!'

However, both she and Rudolf were soon dismissed; as Jews, they were not allowed to work professionally. In June 1940 they decided, while they were not yet forbidden, to travel away from Prague. Being out of the capital meant that they were less likely to be intimidated by the occupation forces or picked up by the Gestapo; living in the country was less dangerous.

They went by train to spend some time in the village of Nová Huť pod Nižborem near Beroun, about thirty kilometres to the west of Prague. This village lies on the river Berounka with the 13th-century Nižbor Castle and the high Hradiště Hill dominating the local landscape. Rudolf found some work as a farmhand with the farmer Kadlec in nearby Stradonice on the opposite bank of the river. They stayed in Heda's parents' three-storey country house built in 1924 for themselves and the Kafka family but now empty.

Heda kept herself occupied by inventing dust jacket and binding designs using a pile of books stored in the loft as examples; she found a set of watercolour paints and discarded, yellowing drawing paper. Unfortunately she sat on her glasses and broke the frame; Rudolf had to repair them using a bit of wire. They were crooked and he laughed, seeing Heda perching them on her nose. In the evenings they stayed in and Rudolf played Beethoven and Brahms pieces on an upright piano.

A friendly white and tabby kitten fell in love with Rudolf. Suddenly he was struck with bad flu, with an inflamed throat and a high temperature. Heda did not know what to do, she was too young and inexperienced; nor were they allowed to see a local doctor, who would not dare to come and care for Jewish patients. Heda locked the kitten out of the house for 'hygienic' reasons and tortured Rudolf with cold compresses. Rudolf became fed up; the compresses were awkward and did not 'work': 'You know what, give me the kitten and I'll put him round my neck and that will be a better medicine!' Heda opened the door; the kitten, pleased, jumped on the bed and curled on Rudolf's throat like an experienced medic. The kitten kept him warm and its purring sent Rudolf to sleep. This treatment lasted two days and he felt much better on the third.

They lived in Huť until 8 September. On the previous day, the Luftwaffe carried an all-night bombing raid on London and the Blitz began. They heard this triumphant German news on the radio and decided to return to Prague.

From the autumn of 1940 until June 1941 Rudolf attended a course in optics and precision tool mechanics organized by the Prague Jewish Religious Council – Jüdische Kultusgemeinde Prag based in Maiselova Street – now Philip de Montegasse. Afterwards he was employed in the optical factory Laopta in Libeň as a skilled labourer until October 1941. That was all he was allowed to do under the repressive political regime despite being a qualified lawyer.

Transport to Łódź 11

We took down mournful masks from the days
within them palms of hands burned by the message
  of fire
lying in the wake and the line of life
with a freezing finger was covered up by death.

František Halas, *Panychida*, 1938

The Blochs received a letter from the Central Office of Jewish Emigration – Zentralstelle für jüdische Auswanderung – in Dělostřelecká Street, renamed Schillstrasse, in the suburb of Střešovice (Streschowitz) to attend an interview and discuss the state of their properties, possessions and belongings. Ervín went to the Office but was not allowed to tread on the carpet stretched along the halls and corridors and had to walk along the narrow strip left between the carpet and the wall. The interview room looked like a bank; there were glass security screens with opening slots above a counter and German clerks sitting behind them.

Ervín was asked: 'Have you got the list of your possessions we requested? Are you certain everything you have is listed here to the smallest item, every piece of jewellery, gold, diamonds, pearls, pictures, books, furs, carpets, money, bonds, foreign currency, shares, coffee, cocoa, tea? Nothing must be concealed or withheld. We need to have knowledge of all you have.'

Ervín sighed and passed the list through the slot, thinking it was good that they had friends, the Musils, in their building who had promised to look after some of the Persian carpets and pictures, claiming them as theirs.

The German looked up from the long list with less suspicious eyes. 'Good, it looks like you're not a stupid Jew like some who pretend they've nothing and lie to us. But don't worry, we'll come and check.'

'Do as you please,' Ervín commented. 'What's on the list is all we have.' However, Marta had sewn 500 marks into the lining of both his and Rudolf's coats; they had to have something to survive.

New letters arrived. They heard the ominous thud of paper on to the doormat in the hall and looked at each other before Ervín decided to investigate. All four of them were required to report to the wooden barracks on the Prague Trade Fair Palace – Prager Mustermessepalast – grounds in Bělského Avenue (Belskystrasse) with a single suitcase each, weighing not more than 50 kg, on 19 October 1941 by 4 p.m. Should they fail to turn up they would be charged with committing sabotage against the German Reich.

On Friday, 18 October Rudolf's parents, Vítězslav and Berta, came to visit them. Rudolf, Heda and Heda's parents were to be transported to live and work in Litzmannstadt. Where was this town? They had never heard of it. Jiří Toman, Rudolf's former schoolfriend, who assured both Heda and Rudolf that he would do anything to protect and look after them if they ever needed it, discovered this through his business dealings with the Germans. It sounded quite elegant and superior, and possibly located in Germany rather than somewhere in Eastern Europe. They believed this was good luck, especially when they found that in the same transport – selected on the orders of the Protectorate authorities by the Prague Jewish Religious Council – were many university graduates, writers, musicians and successful businessmen. Ervín, as factory director, kept going to Waldes right up to the last moment of their time in Prague, handing over production to the new German management.

The worried-looking Vítězslav and Berta came for chicory coffee and to say their goodbyes. In the hall on the hooks hung six coats, each with a yellow star on the left-hand side.

Vítězslav told a story about how three years ago he had overheard Margit Klaubert begging her father to get her a radio when he had visited his German supplier Alexander Klaubert, who was the director of the J. C. Klaubert factory. This had been in November 1938. When he got back to Prague Vítězslav went to see his friend Hugo Roubitschek who had a shop called Neuradio

Vítězslav Margolius, Prague 1941

in Spálená Street, renamed Brenntegasse during the Protectorate. 'This is an English catalogue of the latest Philips models; the portable battery type in blue leatherette will be the best for a youngster as it can be carried around the house or used outside in the garden,' Roubitschek had recommended. Vítězslav paid for the radio and made sure Roubitschek delivered it to Margit for Christmas. Vítězslav was bewildered: 'We always got on with the Germans in business and in leisure. They respected us, you did a favour for them and they returned it in kind. There was never any trouble. It was Konrad Henlein's Sudetendeutsche Partei push for self-determination, his aggressive leadership of the Sudeten Germans, his insistence on the incorporation of Sudetenland into the Third Reich, and his links with Hitler that created the bad blood between the Czechs and the minority. Now the Czechs and especially us, the Czech Jews, are on the other side of the fence and in the gutter.'

They talked together in subdued voices, not daring to look into each others' eyes and discuss the future. They all knew the worst was coming, fearing the true purpose of the transports, but did not want to show their worries openly. It was almost like a comedy, they kept assuring themselves that they were going toward a new life, that everything would turn out well and that they would all meet again soon. 'They'll probably try to kill us all, but no need to get too anxious,' Vítězslav tried to joke, badly.

Marta was upset about her son Jiří, who was staying for long-term treatment far away in a sanatorium in Kelč near Hranice in Moravia. They could not travel to see him for almost a year – under the Protectorate rules for Jews they had not been allowed to leave Prague since 1 November 1940. Marta mentioned that she had received a letter from the head gardener at the sanatorium. He wrote that Jiří helped in the sanatorium gardens in the afternoons and continuously sang arias from operas while working; Puccini's *Tosca* was his favourite.

After his parents went home to Masná Street (Fleichschmarktgasse), Rudolf left the living room and ran into the privacy of the bedroom. After a while Heda found him there, staring out of the window on to the bleak green plain outside with tears in his eyes. 'I know I'll never see them again,' he said.

The following day they handed over the keys to their apartment. With a suitcase each and their transport numbers (B 624 and 625 for Ervín and Marta, B 820 and 821 for Rudolf and Heda – B being the designation for the particular transport), elegantly dressed, full of expectations but forebodings, they all went to the Trade Fair Palace assembly grounds barracks at Letná (Sommerberg). Both Ervín and Rudolf had put hammers in their cases, thinking they might be taken to a labour camp after all.

Věra Musilová, daughter of Kristina and František Musil, the acting concierge for the Zlatokorunská apartment building, accompanied them all to the tram stop at Na Veselí. There the travellers boarded the last carriage of the number 18 tram. Věra hugged Ervín and Marta and thanked them for all the books they had lent to her, especially the *Filosofská historie* by Alois Jirásek, about the 1848 Czech uprising against the Austrians in Bohemia –

her first proper reading book. She also mentioned the German lessons and the lovely cakes, chocolate eggs and pocket money given as presents. Věra said goodbye to them as if they had been her own grandparents ... After the war and the complete destruction of the older generation of my family, the Musils became my surrogate grandparents: the roles switched.

In the barracks, the thousand who came were registered. Their identity cards were stamped with 'Evakuiert 21.10.1941'. They were counted, put into groups and allocated a small area of floor to sleep on. This took almost two days, in growing pandemonium. They also had to file past the SS Obersturmführer Richard Fiedler, the officer in charge of the transports, who confiscated any luxury goods or musical instruments carried.

They observed a Gestapo officer shouting the name 'Pollak!' A distinguished man stood up to attention, citing his full name in return.

'Your visa for Singapore has arrived,' screamed the officer.

Dr Pollak extended his hand for the piece of paper. The Gestapo officer smiled, tore the paper into small bits, dropped them to the floor and ground them with the heel of his polished boot, then turned and marched out of the building.

Then early in the morning, at 5.30 so as not to arouse attention, all one thousand of them were marched in columns along the streets of Prague, accompanied by thirty Czech police officers, to the nearby Holešovice-Bubny (Bahnhof Bubny) railway station. There they were squeezed onto a passenger train with boarded-up windows, destined to arrive not in Germany but in the Łódź Ghetto in Poland, eighty miles south-west of Warsaw. This was Litzmannstadt; the Germans had renamed the town after their General Karl Litzmann who led a battle against the Russians there during the First World War.

They left Prague at 1 p.m. on Monday, 21 October 1941 in the second transport. The train went on a strange route, via Dresden, Görlitz, Liegnitz and Breslau, and arrived in the Marysin Station, Łódź the next day at 3.30 p.m. It took half an hour to disembark, to the loud screaming of '*Alle Juden raus*'. The journey

Holešovice-Bubny Railway Station (Kaplan Productions Archive)

lasted over twenty-six hours and only once was a small amount of water distributed.

A few days earlier a scene had occurred that could only happen in Prague, the city of contrasts and unpredictable events. When the first transport, A, left the Holešovice-Bubny Station on 16 October, the famous German circus Krone, which was leaving after visiting Prague, was being loaded onto another train at the same station. Theirs was an express train, fully equipped with all modern conveniences for both the circus artists and their animals. Utmost care was taken during the loading to make sure their journey would be the most comfortable possible, while on the adjacent platform deportees were being roughly herded on to a boarded-up passenger train. So at the same time two trains left Holešovice-Bubny Station: the special circus train heading back to Munich, and a packed, sealed train with 1,000 Prague Jews going to the Łódź Ghetto in occupied Poland.

Jiří Bloch was transported from Kelč to the Theresienstadt Ghetto in June 1942 and from there to the extermination camp of Malý Trostinec near Minsk in Belorussia. Kateřina Blochová, Ervín's mother, a frail old woman who would not harm a fly, was deported from Ostředek to the Theresienstadt Ghetto in September 1942 and a month later to the Treblinka extermination camp fifty miles north-east of Warsaw.

Vítězslav and Berta were taken from Prague in December 1941 to the Theresienstadt Ghetto (their transport numbers were M 375 and 376 – transport M) and a month later, in the cruellest of winters, they were transported, half dead with no food or water, in a sealed freight train to Riga in Latvia – at least a three-day journey. On arrival at Riga railway station they were put onto trucks and driven eight kilometres to an execution site in the Rumbuli Forest. Teetering on the edge of freshly excavated trenches, they were shot in the back of their heads.

Why transport them all the way to Riga to a fate worse than that of animals? In those early days of the war the Nazis did not want to create any suspicion in people left behind, or in observers from abroad, so they chose to display their actions, the elimination of the Jewish population, away from the areas the people had originally come from. The true Nazi atrocities were only discovered after the war and to this day many still refuse to believe them.

When the Blochs, Heda and Rudolf arrived at Łódź, they were sent to temporary reception accommodation in a school building. There were many people allocated to each room, rooms which were full of bunk beds and had no space to walk about in. Two people slept in one bunk on their sides, each curled up in a position like a baby in its mother's womb but without its warmth and comfort. There was no room to stretch at all and once awake it took ages for the resulting cramp to pass. Later Rudolf and Heda found a small ledge under the roof and managed to sit up and sleep like that, making their overnight rest tolerable. After a week they all had to find their own accommodation. They discovered a half-demolished apartment house in Lagiewnicka Street with cracked walls but with a basement cellar and one empty room in which they lived for the next three years. Marta and Ervín hid in the cellar several times to escape deportation when people were rounded up in unannounced searches.

In Łódź Rudolf worked in supplies transport, building demolition and guarded firewood supplies at night; he also worked as a fireman, on station patrol and in agriculture on the Ghetto fields. Heda toiled in a factory making mats so that Wehrmacht tank crews could keep their feet warm while fighting the enemy. From old rags, clothes and other cloths and fabric – some covered in blood and sweat stains as they were collected from prisoners and deportees on arrival – thin strips were torn and woven on the frames into mats. Marta was supposed to work in the same factory but had no strength to go there. Heda brought her the cloths and Marta tore them into strips for Heda to take to work the next day. Everyone had to work in Łódź and this had to be indicated on the individuals' identity cards. Without proof of work there was the constant danger of instant deportation. Searches were made through the Łódź Ghetto buildings and the elderly or ill were randomly selected, so Heda knew she had to make Marta's work official. One day while at work, she noticed an empty manager's office; he was showing visitors round the factory. Heda climbed in through the window, found the

factory's rubber stamp and impressed it onto Marta's identity card.
Now Marta was properly employed.

Ervín was ploughing the fields outside the Ghetto,
walking all day behind the thin horse. Heda went to see him once
bringing him a small piece of bread. 'The heart feels so painful now
spring is here,' he observed to her.

After a month, Heda came running to Rudolf's guard
shed, crying and waving a piece of paper. Ervín had received his
deportation order. Rudolf tried to calm her down. Suddenly Chaim
Rumkowski, the feared and all-powerful Jewish leader of the Ghetto,
walked in. He was inspecting the state of the food depot, and roughly
asked Heda what she was doing there. Heda tearfully explained.
Without a further word, Rumkowski took the paper, wrote across it
'Zwolnic', and signed it. Ervín was saved for several more days.

The Ghetto was grey, black and brown. Hardly any other
colour. Render was peeling off the building walls, exposing the bare
brickwork and concrete hidden beneath; the walls were cracked from
the roofs down to the cellars. The sky was always a dirty yellow,
complementing the hues of the Ghetto, and rarely blue; that colour
that was lost to them and faded from their memories. The open
ground between the buildings was covered with patches of burnt-
sienna-coloured grass. Was there another colour in the world? If
you live in this environment continuously for three years you
become conditioned to it, even though you try to resist it with your
mind.

In the distance the sound of a heavy truck powered by
diesel engines promised a flash of the khaki colour of an army
vehicle. It thundered along the Łódź streets disregarding the traffic
rules. What was its cargo this time? It was usually overloaded with
emaciated corpses. When it came under Heda's dirty broken window
she saw it was full, full to the brim with cut red carnations. Red
carnations in Łódź! For whom were these intended? The whole
truck ... As it passed along her block Heda heard the sound of
someone playing the Brahms Violin Concerto from the floor above
where a Jewish woman lived; by some miracle she had been allowed
to keep her instrument. Heda felt that the music rather than the
truck engine was accompanying the flowers on their journey to

their unknown destination. They were dying of hunger, were dirty, weak and ill. They saw only misery and strife around them. It was a shock to find that there was still any beauty left in the world.

The wooden Hohensteiner Bridge, rising like a hump from street level over a tramline and dropping down on the other side, connected the two halves of the Ghetto which the tramline divided. The tram was a link with the living city outside the Ghetto boundaries and the bridge had to be crossed to get to work in the Ghetto factories. Despite their constant weakness and hunger, people liked to walk over the bridge and watch the trams and observe the well-dressed, well-fed passengers, but they were not allowed to stop and stare. They shuffled slowly and painfully across in their dirty, torn clothing with rags round their swollen legs and infected feet.

Life, friendship and death occurred here, in this appalling place, as anywhere – but more poignantly. A Polish woman was in love with one of the Ghetto inhabitants, a Polish Jew. To see him she used to ride on the open platform of the tram. He would try to be on the bridge at the same time, just so that their eyes could make contact for a few seconds. It became a weekly routine. There was no

Hohensteiner Bridge in Łódź (USHMM)

food, the man was getting weaker and his health was deteriorating, yet he hauled himself to the bridge every week and each time she noticed his thinner body, his pale face and his dark eyes. The man became very ill; there was no health care or medicine available and he passed away. A friend of his walked up to the bridge, going slowly to reach the top. The woman, standing on the platform, was leaning out to see her man as soon as she could and keep eye contact with him for as long as possible. That day the friend on the top of the bridge opened his coat and waved a black rag. She froze – it took a second for her to understand – then screamed and lost her balance. The tram continued, slowed down by the body that was being dragged between its wheels.

However, there were some good moments even if they did not last long. One day Rudolf barely noticed a faint knock on the door, yet he almost shouted to encourage his visitor to enter. He heard the door open creakily on its only hinge and then the crashing down of bony knees on the grimy floor of their Łódź hovel. In front of Rudolf knelt an old woman, her head covered in a stained scarf, her whole weak body shaking with emotion. Rudolf, startled and confused by this unusual situation, begged her to get up immediately. The old woman kept whispering continuously, as if praying, and avoiding his questioning glance. 'Why are you here?' he asked, bidding her to get up again.

'Don't you remember?' she replied.

'No.' He was puzzled.

'Here, in Łódź, the railway station, the train, and the last wagon ...' she recounted. 'You were supposed to stand and watch over us and you were behind the SS guard, then you crept inside and opened the wagon door at the back and told us to run off across the fields. The guards were shouting orders, counting new arrivals and had no time to look behind them. My brother and I got back safely to our room in Łódź. I wanted to thank you and this is the first chance I had.'

'Come on, please, get up.'

She raised herself reluctantly and perched gingerly on the edge of a nearby chair. He did not say anything. He took her by the elbow and led her silently out of the building. Outside was a normal overcast day but there was something in the air, making one breathe freely and easily. 'Look at that old doorway across the street,' he bid her. 'Look at that tree with bare branches, look at that little boy sliding on the frozen puddle, look at that dark cloud slowly approaching from the horizon.' Every time he squeezed her elbow.

'Thank you,' she whispered again and Rudolf pushed her gently into the street and returned to his dark room inside. Later Rudolf found out that both the old woman and her brother were deported from Łódź once more and lost their lives in Auschwitz.

In the summer of 1944, after three years of empty and miserable lives in Łódź, all the Ghetto inhabitants were herded to the Łódź assembly grounds and ordered to stand to attention and listen to a group of meticulously groomed German Army officers. Their leader addressed them.

'*Ich gebe euch mein Ehrenwort eines deutschen Offiziers* ... I give you the word of a German Army officer that nothing bad will come to you. Eventually all of you will be moved out of the Ghetto to another place to work and live.'

Ervín, having served in the well-regimented Austro-Hungarian Army and remembering past times, was suddenly happier. He believed German officers when they made promises such as these. 'We'll be all right,' he told the others quietly. However, times had changed from the First World War, when peoples and soldiers of all religions and nationalities were still held in respect.

A Stumble out of Auschwitz-Birkenau

Death soon will kick open my door
and enter.
With startled terror I'll catch my breath
and forget to breathe again.

Jaroslav Seifert, *Autobiografie/Autobiography*, 1979 (translated by Ewald Osers)

The Nazi concentration camps were purposefully placed in the most inhospitable parts of Germany and the occupied territories – the marshy and cold Dachau; the windy and cool Sachsenhausen; the heavy-clay-based and misty Neuengamme; the stony Mauthausen beaten by icy winds; the rainy, often shrouded in fog, north-facing hilly position of Buchenwald; and the boggy, flat, exposed, sandy and hot Auschwitz and Birkenau. As there was no local drinking water, diseases and infection were naturally present.

The inmates lived like animals. Many camp huts were originally built as farm buildings, and the Nazis admitted that they were not even suitable for housing cows. More care was taken to house the savage guard dogs. On orders from Berlin, dog kennels were erected in Birkenau for 250 animals; they included all modern facilities, a specially equipped kitchen, medical room and large lawns outside for exercise. These cost 81,000DM.

The accommodation for humans was arranged in predominantly wooden barracks without windows; fresh air was brought in through the roof vents. The three-level bunks were only suitable for lying down; the lowest was just above the floor. Each prisoner had 0.8 square metres to live in: to eat, sleep and store his possessions, and there were 400 to 500 people living in each barrack. There were no toilets or washrooms in the hut, just two open barrels, which often overflowed with waste. The washroom was in a separate building with lines of open concrete holes and wooden troughs for washing. However, there was no soap, no towels or toilet paper. Initially there was a single tap for drinking water in the whole camp, and water was so precious that it was sold for bread. Prisoners used their battered metal food bowls for eating, drinking, washing and relieving themselves – another reason why there were many diseases.

Rudolf, Heda, Ervín, and Marta were put on a freight train from the Łódź Ghetto to Auschwitz-Birkenau on Monday, 14 August 1944, in one of the last transports, and arrived the next day. All the 70,000 remaining residents of the Łódź Ghetto were moved out in this way.

The wheels screeched on the rails as the freight train entered the concentration camp. The sealed wagons were unbearably crowded, but the journey from Łódź to Auschwitz was comparatively short. The doors slid open and, amid loud shouting, everyone was ordered to form into lines on the ramp. Camp guards organized the crowds. Almost unconsciously, they were sorted into columns, one on the left and one on the right. Initially there was considerable confusion before the guards brought some order to the bewildered group of travellers.

Men and women were separated. Heda and Rudolf, who had been holding hands, were torn apart and lost track of each other in the confusion almost immediately. Ervín disappeared in a crowd of older men destined for the showers and the gas chambers. Heda slipped a tube of strong sleeping tablets that she had carried with her all the way from Prague into Marta's pocket. Heda took her hand and was marched with the rest toward the podium where Dr Josef Mengele stood. A guard grabbed Heda by her shoulders and threw her on the ground. When she got up she saw her mother a long way ahead, being taken away with the older women and extending her hands toward her daughter.

Later, as Heda sat dumbfounded on her bunk in the barrack she saw a dandelion seed slowly floating in the air toward her. She raised her hand and it settled very gently on her palm. 'That was Marta, my mother, saying goodbye,' she thought.

The conditions in the camp were intolerable and incomprehensible to anyone with a normal mind. What followed does not need to be described in any detail.

The one thing I have left of Ervín's is a small diamond ring he received from the Waldes company after twenty-five years of loyal service in 1933 and an envelope sent to him from the 1928 Graf Zeppelin airship crossing to the United States – my grandmother Marta, unusually, was a zealous stamp collector. In 1945, Heda walked through her native street in Prague again and met two former students whom Marta supported. On discovering Marta's fate they burst into tears in the middle of Chodská. Without Marta they would not have completed their studies.

In the latter part of 1944, there was a great shortage of people to form the workforce of the Reich. Hitler had called up all remaining German males for army service due to the fighting on all fronts which had resulted in the Wehrmacht becoming increasingly

Ervín and Marta Bloch

stretched. The concentration camp guards who were not recalled to the various fronts were unable to cope with the ever-increasing influx of transports. These were frantically continued by the Reich, which was bent on completing the annihilation of Jewry in occupied lands. The Nazis, who were collecting all the deportees from other ghettos and labour camps, could not manage to send them all to the gas chambers – where they were originally intended to end – on their arrival. There was no work for the new prisoners in Auschwitz-Birkenau. One proof of that was that neither Heda nor Rudolf had a prisoner number tattooed on their arms; they were not intended to 'stay on'. Prisoners stood or knelt at the frequent, two- or three-hour-long roll calls on the sandy soil of the appelplatz while the kapos smacked their whips over them. It was unbearably hot; there was no water, and only once a day a small tin pot of thin soup was passed around for five people to share. Heda and Rudolf were in Auschwitz for about a fortnight, and each was unaware of the other's fate.

There was overcrowding as more and more people were brought in. Conditions had to be improved and some inmates were moved out again as otherwise chaos would have ensued. If a train arrived bringing new 'cargo', then that same train was used to take younger people out to the labour camps in the west. If Heda prayed for a miracle, she would be on a train to Gross Rosen. It could be Dachau for Rudolf, if he was very lucky. There was now no room in the gas chambers for young men and women. Mothers, children, older people, the infirm were of no use for the Reich; they were still being gassed on arrival at Auschwitz and burned. The crematoria chimneys smoked continuously, day and night.

Heda remembered sneaking outside on one quiet night when the other prisoners were already in their bunks. She did not care if she was shot, and got outside the barrack into a beautiful night. The sky was as full of stars as if she had been in the mountains and the electric wires stretched around the camp were singing. The wind was blowing, and she could hear the wires vibrating. Heda lay there thinking: 'God, the world is so beautiful with all those stars and music and here I am, lying in the dirt like a worm.'

The Red Army neared the former Czechoslovak borders in the east and the Allies were getting ready to enter German territories after the Second Front opened with the landings in Normandy in June 1944. The Nazis were under pressure to act. The guards began preparing the young male and female prisoners for transport out of Auschwitz-Birkenau and into labour camps where the German war-support industries were located. Their kapos warned them that the next day they would be moved out and that if it did not work out they would then go to the gas. The prisoners always walked within the camp in groups of five, because that was the way they were counted: if one of them went missing the other four were sent straight to the gas chambers. Suddenly Heda noticed that she was standing in a group of six women in the formation ready to march off to the train. She stared incomprehensibly around, not understanding what had happened. Then another woman pushed her from behind; unconsciously Heda stumbled several rows forward and by a miracle joined a line of four women. The freight wagons filled up with women. At Heda's line of five the loading stopped as the last wagon was full. She was destined to stay in Auschwitz.

There was a hoarse shout from the train: '*Senden Sie noch eine!*' as one of the women fainted and they threw her out onto the tracks. Now Heda was standing at the end of the line of five, by the German guard who directed the embarkation. He screamed in her ear '*Schnell!*' adding, in an almost-friendly whisper, '*Leben Sie wohl,*' and pushed her roughly forward to join the train as a replacement. Had Heda turned back she would have seen the remaining group being moved by the guards' rifle butts towards the 'showers'.

This way the young women were transported in sealed trains further west to the Christianstadt camp at Gross Rosen in Poland, where they arrived in September 1944.

There Heda was allocated to the underground munitions factory outside the camp. She worked at a carousel table, filling cartridge cases with a highly volatile mixture consisting of three different explosives. Many times, while she was not supervised, she deliberately mixed the wrong proportions on purpose and, in this small way, sabotaged the war effort. Later she was requisitioned, with other camp inmates, to work in the brickworks and on a farm.

A young German farmer, who could not have been more than twenty-five, befriended her – not to exploit her in any way but out of admiration for all her suffering. There was no implied threat, no malice in his actions; he did not seek any favours from her. He gave her a knife. Owning it was forbidden, punishable by death. However, the knife was extremely valuable in the camp as food could be divided properly and equally; otherwise the small piece of bread which had to be shared among five of them would crumble into dust. The knife, which she kept hidden in the wall of the barrack behind a loose board, could be also used for repairs and defence. That is why the other women called the farmer Kudla (colloquially 'knife' in Czech); even Heda did not know his real name. He could not risk telling her. Had Heda been tortured, his actions would have been discovered by the SS. Sometimes he spread a white napkin on the table, put an apple on it and watched Heda eat it. He enjoyed watching her and it gave him pleasure that he could help in these little ways.

One day there was shouting outside the barracks: 'Heda, Heda, Kudla is looking for you!' Heda ran out and saw Kudla riding a green-painted open cart pulled by a small pony which was circling round the camp exercise yard. In the wagon was a large sack of potatoes which shook violently as the cartwheels rode over the rough ground of the camp. How Kudla had got inside the camp with the cart was a mystery as normally he was only allowed to be at the farm were the inmates worked. As soon as he saw Heda, he swerved the pony and cart towards her, dropped the sack at her feet and rode out of the camp. The women grabbed the torn sack and its spilled contents, and rushed into the barrack before the guards noticed anything unusual. This food was an unbelievable deliverance for their starving bodies and many shared in this unexpected gift. In fact, this bonus saved their lives. Within days the camp was liquidated and the young women, in the cold month of February, were sent on a death march to Bergen-Belsen, the guards pushing them away from the nearing eastern front and the advancing Red Army.

Return to Prague   13

How the street changes without walkers
and through windows stars fly into mirrors
when rocked into sleep the tenants
enter novels resting shut on the night tables.

Vítězslav Nezval, *Pražský chodec/Prague Walker*, 1948

The Riederloh concentration camp was located near the town of
Kaufbeuern in Germany. Rudolf was moved there from Auschwitz-
Birkenau in September, at the same time as Heda left for
Christianstadt. Rudolf and his fellow inmates were cutting down
trees and clearing the local forest for new roads, digging trenches
and building underground factories. It was terribly hard work for
such weakened people, both physically and mentally. Rudolf kept
describing the beautiful local countryside, high mountains and
forests. He said how painful it was to see all the beauty round him
and at the same time be conscious of their awful misery, loneliness
and humiliation. This was a very common reaction; every time
a prisoner was reminded about the passive, indifferent beauty of
nature he acknowledged his own humility and loneliness, comparing
it to his own miserable condition in such a callous world.

At the beginning of January 1945, Rudolf was transported
to the Dachau camp, where there were 67,600 prisoners, which
included 22,000 Jews. After a fortnight's stay in Blocks 21 and 19
he was moved to the Mühldorf camp, arriving with typhoid fever
caught during the then-current Dachau epidemic. He worked for a
week in the building of secret underground hangars, then was sent
back to Dachau where he was kept in the invalid block and in the
infirmary ward. He had a fever as high as 40 °C and felt very weak,
with stomach pains and a headache. He also developed a rash of flat,
rose-coloured spots. He was seriously ill, but with his language skills
he befriended a French doctor who helped him to recover, and he

returned to Block 24. Every day he was then marched to repair the railway line near Munich which had been damaged by Allied bombing. Afterwards he worked at the stores and in the garden of the Todt Organization in Dachau. He wondered many times why the Allies never bombed the concentration camps or the railway tracks leading to them. Obviously, some of the inmates would die but the great majority would be able to escape and save themselves, and the transports would be suspended.

On 23 April 1945 Rapportführer Ruppert and Vernehmungsführer Bach reduced the bread ration in Dachau from an eighth to a tenth size per person. At one o'clock, an order was given for all Jews to report to the appelplatz and stand to attention. The ill and weak lay on the ground. The cold and windy night came and they had to remain standing. Many more collapsed. Several other transports arrived from other camps and joined the vigil. In the morning, there were sixty dead. Most of the sick were lugged to the forty railway freight wagons standing outside the main gate. After loading, the train was sealed but there was no locomotive to take the wagons away. Unsupplied with water or bread, the wagons remained unopened until the Americans arrived five days later and were confronted with a ghastly spectacle.

On 26 April 1945, when the fronts of the American and Russian offensives had become very close, Rudolf was selected into the first march out of the Dachau camp and taken in the direction of the Austrian border. During the first night, he escaped into the forests with other prisoners. Had he stayed with the march of about 6,700 Russian, German and Jewish prisoners he would have been shot by machine guns aimed at the column on the road toward Tegern Lake. This order was carried out on Himmler's instructions.

After several days of hiding and moving north, Rudolf encountered American troops from General George S. Patton's Third Army on 1 May 1945. The Americans were on the offensive against a small group of elderly German troops still defending the forests on the German–Austrian border. Rudolf lay at the bottom of a grenade crater with another prisoner, Václav Vacek, also from Prague. Bullets hissed above their heads as they crouched, defenceless, in the muddy puddle. It felt like an eternity. The end of the war was right there and yet it seemed distant at that precise moment. They waited patiently, counting the minutes, and soon heard running boots pounding the earth between the grenade craters. The American soldiers were coming. Not minding the continuous firing, Rudolf and Václav – in their dirty striped prisoner's garb and shortly cropped hair – came out of their hiding place with their hands up, flagging down the Americans. Hugging them and unable to contain their joy, Rudolf began explaining where they came from and describing their escape from Dachau.

They camped with the soldiers near the Bavarian–Austrian border and later were taken to the temporary survivors' collection camp at Garmisch-Partenkirchen. Over 1,000 people were gathered there. From the first day, Rudolf acted as an interpreter and the Americans appointed him the leader of the camp. He remained there until all the Czech prisoners went back: the first half at the end of May, the second – which included Rudolf – arriving in Prague on 8 June 1945.

Rudolf had found out that a member of his family had survived the war from a broadcast on Czechoslovak Radio which had mentioned his name, but the message had remained unfinished as it was interrupted half way through by a local power cut. When his special train arrived in Prague, all his fellow passengers made bets that it would be Heda and waited inside until Rudolf phoned the radio station to find out. 'Was it Heda?' they asked.

'Yes,' he replied, elated, and everyone got off to find their own loved ones.

Heda's salvation at the end of the war was as miraculous as Rudolf's.

On 22 February, while the detainees were pulled back westwards, Heda escaped from the death march leading from the Christianstadt concentration camp in Poland to the Bergen-Belsen camp in Germany.

They were nearing the Czech border and Heda saw a sign reading 'Nach Prag' by the roadside junction, pointing south. This was the place to get away. Her hair was short and her coat had a square of striped cloth set into the back to identify her as a prisoner. She had to get rid of it. She also had to find some shoes as she was walking in the snow with her feet wrapped in cloth. Luckily, their German guards were old men as all the younger ones had been called up to the shrinking fronts. The old men did not care much about their charges and went to rest and sleep after herding them into barns which they requisitioned for the night along the way. On the previous evening a young Frenchman, Lucian, had found a needle and thread for Heda. She removed the striped square and with Kudla's knife cut the fabric from the back of lapels and returns to fill the hole until finally her coat looked almost normal from a distance. Then she was given a pair of leather shoes with soles wired to the uppers that would be strong enough for her journey.

Early in the morning, when it was still dark, she got up with three other young women, opened the barn door – she had previously loosened the hasp with her knife – and scrambled over the surrounding fence before the guards heard the commotion and started shooting, stopping several more who tried to do the same. Now it was important to get to Prague without being caught and find a hideout. The women walked mostly at night, helped by kind strangers. A brave young girl led them through her village and the surrounding countryside and showed them the way. Finally, an elderly Czech man with a horse and cart took them to Prague.

They reached freedom after three and a half years of detention. They arrived a week after an American bombing raid on 14 February 1945, when over sixty flying fortresses of the 8th US Air Force dropped 152 tons of bombs on many populated parts of Prague – probably by mistake, some reports giving the explanation that the bombers mistook Prague for Dresden. About a hundred houses and historical sites were destroyed. All the casualties were civilians, and not one of the city's factories which could have been of use to the Wehrmacht was damaged. The five-minute raid left the city bewildered by the sudden senseless destruction.

Heda's companions were in luck and were hidden by friends at their first attempt although Heda was not so fortunate. She arrived hungry, exhausted and hardly recognisable, and without any documents. The Gestapo frequently patrolled the streets. Under cover of darkness, cautiously walking through the city, she approached all the friends of her family one by one to ask for refuge for a few days to gather her strength and recover. Sheltering escaped prisoners from the concentration camps was punishable with immediate execution of the whole family by the occupying German authorities.

Rudolf's best friend was Jiří Toman. They were at high school together, joined the Czech section of YMCA in 1929 and went everywhere on holidays, travelled in European countries and the USA. You could not ask for a better friend. He would jump into a fire for you. But how times and situations change people . . .

Heda was aware of the danger she presented to the people she contacted and tried to visit only her closest friends, avoiding families with children. She had no luck as everyone was too frightened to take her. For one night, the Musils had her in and then Ervín's former secretary Mrs Osvaldová accommodated her. Next, Heda came to Jiří Toman's door. He poked his head through the gap and was terrified when he saw her. Even though he was single, a major in the Czechoslovak Army and highly trained to cope with emergencies, and in spite of his pre-war promises, he was too scared to offer any help. After interrogating her about life during her captivity, he pushed her back onto the street. Heda had to carry on, finding another way and eventually locating an empty apartment in Heřmanova Street (Hermanngasse) at Letná that belonged to Rudolf Brada who used the space to hide people on the run. A domestic help of the Bradas, Helena, came to check over it, which she did every six months or so. By an amazing coincidence she was there on that very same night; Heda reached the apartment and surprised Helena, who was on the way out but let her in. Heda stayed inside for several days and was then moved to Rudolf Syrovátka's more secure apartment in Dr Albín Bráf Street (Albin Brafstrasse) in Dejvice. Heda stayed there until the beginning of May. She had to spend days sitting in the bath so that no sound of movement could be heard and her presence be detected by the nosy neighbours who were bound to report anything unusual. After the war, the inquisitive concierge was annoyed when he found out that she had lived there without him knowing. Heda fed on large quantities of dried peas which were full of worms. She carefully removed each worm before soaking and eating the peas but was later told that she had missed out on her diet, as the worms were a good source of protein. During her stay, Syrovátka brought in a badly wounded Russian partisan and Heda looked after him. The Gestapo agents followed Syrovátka to the apartment during one of his visits and interrogated him while Heda hid in the bathroom.

Then when the Prague uprising started, on 5 May, Heda went out to help on the barricades. Elderly men and women were still erecting the first one she came to. Busily they tore out granite cobbles from the surface of the road and piled them high to block access through the street. The only young man there was lying wounded and shielded himself behind the rising barricade with a captured Panzerschreck resting next to him. He was pointing at the weapon and gesticulating to Heda to take it and stand in the nearby doorway. Armoured cars belonging to the defiant SS were rumbling down the street. She took it and ran up to the house without getting

Prague barricade, May 1945 (Kaplan Productions Archive)

further instructions and fired the Panzerschreck, the tube resting on her shoulder, in the direction of the cars. She stood with a wall behind her and was blown off her feet by the Panzerschreck as she fired; the rocket went the correct way but over the target. Despite that, the convoy turned away. After recovering from the shock Heda decided she was not up to real fighting and explored further down towards the city centre to join the Red Cross. Wearing the armband of a nurse she tended the wounded and took weapons hidden in baskets under piles of medicines through the enemy-occupied streets.

The cornered and desperate members of the SS set fire to apartment buildings and drove the Czechs in front of their tanks. Small children were dragged out of air-raid shelters, bayoneted, their heads cut off and eyes gouged out; pregnant women had their bodies ripped open. Almost 1,700 Czechs lost their lives in the Prague uprising.

However, in the last days of the war after Hitler's suicide, the Wehrmacht high command wanted to avoid placing themselves in difficulties. The German army saw Prague as a vital communication centre, forming an evacuation route westwards for German civilians and their remaining units fleeing from the advancing Red Army of Field Marshall Koniev coming from Dresden. The American Third Army waited in Pilsen, fifty kilometres west of Prague, on Eisenhower's orders. The Soviets preferred this arrangement, claiming that they wanted to prevent any confusion of armed forces in the area. Stalin always planned ahead for the post-war era and never wanted to leave Prague to the Americans. Though there was no opposition anywhere, General Patton was furious that he was not allowed to proceed and liberate Prague. Eisenhower had told the Soviets that Prague was in their zone and that the Americans would halt on a pre-arranged line southwest of Berlin.

In Kralovice, a small town north of Pilsen, a US military reconnaissance jeep came into the town square on 6 May 1945. The American major and his driver stopped and local people gathered round the car, welcoming them. Suddenly the field phone rang and the major answered. He put the phone down in a hurry and ordered the jeep to turn round immediately and return to the Pilsen demarcation line. However, the Americans secretly sent a couple of jeeps to drive to Prague and secure the US Embassy before the Soviets entered the city early in the morning of 9 May. Should the US Army have continued on its course it would have reached Prague two days earlier than the Red Army, many more lives would have been saved and Central Europe would have come under the wing of Western democracy. Patton vigorously disagreed with Truman and Eisenhower's policy, but he was helpless. He maintained that 'we have had a victory over the Germans and disarmed them, but we have failed in the liberation of Europe; we have lost the war!' Following the end of the war the main political influence was not the Yalta Agreement but the final victorious position and presence of the Red Army. After Vienna, Prague was the first capital of Europe to be captured and the last to be liberated.

On Rudolf's return, Heda did not mention the full truth about Jiří's behaviour to him. She said that he had tried to help but could not because he had visitors that day. Rudolf stayed with Jiří at his apartment in Blanická after returning in June 1945 before they found – with Heda – a small apartment in Přemyslovská Street in Vinohrady. Jiří apologised to him, begging on his knees, confessing

A Russian tank in Prague, 9 May 1945 (Kaplan Productions Archive)

that he had been a coward right through the war and had hardly ever left his rooms. Later Rudolf used to meet him but the atmosphere was strained between them, and it was even more so when Heda was also there. In 1947 they all went to a cinema to see an English film, Carol Reed's *Odd Man Out* with James Mason and Robert Newton, a dramatisation of a book of the same name by F. L. Green. The story is set in Belfast and is about a wounded Irishman, a member of the IRA, on the run. After a bungled robbery at a factory mill, the British police pursued him. Wherever he turned, he was refused shelter and was thrown back on the street. Sitting next to Rudolf, Heda felt him stiffen during every minute of the story. The theme of the film, so evocative of Heda's situation when she had walked half-dead round Prague without help, made Rudolf realize the coincidental parallel. Without looking at Jiří he grabbed Heda's hand and pulled her out of the cinema even as the last scene of the film – the shooting of the hero Johnny and his lover Kathleen – was illuminating the silver screen.

They never saw Jiří after that evening.

In June 1945, Rudolf tried to find work and heard that the Czechoslovak Military Police was looking for people with a good knowledge of foreign languages. He spoke fluent English, French, German, Polish and some Russian and Spanish. On 13 June 1945 he joined the unit, and stayed until 30 November. The main purpose of his work was to look for important people who might have survived the war but who were so far unaccounted for. The first major task he was given was to trace the artist and writer Josef Čapek, brother of Karel. Immediately Rudolf remembered the Christmas walk through Prague with his father in 1933 and was pleased to be connected with the Čapeks directly. Going back to Germany and being reminded of his own experiences of suffering was not very appealing but it was a job, and he wanted to help Jarmila Čapková, Josef's wife.

Karel Čapek died in Prague on 25 December 1938, another Christmas Day, when the Sudetenland part of Bohemia was already occupied. Both brothers were on the Gestapo list, two of the first people they planned to arrest for their openly anti-Nazi attitude.

Josef travelled to the village of Želiv to spend the summer in the country, which was by then under the rule of the Third Reich. On 1 September 1939 the German police arrested him there. Jarmila had packed some clothes into a sports bag for him while he changed and washed. Then he was taken to the Pankrác Prison in Prague and from there to Dachau, Buchenwald and Sachsenhausen concentration camps and at the end to Bergen-Belsen where he was seen almost until the last day of the war.

Jarmila had heard from several witnesses – fellow camp detainees – that he had died but wanted to know for sure and asked Antonín Sameš, head of the Military Police, for help. Sameš offered his own car, together with his private supply of petrol and his driver, and cleared all the formalities for them to reach Bergen-Belsen. On 23 June they set out with Jarmila and drove via Pilsen. While stopping there Rudolf talked to camp returnees who assured him that Čapek was still alive. Full of hope, they continued to Cheb, across the border and through the Anglo-American zone to Braunschweig, a devastated town where they spent the night in the camp detainees' collection centre. The next day they carried on to Celle and Bergen-Belsen. They interviewed those survivors still there but they failed to recognize Čapek from photographs shown to them. By mid-July, as they had found no positive news of Čapek, they returned to Prague. Much later, it was established that Čapek had died in the typhoid epidemic that raged through the Bergen-Belsen camp in the last weeks of April 1945. Rudolf made a similar second journey to try to find the son and brother of the Czech General Liška in south-east Germany and south-west Poland.

From Idealism into Self-Destruction

14

●

●

> People with ideals should not be given an opportunity to influence affairs of this world.

Karel Čapek, *RUR Rossum's Universal Robots*, 1920

The Czech writer, Arnošt Lustig, wrote recently about the post-war period:

> 'We all believed – wanted to believe, forced ourselves to believe
> – that now there would be an age of justice, that all evil would
> be punished, the righteousness would be rewarded. The world
> would be how it should be, without wars and injustice, blood,
> defeats, humiliation. We saw another map of the world than
> the one that existed. What it could be, what we wished it to
> be and what it could have been at least in part already. The
> illusion appeared as the truth. We helped as much as we
> could. This vision could have been compared to a beautiful
> woman, to a sweet temptation, to a deserved satisfaction.'

Another well-respected Czech writer and journalist, Ota Pavel, in his beautiful story *A Race through Prague* about his father, Leo Popper, that was originally written in 1971, circulated in samizdat copies and published in Czechoslovakia after the Velvet Revolution, began:

> 'After the war when the Communists became one of the
> leading political Parties my father immediately applied for
> membership. He took my mother and my brothers along with
> him. I was the only one too young for such matters. He joined
> that Party enchanted, as were many others, by the Red Army.
> In this case, the moment of enchantment had taken place on

127

the box-seat of a horse-drawn wagon driven by a long-haired Russian soldier, who was giving him a ride to Buštěhrad. Father also believed that here at last were just and decent people who would not divide mankind up into white and black, Jews and non-Jews. At least that is what they all promised in their books and speeches, all the way back to Lenin.'

Rudolf had the same attitude as Lustig, Popper and many others. He was proud to believe in Communism, to serve the cause of humanity, to be present at the beginning of a better future. To establish a classless society after the horrors of the Second World War; at last the world seemed to be taking on a semblance of order. What a beautiful order it promised to be. The ruins left by the war had already disappeared; the process of rebuilding the nation was well under way. To Rudolf, the Party was a vital and consuming part of his life. He was happy and secure, proud that the Party – and through it, the nation – could use his talents. During the war, the most powerful, unyielding underground opposition to Hitler had come from the left. Socialism offered the alternative to an unjust society, to anti-Semitism, poverty, oppression, and with its peaceful policies it claimed to eradicate wars and conflicts.

Rudolf did not waver when Pavel Tigrid came to see him soon after his return from Garmisch-Partenkirchen and attempted to discourage him from his support for the Party. There had always been tension between the two men because of Heda, whom Tigrid also admired. Tigrid's exile in the West during the war gave him a good political perspective but he had escaped actual suffering and therefore had a very different view to that of Rudolf. Tigrid did not understand that Rudolf's witnessing the dreadfulness of the concentration camps and Nazi atrocities had reinforced his support for the Communists. He tried to dissuade him, but Rudolf was determined, even after they heard a woman calling for help outside the apartment and saw that a Soviet soldier was abusing her. Tigrid tried to use the event to illustrate what the Soviets were really like and gave Rudolf Arthur Koestler's *Darkness at Noon* to read. However, they vehemently disagreed and Tigrid left, never to see Rudolf again.

In November 1945, Rudolf met Otto Klička, a former fellow student from the high school and a member of the Communist Party, who persuaded him that the Federation of Czechoslovak Industry located at 14 Na Příkopě Street was looking for able people with language skills to help to reconstruct the country's post-war economy. Rudolf resigned from the Military Police and joined the Federation. He decided that his task in life was to help to rebuild the country. He believed that this was a better opportunity for him, and was his destiny. His attitude was reinforced by the sense of guilt he felt in surviving the concentration camps rather than his parents, relatives or friends. He owed them; they died in his place. It left him with an undertaking to accomplish what they themselves were not able to achieve on their behalf. For their sake, he had to fulfil their hopes, hopes that had been cut short, and create a new world in which no similar circumstances could ever occur again. He was one of the lost generation who miraculously survived. He wanted to sacrifice what was left of his life for the children of the future in the memory of his murdered parents.

At that time, Communism, with its classless, unselfish attitudes encompassing all religions and races without exceptions and prejudice, was the one political system that seemed to be able to assure this outcome. Rudolf believed that Communism had matured from the pre-war time of terror during the late 1930s, although he had heard that almost eight million people had been arrested by the secret police in the Soviet Union by then. That was a necessary stage in the political development of any radical system in order to achieve perfection and that bloody era was left behind, never to be repeated. Rudolf denounced all personal property and urged Heda to sell anything she had inherited from her parents. He wanted nothing for himself. He brought friends to their apartment where they discussed the political and economic issues of the post-war situation in Czechoslovakia late into the night. Rudolf, who before the war was not politically involved or interested, was especially impressed by the Communists and their courage during the war and what they did in the camps, resisting and fighting the enemy. Their underground was well organized and their aims seemed to be honest and well intentioned. He even joined an illegal

Communist cell while in Dachau in order to help fellow inmates survive.

Heda and Rudolf went to visit Rudolf's distant relatives, Hedvika and Vlastimil Borek, well-educated intellectuals, who spent the war years in Moscow. Borek, a friend of Gottwald who made propaganda broadcasts on Moscow radio, was Deputy Minister of Foreign Affairs. They said they were greatly impressed with life in the Soviet Union. They described the self-sacrifice, idealism, the patriotism and feeling of brotherhood of the Russians, their endurance and determination to succeed in the war against Nazism. They praised the equality of various nationalities and races, their fortitude and willingness to work hard for little reward, their friendly acceptance of foreign refugees. What impressed them most was the solicitude of the Soviet Communist Party and the Soviet government. It almost appeared as though the Boreks recruited them into the Party.

Heda and Rudolf were encouraged. In late November, Rudolf brought home the Communist Party applications and they were accepted into the Party in December 1945. Ten years later

Czechoslovak Communist Party badge

Hedvika Borková confessed to Heda that while in the Soviet Union they had suffered hard times, people had been afraid to talk to them, they had experienced collaboration, food shortages, black marketeering and anti-Semitism: the complete opposite to what they had described earlier. They had not told them the truth then out of fear.

Rudolf worked as Trade Secretary at the Federation until 31 March 1949. While there he travelled to Poland for trade negotiations in 1947 and the following year, at the request of the Ministry of Foreign Trade, he flew to Moscow with the Minister of Foreign Trade, Antonín Gregor. Further trade business took him to France and Belgium. From 1 April 1949, he was employed as the Chief of the Minister's Cabinet and was promoted to Deputy Minister of Foreign Trade in August 1949. At the Ministry Rudolf originated the so-called Dollar Offensive and other programmes that were to establish and improve the hard currency reserves of the Czechoslovak economy. At that time of the Cold War, any contact or negotiation with Western nationals had to be reported in writing to the Ministry's Section for Political Affairs and the same information was also passed on to State Security.

Ironically the Ministry of Foreign Trade had offices at 20 Politických vězňů Street in the New Town. It is a dark, forbidding, roughly stone-clad building with a very distressing history. Before the war it had been the head office of the Petschek & Co. Bank; during the Protectorate it was requisitioned by the Gestapo as their Prague headquarters and colloquially called Pečkárna after its previous owner. He was a Jewish financier and coalmine owner who fled the country after Munich and emigrated to Britain. The Gestapo used it for offices and interrogations, and in the basement were holding rooms and torture cells.

The Ministry of Foreign Trade consisted of the Presidium and seven sectors: planning, trade-political, import-export with capitalist countries, trade with the people's democratic countries, trade with the Soviet Union, administration, and the control and financial sector. Rudolf, as the Deputy Minister, headed the sector for trade with capitalist countries.

Rudolf went to a picture auction on the advice of Dr Rudolf Škeřík who had a vast art collection in his apartment at Na Perštýně; no empty wall space could be found there, pictures were jammed in frame to frame. Rudolf wanted to buy Heda something appropriate by a Czech artist for the new apartment in Přemyslovská. All their possessions were lost, as were their parents', apart from several precious pieces saved by the Musils when the Nazis requisitioned them. They had to start from scratch to furnish their new accommodation and make it look like their new home. Rudolf, wanting a small figurine, had already contacted the sculptor Jan Štursa's nephew, Dr Rudolf Štursa, in order to buy a plaster cast of a *Melancholic Girl* (1906). This represented the pinnacle of Štursa's work in exploring a permanent poetic embodiment of youth, and reminded them of their pre-war courting.

What struck Rudolf at the auction preview was a seascape from the coast of France, a view of the sea with a warehouse and the French flag in the foreground, by Kamil Lhoták. He loved the sea; he remembered his journeys by ship, from Hamburg to New York on the *SS George Washington*; from Varna to Haifa and to Naples on the *Bourgas*; his wanderings around the Mediterranean to Nice, Marseilles and Mallorca's rugged coast, which he admired when hitchhiking through Europe as a student in the 1930s. Lhoták's painting symbolized the great expanse of water changing colour with the sky and its pretended innocence which could suddenly transform into a treacherous killer as quickly as human nature. The Czechs, being a nation without access to the sea, are fascinated by it once they have a chance to discover it for themselves.

Lhoták's picture was most suitable and Rudolf knew Heda would also approve. It is one of the few things including the Štursa sculpture, a small ebony figurine of a Negro bought in Paris, Jan Slavíček's sepia watercolour view of Venice and Jan Zrzavý's primitive but beautiful lithograph of his typical rounded boats on the sea, that survive from Rudolf's collection. Recently in Prague I found the same Cubist glass that Zrzavý used in his picture and that brought me closer to the past.

Towards the end of March 1946 Heda persuaded Rudolf to drive north to the Krkonoše Mountains for a long skiing weekend. They loaded a car they had borrowed for the trip and drove off northward. Soon after Prague the tempting sunny weather, which partly prompted them to leave, changed into a snowstorm. The visibility was zero. Rudolf could hardly see the front of the bonnet. He opened the door and watched the road surface under the car while crawling along in first gear. 'You know this is the first time I've forgotten work at the office, Heda,' he observed.

Soon he saw the red rear lights of another car in front and relaxed. Now he could shut the door, sit back, follow the lights and keep a comfortable distance. Eventually they reached their destination late at night. It was an old wooden high-mountain chalet with thick walls made from large tree trunks; it had small windows and a steeply sloping roof. It was very cold and they had to make a fire in the stove to get warm after their exhausting journey. Luckily, the blankets on the bed were thick and soon they went to sleep. Despite the lit stove, their warm breath showed in the cold air of the bedroom.

In the morning they woke up, poking their noses from underneath the covers to see that the sun was up and was coming in through the white frost that had 'painted' pretty patterns on the inside of the windowpanes. It was a struggle to venture into the cold. Rudolf rushed into the small bathroom to wash and have a shave, but the water left in the basin was frozen at the bottom. It was colder inside than outside, he noticed when he went out into the sunshine to fill a jug with water from the deep well. The pump was wrapped in a blanket and the lever squealed, the noise echoing from the nearby hills.

Heda refused to move from the comfort of the warm bed and looked at the frosted windows. She saw Petr Blass mirrored in them: the white colour brought the memory back. Heda used to visit Míša Kafková-Blassová, elder daughter of her mother's sister Hedvika, after whom she was named, to play with Míša's young son Petr. She usually went wearing a white blouse because he was always so pleased to see her in white: 'What a lovely colour, auntie!' They had also been taken to Łódź. As with the rest of the Ghetto, the Blass and Kafka families were transported to Auschwitz on evacuation. When they arrived the guard tore the six-year-old Petr out of Míša's hands and threw him on to a cart to be taken to the gas chambers with the other children. From that day, Míša had wandered distraught around the camp like someone deaf and dumb, oblivious to the outside world, and one day she disappeared. On the ramp her sister Máňa refused to leave her mother Hedvika in the older group and stepped with her into the void – voluntarily. Heda always considered her sight of the line of mothers holding their children's hands and slowly walking unknowingly toward the gas chambers to be the most horrific experience of her life.

Heda buried her face in the warm blanket, not daring to look up for a long while.

When Rudolf finished pumping the water, icicles formed on the pump spout. He looked towards the forest over the glistening crystals of freshly fallen snow and saw some deer looking out cautiously from under the branches, as if reluctant to break the new beautiful cover over the landscape. A rabbit hopped about their legs and Rudolf recalled a scene from three years back. With a fellow Ghetto resident, he had been on guard outside a food storage depot on the perimeter of Łódź. It was the middle of winter. Snow was everywhere. The frost was heavy. They shivered in their torn ragged coats and wet shoes which were breaking apart. There was nothing to eat to assuage the all-prevailing hunger. Suddenly a thin rabbit, itself looking for food, crossed the white field in front of them. They both chased it for a while but the animal's strength was even less than that of the men. Rudolf got to it first and killed the rabbit, striking it with the edge of his palm, and put it under his coat. Then they surreptitiously ran home where Marta divided the loot in half so it could be shared with Rudolf's friend's family. Despite his hunger, Rudolf had been upset as this was the first animal he had ever killed. As a boy he had been horrified when he caught a green lizard by its tail. The creature had wriggled and disappeared, seemingly unharmed, but its tail was left in his hand. His war experiences, though, had tamed his sensibility toward animals as he lived through and observed all the human suffering.

A recipe for a roasted rabbit in the Łódź Ghetto:

Find a rabbit, kill it and bring it to your place of habitation without getting caught. If you are discovered with a rabbit, you will be shot dead on the spot. Skin the rabbit carefully without wasting a gram of meat. Gather, and if necessary steal, enough flammable material to make a fire, for long enough to roast the rabbit. Roast on a spike on an open fire but make sure you are not found out. When ready to eat, no utensils, further ingredients or salt or spices are required. Share with your family, lick and chew the bones dry. You will not eat anything like it again. A feast like this comes once in a lifetime. Ingredients: half a rabbit, portions: hardly sufficient for four people to share.

So soon after the war, the recollections were coming back.

Rudolf wanted to cheer up Heda, to stop her remembering their worst time, the loss of her parents, brother and relatives, and start looking forward to their new life together, to a better, secure future and to having a family. He found out from an acquaintance that an old woman was selling puppies in one of the medieval courtyard houses in the Old Town at Anenské Square and sent Heda there to choose one. Heda discovered the four-storey house quite easily, opened the heavy gate and found herself in a dark enclosed triangular courtyard with three levels of access galleries – pavlače – running on one side of the building. On the galleries sat young women, scantily dressed. Water was dripping from the outside taps. Women kept coming with water jugs, filling the metal containers. Heda, inexperienced and bewildered, walked upstairs and found the woman selling puppies on the top floor. She had them scattered on the floor of her apartment all frantically running around except one little black, weak creature, a Scotch terrier, sitting sadly in the middle. Heda picked him up and he cuddled immediately in her hand. This was the one she took home. Later she realized that the pavlače house must have been a brothel.

The dog – they called him Ďas, Little Devil – grew and they had a lot of pleasure with him. Ďas became a member of their small family. Once they all went for a long walk and it started to rain. The only way back to their Vinohrady apartment was to take the tram. In those days, soon after the war, dogs were not allowed

Ďas

to ride in the streetcar. The old carriage design was different, with open platforms at either end and the enclosed cabin in the middle. Rain was coming down even more heavily and they saw a tram arriving at the nearby stop. Running with Ďas under Rudolf's arm they boarded the tram. The tram set off and they huddled into the crowded and damp cabin. Ďas was whimpering in confusion as the rain lashed at the windows. The ticket conductor was struggling through the crowd, getting nearer. Rudolf tried to conceal Ďas under his coat, but the dog was frightened and yapped. Before the conductor reached them, Rudolf asked Heda for her scarf, wrapped Ďas in it and stretched his arm out of the cabin onto the open platform.

The conductor came and demanded that they leave the tram at the next stop. Rudolf started to argue like a true lawyer that the dog was not 'inside' the tram and that therefore no regulations were being broken. In the meantime, the tram was making its way through the cobbled streets of Prague and Ďas was dangling 'outside' on the end of Rudolf's arm. The conductor continued arguing and the whole tram awaited the outcome. Rudolf kept expounding on the basic laws of citizens, their pets and their freedom of travel. Praguers love their dogs and despite their cramped apartments, many have four-legged friends. The conductor was pulling out the rule book. The Flora stop came and Rudolf and Heda alighted. When they got to their apartment in Přemyslovská Das was dried and fed and their adventure was over.

In the summer of 1946 Heda kept complaining to Rudolf that despite his recent promises he was too busy at work, travelling abroad often, not being at home, not looking after her and that as a young wife she should be pampered and cosseted. Rudolf decided that they would drive to Karlovy Vary, the well-known spa town in western Bohemia, and stay for two or three days in a luxury hotel. He booked the best room in the superb Grand Hotel Pupp in Goethe Street and borrowed a car for the journey. When they arrived, they were shown to a room on the first floor overlooking the park. The room was wallpapered in light-green paper, the furniture was upholstered in light-green fabric, the bed had light-green duvets and pillows and was covered in a light-green bedspread, the curtains were in light-green brocade and on the floor was light-green carpet. In the bathroom, gleaming in the light-green suite, were light-green towels, all there to match the light-green outfit Heda wore – she loved that colour at that time. Das got a basket lined with a light-green blanket. On arrival, Rudolf disappeared and brought back a light-green soap and light-green bath salts to make Heda's stay absolutely flawless.

They went for a walk round the town, sipped the spa waters and observed the mineral water springs. In the evening they had a five-course dinner specially prepared to order by the hotel's best chef, attended by an attentive French maitre d'hotel and Heda elegantly picked at the delicious offering which was beautifully arranged on the best Meissen tableware, accompanied with silver cutlery. Their evening ended by listening to the promenade concert in the town gardens under a starry sky.

The next day, at lunch, Rudolf suddenly said: 'You know what, let's go to Podsedice!' At lightning speed, they packed their bag, and Das, and left all the comfort and luxury behind them.

In Podsedice, standing among the flock of hissing geese in the muddy farmyard strewn with manure was the beaming Vilemína, her hair in disarray and wearing a dusty apron, welcoming them with extended arms covered in flour and butter. At that moment, one of their cows was about to have a calf and everyone was rushed off their feet. Rudolf, even just as he had come from Karlovy Vary in his best suit, tie and polished shoes, ran to the cowshed to offer help and obstructed the vet and his assistant in their work as much as he could with his curiosity and over-enthusiasm. At the same time Vilemína baked typically Czech *buchty*, pieces of yeasty dough filled with plum jam or crushed poppy seeds, which got badly burned due to all the goings on, but everyone – including Micula and her Rudolf Brada who were also there – enjoyed eating them immensely.

Afterwards Rudolf excitedly explained to Heda in minute-by-minute detail how the calf had come to be born, with extraordinary efforts on the part of the vet. Heda believed that this calf was the indirect inspiration for my conception.

I was born in February the following year after a long and extended labour. In those days men were not allowed into the delivery room, so Rudolf paced the sanatorium corridors and in the process kept wearing out the flower bouquets he bought – they faded, one by one – as he waited. I was over fourteen days late. Consequently, to my great regret, Heda was advised not to have any more children.

Heda brought home the little bundle after a week's stay in Doctor Záhorský Sanatorium and put me in a drawer taken from the bottom of the wardrobe. They had not had time to buy a cot yet. Ďas was beside himself with jealousy; his beloved mistress had acquired another 'dog' without consulting him, and suddenly he had a rival! He would not listen or obey, he would not eat and he sulked in his basket, slept and stopped playing. On our first walk outside, Heda and Rudolf wheeled me in a pram, Ďas trotted ahead on his little legs and despite being called back he ran and ran along the pavement. He was far ahead when a car slowed down beside him, the door opened, Ďas jumped in and the car sped off. From a distance, Rudolf and Heda watched in disbelief. Ďas had himself stolen, just like that, and was never seen again.

Heda wanted to call her son Martin (meaning 'Marta's' in Czech) in memory of her mother but Rudolf was so happy with the successful birth that he went to celebrate with his friend Ivan Wiesenberger, a member of an old aristocratic Austro-Hungarian family. First they drank in a café and then they decided to register

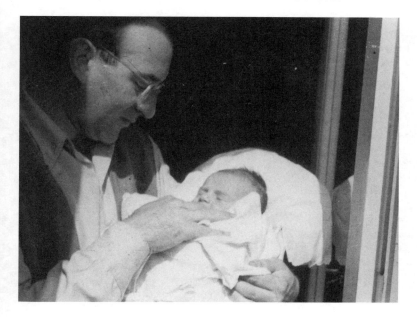

Rudolf and Ivan, February 1947

the birth. They became quite jolly and Ivan stubbornly insisted that the new arrival must be named after his 'godfather'. At the registry, Rudolf did not want to disappoint Heda and wrote down 'Ivan Martin' and both Ivan and he went to bed to sleep it off. Later some people thought that I was given my name because of Rudolf's presumed love of the Soviet Union.

For Rudolf and Heda I was not only their child, I was also the grandson of their murdered parents, a symbol of the survival of their families and Hitler's defeat. Whenever he could, Rudolf hurried home after work to play with me and silently observe me from the bathroom door splashing in the water when I had my bath. Heda commented years later that I used to do the same when I came home and watched my own children being washed.

Sometimes, though very infrequently, Rudolf took me for a walk or stroll in the pram in the nearby Čech Orchards Park. Later, from 1948, when we lived at Letná in Veverkova, Rudolf walked with me to the top of the hill to the 1894 merry-go-round, the oldest such contraption on the European mainland, which had as figurines real stuffed horses. I loved this fairground machine and held on to the horse's mane, spinning round, seeing my father's face in a blur.

Politics Taking Over 15

●
●

What's left of all those beautiful moments?
Lustre of eyes,
a drop of fragrance,
some sighs on the lapel,
breath on a window pane,
a pinch of tears,
a shred of grief.

Jaroslav Seifert, *Song of the Sweepings*, 1965 (translated by Ewald Osers)

In the May 1946 elections, affected by the resentful disappointment of Munich and the country's recent liberation by the Red Army, the Czechoslovak Communist Party won thirty-eight percent of the vote. Edvard Beneš, former Vice-Chairman of the Czechoslovak National Socialist Party, continued as President and Jan Masaryk, a former diplomat, as Foreign Minister. Klement Gottwald, Chairman of the Communist Party, became Prime Minister. Although the Communists held only a minority of portfolios, they were able to gain control over the key Ministries of Information, Trade, Finance, and Interior and State Security. Through these Ministries, the Communists suppressed the non-Communist opposition, placed Party members in positions of power and created a solid base for a takeover.

Beneš had negotiated the Soviet alliance. At the same time, he hoped to establish a neutral and democratic post-war Czechoslovakia to act as a bridge between the East and West, capable of maintaining a balance between both sides. On the other hand, Gottwald was committed to a Communist Party assumption of power by non-violent means.

In January 1948 the Communist-controlled Ministry of the Interior proceeded to purge the Czechoslovak security forces, substituting Communists for non-Communists. Simultaneously, the

Party began agitating for increased nationalization and for new land reform.

National Socialist Ministers, backed by all non-Communist parties, demanded a halt to the Communists' use of the Ministry of the Interior's security forces to suppress non-Communists. However, Gottwald repeatedly forestalled any discussions of the issue. On 20 February the National Socialists resigned from the cabinet in protest. The Catholic People's Party and the Slovak Democratic Party followed suit in an attempt to induce Beneš to call for early elections. Communist losses were anticipated owing to popular disapproval of recent Party tactics. A poll indicated a ten per cent decline in Communist electoral support; however, the democratic parties made no effort to take the advantage. The Ministry of the Interior strengthened its power by deploying the well-equipped people's militia in important industrial areas. On 25 February Beneš capitulated, fearing Soviet intervention. He accepted the abdication of the National Socialist Ministers and received a new cabinet list from Gottwald. The Communist takeover was completed. President Beneš resigned on 7 June 1948 and Gottwald replaced him.

When the British, American and French governments condemned the changes in Czechoslovakia, Gottwald retaliated: 'My Cabinet would not accept lessons on democracy and constitutionalism from those who were responsible for Munich, who bargained about Czechoslovakia's existence with Hitlerite Germany, and who undemocratically and illegally tore up the treaties of alliance and friendship.'

Two days after the takeover the new Minister of Education Zdeněk Nejedlý decreed that a portrait of Stalin must hang in every school classroom. Hurriedly many Czechs and Slovaks left the country before the borders were sealed, justifiably fearing a clampdown on personal freedom in a one-party state controlled by State Security using Soviet practices.

There are wheels within wheels. The story of the birth of dictators and murderers and how they come into this world repeats itself; there are no real surprises. Klement Gottwald's grandfather, Bartoloměj, was a drunk who loved to sit in the pubs. His unmarried daughter Marie was a servant at the farm of Franz Skácel in Hostice, where she became pregnant. On 23 November 1896, she went to see her father Bartoloměj in Dědice, who, as usual, was nursing a big hangover after drinking the previous day and night. He was not in the mood to take in his daughter and her impending arrival and threw her out. Marie decided to see her aunt Bezslezinová instead, crossed the bridge over the Velká Haná river and felt the first contractions. She staggered into the willow bushes by the river and moaned loudly. Thirteen-year-old Franz Zabloudil heard her while carting beetroot scraps through the village and took her to his father's farm.

Klement Gottwald, Czechoslovakia's first Communist President, 'the greatest son of the nation' and its most prolific murderer, was born at the Zabloudils' farm in Dědice and when he grew up followed his grandfather's love of alcohol by spending more time in pubs than at work. He looked very much like Franz Skácel. After the Velvet Revolution, Gottwald's living quarters in Rousínov – where he was apprenticed as a carpenter and which were previously celebrated as the sacrosanct place of birth of Czechoslovak Communism and where young pioneers and militiamen swore allegiance to the Red Star – were rebuilt into a public house and named 'At the Hangman'.

On 1 June 1949 Rudolf had flown to London as the head of the Czechoslovak commercial delegation to negotiate trade agreements with the British government, led by Clement Attlee, as well as initiating the sale of the Swedish Freja mine at the Swedish Embassy in London. Rudolf had sessions with Harold Wilson, then President of the Board of Trade, and other trade officials, held at the Board of Trade offices at 9 Millbank. The negotiations were complex and Rudolf travelled back to Prague for consultations: he wanted to have approval for his decisions at the highest level. On his return to Prague President Gottwald invited him to his private apartment and congratulated him on a job well done.

In August the treaties were signed between Rudolf and Ernest Bevin, Secretary of State for Foreign Affairs and Sir William Strang, Permanent Under-Secretary of State at the Foreign Office. The signing took place at the Foreign Office in King Charles Street.

Rudolf was taken on a tour of the building and was impressed by the elaborate central Durbar Court.

In the first two-year Czechoslovak economic plan, announced in 1947, the aim was to lay the foundations for post-war industrial recovery by replacing worn-out machinery and reconstructing obsolete and damaged manufacturing enterprises. Czechoslovakia was traditionally an importer of many raw materials, particularly for the textile, rubber and leather industries, as well as rare metals and alloys. At that time, the shortage of dollar and sterling reserves prevented any Czechoslovak imports from Western countries. Over fifty per cent of imported items came from the Communist countries and Czechoslovakia used her hard currency for supplies that were essential and could only be bought in the free markets. Under the agreements signed in London in September 1949, Czechoslovakia had undertaken to pay a sum of £8 million during the next ten years in compensation for British property affected by Czechoslovak nationalization as well as repayment of £28 million of Czechoslovak government debt. In order to help Czechoslovakia meet these payments the United Kingdom agreed to permit annual imports of Czechoslovak-manufactured goods to the value of of £5.75 million. All these exchanges would ensure a supply of sterling for Czechoslovakia which could be used for the purchase of machinery and raw materials. That was Rudolf's prime objective: to obtain sufficient hard currency reserves for Czechoslovakia to be able to trade successfully on world markets.

Between the wars, Czechoslovakia had belonged to the club of the most developed industrial nations in the world. The heavy and armament industries ranked among the best and this power base remained, despite the Nazi occupation and the American bombing of the Škoda Works complex in Pilsen at the close of the war. Additionally, Czechoslovakia had one of the world's largest sources of uranium, located in Western Bohemia in Jáchymov. Inevitably these facts added enormous extra interest to the ultimate political destiny of the country. By May 1945, the Red Army had permanently occupied the Jáchymov area. Access to it was highly restricted. Soviet personnel remained there and were increased in number by bringing in experts from the homeland who were not allowed to mix with the local population. A large number of war and political prisoners worked in the mines, living under appalling conditions. Two special transport trains loaded with uranium ore left daily for the Soviet Union. Later the Czechoslovak State Security section took over to safeguard the region. Czechoslovakia was not compensated properly by the Soviets for the vast tonnage of material taken; instead the country was given obsolete army equipment.

The London *Times* carried an article on 16 June 1949 while Rudolf was in Britain:

'CZECH ECONOMIC CRISIS. HOPES OF TRADE WITH THE WEST. There are unmistakable indications that the economic crisis in Czechoslovakia is deepening in a way to cause authorities grave concern. Supplies of raw materials from Russia are coming forward more slowly than was expected. At the same time, Russia is pressing for deliveries of the finished goods that Czechoslovakia provides in exchange. Czechoslovakia often has to sell finished goods to the West, and, indeed, to Russia, at prices far below the cost of production in order to get the raw materials to keep her factories going. Such losses would cause grave alarm in countries with a normal financial system ... '

In between the sessions, over the weekends, Rudolf travelled out of London to see the parts of the country he had missed when he had last visited Britain in 1930. Then a seventeen-year-old, he had arrived with Jiří Toman on the newly built steamer *Melrose Abbey* of the Hull & Netherlands Steamship Co which ran a service from Rotterdam to Hull, and from there he had journeyed to the YMCA camp in Beverley: YMCA Vatra club in Prague had organized the trip. The view of the North Sea from Flamborough Head was a precious memory; he loved that setting. A group of boys were driven there for a day trip and Rudolf had sat on the cliff edge for half a day, never tiring of the outlook. This time he took a train to Hastings and Brighton to look at his beloved sea.

On the evening of Wednesday, 27 July 1949, Rudolf went to St Martin's Theatre in St Martin's Lane in the West End of

London. He saw a play by an American author, N. Richard Nash, called *The Young and Fair*. It had been written in 1948 and the leading roles were played by Marie Ney as Sara Cantry and Jane Baxter as Frances Morritt. Willard Stoker directed it. *The New York Times* review said that 'the play had a habit of living in a state of tension and excitement.' The play's meaning could be interpreted in terms of the contemporary world, of the underhand machinations of a government; it was ugly and insidious, and it was about guilt, innocence and truth, cowardice, hatred and intrigue – very much a scenario that Rudolf was involved in then. He kept the ticket from the play in his wallet as a souvenir; it must have impressed him at the time. St Martin's Theatre was also the place where the London premiere of Karel Čapek's *RUR Rossum's Universal Robots* was staged in April 1923.

Stranded in the Forcefully Distorted Economy

16

●

●

Dear Comrade!
Your news – that in your factory, Gottwald Works Brno Machine Shop, and in your shock-working shift you achieved by the new approach and organization seven times the normal output on your machine – pleased me very much. I believe that you will not only maintain this output and all you have accomplished with the new use of your work time, but that your methods will also be transferred to other machinists in the company. Congratulations on your success. I wish you all the best in your further effort for better productivity. Salute to Our Work!

Klement Gottwald, 1950

Karel Poláček brought me back from one of our Sunday walks and found Rudolf at home and verbally assaulted him: 'You idiots, what are you trying to do to us? When one of my cows produced less than ten litres of milk, I sent her to the slaughterhouse because she consumed more than she produced. Now they are giving a medal to a cow producing four litres!'

'Karel, come on, sit down, let me explain,' and Rudolf pointed at the comfortable red sofa. 'You and I know that at present any contribution to our economy, however small, must be appreciated; the current situation isn't what people were expecting. It's obvious that their high hopes for the future have been dashed.'

In 1949, the local economic recovery was successful and it became clear that the Czechs and Slovaks eagerly anticipated having food coupons discontinued. However, in the second half of

147

1950 there came a sharp decline. This was due to Soviet pressure to re-orientate the Czechoslovak industrial economy in order to supply them with the useful products they needed – heavy machinery, raw materials and armaments – in exchange for basic food and grain supplies. This was contrary to the original Czechoslovak five-year plan for 1949–1953. Then, from the February 1951 meeting of the Party Central Committee, came a directive to sharpen attitudes against the so-called 'class enemies' of the Party, and economic targets were raised in an unrealistic way. The centralized economic model was tightened; the remnants of the remaining private enterprises in retail, industry and agriculture were forcefully eliminated, collectivization was enforced and all production was nationalised.

'Rudolf, placing control into one central government body and closing down small private entrepreneurs surely doesn't bring better results,' interrupted Karel.

Rudolf agreed. Decentralizing the economy and giving factory workers and management independence from state control would enhance productivity. Getting rid of small private companies or farms did not help, especially in agriculture. People work better for themselves than for faceless and inflexible state companies.

Additionally the Communist Party was under pressure from the Soviets to reduce their trade with capitalist countries. In July 1947 the Soviets forbade the Czechs to join the Marshall Plan; Stalin insisted that they choose between them and the West. After the Munich debacle and Western betrayal, it was inevitable, even before the Communist Coup, that Czechoslovakia would turn to the Soviets for help.

Five-Year Economic Plan propaganda

In 1947 the official policy from the government was to trade with both capitalist and socialist countries on a fifty-fifty basis to avoid being dependent on either. Now, though, the directive was to reduce trade with the West substantially. At the same time the import and export structure had to improve to increase hard currency reserves without which debts could not be repaid nor goods and foodstuff obtained that the Soviet Union did not have.

There was also a deterioration of the international situation and the aftermath of the Korean War which resulted in the redirection of essential supplies. Perhaps the Russians were leaning on the Czechs too much, but they had suffered enormously during the Second World War, losing millions of their population, and received untold damage to their fragile economy which was based on the feudal system of the previous century. They never experienced true capitalism and missed that stage of economic development. Because of their sacrifices the Czechs owed them a debt in return.

Rudolf believed that all these current circumstances and pressures undermined Czechoslovak society that itself was still learning to come to terms with the turnaround from the successful pre-war capitalist form they had all experienced to the new, yet unproven, socialist centralized system. This sudden change exposed society's faults, forcing it into a deep moral crisis. With economic failures, people's standard of living and fundamental values were being diminished, eroding their faith in the Party's competence. Honour, responsibility, comradeship, friendship, and the sense of justice and truth ceased to be important human aims and goals. The wave of arrests of leading Communists accused of sabotage and spying confirmed this fragile situation, and led to a general mistrust of political figures and state institutions.

'I sense that I'm being watched every minute of the day for any mistake I could make,' Rudolf added.

'Surely you must find this very difficult? I've known your parents and your upbringing, your standpoint was always very direct, honest and truthful,' Karel conceded.

'For a long time I've felt very vulnerable although I don't fear for myself. At present there are hardly any experts left at the

Ministry. For people who are involved in the economy of the country this situation is dangerous; scapegoats are sought by the Party and its leaders to justify the current difficulties ... it's especially hard for us, Jews, we're always the first in line to be accused if any problems arise. If anything happens to me, Karel, please promise to look after Heda and Ivan.' Rudolf added in a whisper: 'But not a word to Heda about my worries, please!'

Two years prior to this, Evžen Löbl, his colleague from the Ministry, also a Deputy Minister, came to see Rudolf. He was greatly disturbed, thought he was being followed and wanted to hide in the Veverkova apartment to calm down. Then Heda was not at home.

Only days later Löbl was arrested.

The Soviets Arrive 17

Salute our most beloved Party,
long live Stalin, our shining ideal ...
Long live Klement Gottwald, our leader,
in that is your strength, in that is your celebrity!

Vítězslav Nezval, *Hymna komunistické straně/A Hymn to the Communist Party*, 1951

After the February Coup, the Party General Secretary Rudolf Slánský announced: 'The main aim of the Communist Party is to safeguard the successful completion of the five-year economic plan. The Party must acknowledge the great political significance of this assignment. To fulfil the five-year plan successfully first depends on how quickly we shall be able to realize the changeover to Socialism in our country. The assignment depends on the Party to learn to organize and direct labour in all sectors of our economy.'

Many Czechoslovaks entered the ranks of the Communist Party, recognizing that to be able to survive under their new masters it was essential to join them rather than oppose them.

In Party meetings, national broadcasts and newspapers the Czechoslovak public began to be bombarded with the strict requirements of Soviet-style life: 'The Party demands truthfulness and honesty, unswerving observance of duty to Party and state of all its members, and especially of those in leading positions. It cannot trust people who go against the interests of the state, who play false with the government and try to deceive Party and state. Deceiving the Party or state in any form whatsoever, any attempt at deceit, whether by concealing or by distorting the truth, cannot be regarded otherwise than as a severe offence against the Party. It is time it was understood that there is only one discipline in our Party ... ' All the people's democratic countries and their citizens had to stand behind the Soviet Union and conform to the same strict doctrines, and beware those who stepped off the given path.

However, in June 1948 came the break between Stalin and Tito; this had enormous repercussions throughout the Communist camp. Josip Broz Tito, Yugoslav Communist Party General Secretary, had led the Yugoslav partisans' fight against the Nazi aggressors during the war. Aided by the Red Army, which was allowed temporary entry into Yugoslavia, the Yugoslav partisans liberated their country and the Red Army departed. After elections in November 1945 Tito became the Prime Minister of Democratic Federal Yugoslavia and the Soviets endeavoured to ensure that the new state came fully under their political influence.

The dispute was founded on the interpretation of relations between the socialist countries. Tito insisted that the relations must be close and fraternal, but not those of the exploiter and exploited or potential enemies, as was the case with capitalist countries. They had to be based on equal rights and the common interests of all partners, whether great or small countries. He resisted pressure from Stalin to intervene in Yugoslav affairs. Milovan Djilas, one of the secretaries of the Yugoslav Communist Party, pointed out that the socialist state, which was established on the dictatorship of the proletariat, representing those who had won the socialist revolution, took over the means of production. This phase could have been perceived as capitalism carried out by the state. It must give way to measures of democratization and workers' management, or it would harden into bureaucracy, and in time would become a totalitarian tyranny, as had happened under Stalin.

Tito confirmed: 'I'm glad it has fallen to us to settle this issue once for all. Any other Communist Party would have broken before Stalin. But we shan't. We're going to stand up to him.' He assured the world that the Yugoslavs would fight if attacked and go on fighting, even if they had to take to the mountains until their country was free again. Later Nikita Khrushchev revealed Stalin's boast that he would shake his little finger and Tito would disappear and said: 'In the end Stalin shook everything he could shake, but Tito didn't budge.'

Stalin feared that other peace camp countries would follow the independent Yugoslav model and break away from the influential sphere of the Soviet Union. He instigated the terror of political trials to uncover 'enemies' within each Communist Party in order to discourage dissent. Victims were sought out and accused of connection with Tito's opposition attitude and treachery. In later cases, the Soviets turned to Zionism and its supposed link with Western imperialists as the cause of the Communist betrayal.

The show trial was a propaganda arm of political terror. Its aim was to personalize an abstract political enemy, to place it in the dock in flesh and blood and, with the aid of a perverted system of justice, to transform abstract political-ideological differences into easily intelligible common crimes. It both incited the masses against the evil embodied by the defendants and frightened them away from supporting any potential opposition. Other East European countries, such as Hungary, were putting pressure on Czechoslovakia to take action; they even supplied a list of suspected Czechs to be arrested. Hungarians expressed fears about the country's internal stability because Czechoslovakia was the only European Communist state without Soviet troops on her soil.

Ironically, it was the Party General Secretary Rudolf Slánský who drafted a telegram for President Gottwald to sign which was sent to Moscow on the day the 'László Rajk and his Accomplices Trial' opened in Budapest on 16 September 1949. The telegram officially requested the Soviets to despatch advisors, later called 'teachers' by Czechoslovak State Security, to assist with investigation and search for 'enemies' within the Czechoslovak Communist Party as directed by Stalin and Beria. It said: 'When Rajk's traitorous clique was uncovered in Hungary, some of its contacts led to Czechoslovakia. We request that the Central Committee of the Soviet Party dispatch specialists familiar with the results of the Hungarian legal enquiries to assist us in investigating this matter.'

Slánský, seconded by his associates Karel Šváb, Deputy Minister of State Security and Bedřich Reicin, Deputy Minister of National Defence, was creating a monstrous whirlpool for himself and others who would be pulled down with him without realizing it. Slánský was not without blame in the situation that developed in Czechoslovakia. He and Gottwald were closest to Stalin, both having spent the war years living in Moscow at the Soviets' invitation. Slánský's stay in Moscow was not a happy one. His three-and-a-half-months-old daughter Naděžda was kidnapped from a Moscow park by an unknown woman while being looked after by her eight-year-old brother Ruda and was never found.

It was Slánský who instituted the arrests of non-Communists in 1948. In the same year he proposed that the government build forced labour camps on the model of the Gulag and Nazi camps to act as a good influence upon the proletariat. He believed that educating and politically convincing people was not enough. In 1949, he was planning to purge the Party following the Soviet example to stop the alleged class enemy infiltrating Party ranks. He proposed to scrutinize the background of every Party member, new and old; the purity of the Party had to be maintained. The State Security apparatus increased in number out of all proportion to deal with the planned pressure on the country's population. As the first source, State Security used Street Communes to gain information on possible undesirable elements who might suit the role of class enemy.

The search was aimed at finding the enemy not just at grass roots level, but inevitably higher up the ranks of the Party – eventually reaching its initiators.

On 23 September, a week later, replying to Gottwald quickly, the Soviets sent a message: 'In response to your request, the Ministry of State Security has been instructed to select and send to Prague the necessary specialists.'

Early in October 1949 the Soviets arrived. From then on until the spring of 1950, the Soviet advisors were General N. T. Likhachev and Colonel N. Makarov, the same people who had prepared the Rajk Trial in Budapest in 1949, the first major show trial in Central Europe. They insisted that the Party alone could not be trusted to seek out the opposition; only State Security could uncover it. It was obvious that nobody would confess while at liberty so people had to be arrested, placed in custody and physically and mentally abused in order to make them confess to their 'crimes' against the Party. The Soviets did not only advise but also directly participated in the interrogations, assisting Czechoslovak Security and taking over when the results were not forthcoming quickly enough.

The other Soviet advisors who came to Czechoslovakia were Alexei Beschasnov, Vladimir Boyarsky, Ivan Chernov, Semion Galkin, Georgi Gromov, Grigori Morozov and Boris Yesikov. Following their deadly deeds, many of these operatives – as Lavrenti Beria's henchmen – were liquidated on their return to the Soviet Union. No witnesses were needed to the crimes, subversive machinations and lawless activities committed by the Soviet State outside its borders. The Soviets confessed to their Czech security colleagues that they hardly ever reached retirement.

The Czech public knew nothing about this – that the government invited Soviet agents to reinforce their security departments and unleash terror in the country on the well-tried Soviet model – not even ordinary Party members. The number of arrests increased and people were seized without any knowledge of having done anything against the regime. The most exposed were those people who had lived in the West both before and during the war, the Spanish Civil War veterans, pre-war landowners and industrialists, and the Jews.

Likhachev was a small bald man. His behaviour changed to suit the particular situation required – he could be a friend, diplomat or bully. He was a man able to act many parts convincingly.

To set the scene from the beginning, Likhachev said to Teodor Baláž, the Slovak State Security Director: 'Stalin sent me to prepare a trial and I've no time to waste. I came to Czechoslovakia to see heads roll. I'd rather wring a hundred and fifty other necks than lose my own. I don't care how you get the confessions; I'm not interested in knowing if they're true. I'll believe them but leave all the rest to me. What do you care about some Jewish shit, anyway?'

Baláž objected that before he could do anything he had to consult the Chairman of the Slovak Communist Party, Viliam Široký. 'Why bother? We'll kick his arse as well,' Likhachev assured him.

18
●
●

Journeys of
Misunderstanding

> Poetry is another of those values unassailable in our society.
> I was shocked when, in 1950, the great French Communist
> poet Paul Eluard publicly approved the hanging of his
> friend, the Prague writer, Záviš Kalandra. When Brezhnev
> sends tanks to massacre the Afghans, it is terrible, but it is,
> so to say, normal – it is to be expected. When a great poet
> praises an execution, it is a blow that shatters our whole
> image of the world.
>
> Milan Kundera, in an interview with Olga Carlisle, 1985

Likhachev and Makarov worked fast and helped to stage the first
Czechoslovak political tribunal, 'The Trial with the Leaders of a
Sabotage Conspiracy against the Republic: Milada Horáková and
Accomplices,' held in Prague from 31 May until 8 June 1950.
The thirteen defendants, mostly non-Communist-Party members,
were branded as terrorists, traitors, bandits and nihilists, and
sympathisers of Trotsky and Tito. They were accused of treason and
espionage; four were sentenced to death, four received life sentences
and five long-term imprisonment.

One of the defendants sentenced to death with Horáková
was Záviš Kalandra, a former Communist journalist and essayist
who was thrown out of the Party for his disapproval of Stalinist pre-
war repression in 1936. The French Surrealist writer and artist
André Breton, together with the poet Paul Eluard, met him during
their 1935 Prague lecture tour. On his return to Paris Breton wrote
a letter to Vítězslav Nezval, the Czech poet, who organized his talks:
'Often in the mornings, before we met up for lunch, I would look out
of the window of the room at the rain as beautiful as the sun over
Prague and I would enjoy this very rare certainty that I would take

away from this city and from you all one of the most beautiful memories of my life.'

After Kalandra's sentence was announced Breton sent a telegram pleading for clemency to the Czechoslovak government which was also signed by Jean-Paul Sartre, Albert Camus, Simone de Beauvoir, Max Ernst and others. Winston Churchill, Bertrand Russell and Eleanor Roosevelt issued other protest notes.

Breton also published an 'Open Letter to Paul Eluard, 13 June 1950' printed in *Combat* the following day: 'It is fifteen years since we, you and I, went to Prague at the invitation of our Surrealist friends ... and certainly you will not have forgotten how we were received in Prague then. Recall a man, who hovered around, who used to sit down often with us and really try to understand us, because this was an open man ... I think you will remember this man's name: he is or was called Záviš Kalandra ... according to the newspapers he was sentenced by a Prague court last Thursday to death, self-evidently after prescribed confessions. You know, as well as I, what to think of these confessions ... How can you, in your soul, bear such a degradation of a human being, especially a person who was your friend?'

'I already have too much on my hands with the innocent who proclaim their innocence to worry about the guilty who proclaim their guilt,' answered the French Communist Party member Eluard, not bothering to lift a finger.

Czech intellectuals believed that greater pressure from abroad could have prevented the trials, and for years were appalled by Eluard's reaction. Jan Zábrana, a well-known translator and writer, mentioned in his private diary in 1973: 'And so a poet blessed the murderers bashing the prisoners' teeth, being showered in the reinforced concrete solitary confinement cells. Don't bother me with drivel about the frail soul of Paul Eluard. His soul, wrapped in the shit of cowardice, glows like amber from the nether world.'

Between April 1911 and July 1912 Albert Einstein was appointed as a Professor of Theoretical Physics at the German Department of the Charles University in Prague. He lived in Lesnická Street in Smíchov, lectured in the Klementinum, formerly a Jesuit College and later the Astronomical Institute and National

Library, and spent happy hours in the library of the Physical Institute in Viničná Street. He met Franz Kafka and Max Brod at the pharmacist's wife Berta Fantová's literary salon in the Unicorn Apothecary House at 17 Old Town Square; here spiritualism, Rudolf Steiner's Theosophist movement and philosophy were discussed and music was played. While in Prague, Einstein began his work on a relativistic theory of gravitation. He published eleven papers, six of them concerned with the theory of relativity, papers which are particularly significant in that they paved the way for his general theory of relativity. In the preface for the Czech edition of his *Theory of Special and General Relativity* Einstein remembered: 'I am pleased to see that this little book, which expounds the main ideas of theory of relativity without mathematical elaboration, is now appearing in the native language of the country where I found concentration necessary to finalize into a specific form the general theory of relativity, which I had already conceived in 1908.' Undoubtedly remembering his stay in Prague prompted Einstein to send a telegram to President Gottwald from Princeton on 14 June 1950: 'I please [sic] with you not to carry out the death sentence on Milada Horáková, Záviš Kalandra, Oldřich Pecl and Jan Buchal stop They were victims of Nazism inmates of German concentration camps stop Am deeply convinced that they deserve to live.'

Kalandra and the other three defendants were hanged in Pankrác Prison on 27 June, 1950. It was said of Gottwald that he threw the telegram in the wastepaper basket. Horáková said before she died: 'I lost, I fall like a soldier, with honour, I love my country and her people ... '

Kalandra's interrogator later confessed: 'We pumped him for three days and three nights, we took turns but Kalandra was there all the time. When he could not stand up any more and was lying down on the floor, only then did he agree to sign his confession.'

However, Stalin was not satisfied with the effect of the Horáková case and this time planned a more spectacular show to reveal enemies in high positions within the Czechoslovak Communist Party. This move was intended to strengthen Soviet power and serve as an example to frighten all the satellite countries into further submission, including Tito's Yugoslavia.

Chauffeur Krejčí, used by President Gottwald and his deputy Antonín Zápotocký, recollected: 'On the Sunday afternoon 11 November 1951 I went to watch football at Sparta ČKD Prague at Letná. By half-time in the Czechoslovak Premier League match with ATK (Army Sport Club), Sparta was winning 2–0, and the announcer asked me to come to the eighth section of the stalls over the public address system. My wife waited for me there and said that my superior had phoned, telling me to take my Tatra 87 and drive straight away to the Soviet Embassy.

'There they ordered me to go to Ruzyně Airport and collect the arriving Soviet dignitary. I drove right up to the Ilyushin IL-12 aircraft when it landed. Anastas Mikoyan, member of the Soviet Politburo, Stalin's emissary, came out and got into the back of the car directly from the steps. This was a top-secret visit.

'First we stopped at the Castle. Mikoyan had a discussion with President Gottwald and after that with the Soviet Ambassador Michail A. Silin but not in the Embassy, in the Prague park called Stromovka! This was a strange place for a secret discussion. Now, it was a dark winter evening. The cold wind blew sharply across the asphalt paths and the park was empty. With the pistol deep in my pocket I kept to the prescribed distance and only occasionally overheard a few words. According to security regulations, I immediately increased my distance.

'The discussion between Mikoyan and Silin lasted some hours. When they finished I took Silin back to the Embassy and Mikoyan to see Gottwald again. Afterwards I drove Mikoyan to his aircraft at Ruzyně to fly back to Moscow. I do not understand why they had chosen a Czech driver and why they walked in Stromovka. I assume they worried about both Soviet and Czechoslovak surveillance in their Embassy building.'

This mission was highly classified and Stalin insisted that only very few of the Soviet staff knew the true purpose of Mikoyan's sudden visit. He had sent Mikoyan to force Gottwald to stage another major trial and to detain his friend, the Party General Secretary Slánský.

Gottwald resisted, as no proof was given for Slánský's arrest. When Mikoyan saw Gottwald the second time that day he repeated Stalin's demand and confirmed that he, Gottwald, would be held responsible if Slánský fled abroad. Gottwald realized that there must be some evidence although this was not volunteered, and asked Mikoyan to convey his agreement to Stalin.

Despite pressure from Stalin Gottwald hesitated over Slánský's arrest for the next ten days. On 22 November, the chief Soviet advisor General Alexei Beschasnov demanded to see Gottwald and brought a copy of a letter smuggled from West Germany, allegedly intercepted by Czechoslovak State Security, offering to help Slánský to escape. There are several versions about the origin of this offer: it could have been a genuine proposal coming from Czech émigrés abroad, a plant by Soviet intelligence, or what Gottwald and Zápotocký assumed – tinged by the obsession of the times, though most unlikely – an asylum initiative coming from Israel. With this new evidence, Gottwald had to act.

Earlier, on 14 November, the Soviet Ambassador Silin had been recalled to Moscow and replaced the following day by Anatolij J. Lavrentjev. It was rumoured in Prague that Silin, as a supporter and a friend of Slánský, had been arrested. Similarly, Slánský, Šváb and Reicin were later included in the Trial with the intention of liquidating those who had constructed and participated in the terror staged in Czechoslovakia. They were seen as being Beria's agents rather than Stalin's, and when Beria fell out of favour his men were removed with him. On the other hand, the other chosen defendants, such as Vladimír Clementis, Josef Frank, Ludvík Frejka and André Simone, were long-standing Communists, experts in their professions and had not been involved in the political games or cadre cleansing.

Least of all Rudolf, who was arrested in January. He was a new Party member, and was concerned with purely economic matters and not connected with any Party intrigue. All his decisions were taken with the approval of his superiors.

Towards Manufactured Guilt

19

> One day it will be necessary to draw swords to defend the truth that the grass is green.
>
> Quoted by Ferdinand Peroutka, *Svědectví*, 1972

A priest was sitting in the third class compartment of the crowded Prague-bound train where anecdotes about the Communist regime were being told. The priest was not paying any attention to the discussion. He was absorbed in his prayer book, but nodded his head because of the rhythmic movement of the carriage over the bumpy tracks. When they reached Prague, one of the travellers revealed himself as a State Security agent and arrested all of them, including the priest. Nodding his head cost the priest ten years of his life.

A highly poisonous atmosphere prevailed in Czechoslovak society; an unbearable feeling of fear spread throughout the population. People did not trust their colleagues at work, their friends or even their own family members. No one could be depended upon. You couldn't confide the most trivial details of everyday life to anybody. Simple information given, say, to a foreigner could have led to a serious allegation. You could, for example, have told the traveller that 'the Charles Bridge was the oldest bridge in Central Europe'. Your subsequent potential interrogation by State Security, when you were allowed only to answer 'yes' or 'no', would have proceeded like this:

'Did you give a foreign national information about bridges in Prague?'

'Yes.'

'Are bridges important to the defence of the country?'

'Yes.'

'In case of war would the enemy bombard the bridges?'
'Yes.'

'Is it probable that during the bombing innocent civilians including children living in densely populated areas close by would perish?'

'Yes.'

'You are a traitor and murderer; you have given away vital information essential for the security of the country, you have placed our children in mortal danger.'

A Report on Recommendation for JUDr Rudolf Margolius, Deputy Minister of Foreign Trade, to be included in the selection of additional suspects of the Anti-State Conspiratorial Centre headed by the former General Secretary Rudolf Slánský. Prepared at the request of Ladislav Kopřiva, Minister of State Security, Prague.

Wednesday, 28 November 1951

Dear Comrade Minister
Following files were studied:

People's Street Commune Committee Reports, Veverkova Street, Prague 7 Letná, Reports of the State Security agents from the Ministry of Foreign Trade, An Interrogation Protocol of Evžen Löbl.

A Draft Report on Margolius family living in 6 Veverkova Street, Prague 7, Letná:
21 November 1951

Dear Comrades of the Street Commune,
We've been asked to report on families that do not fit into our community. We believe that the Margolius family is such a case. Neither Comrade Margolius nor Comrade Margoliusová attends the Commune meetings. They have a thoroughly unproletarian attitude. They don't greet their

fellow comrades in the street in the prescribed Communist manner or dress appropriately to conform to other comrades. They don't participate in the brigades organized by the Commune to clean the park and street and improve our environment. They don't decorate their apartment windows with flags of the beloved Soviet Union, our saviours from Fascism, and the Czechoslovak Republic as required on all state occasions and the birthdays of our greatest leaders, Comrades Stalin and Gottwald. Their little boy refuses to play with our children in the street.

They never queue for food and send their domestic help (please note, they have a domestic help!) to do all the citizens' work for them. They have a number of foreign visitors who visit them often and who are entertained into the small hours. They listen to broadcasts from abroad, buy large quantities of books and often go to the theatre or cinema. Comrade Margoliusová even has time to go to the hairdresser. They also own a car and none of the other families we know has one. We've heard that both Margoliusová's and Margolius's fathers were Jewish capitalists who exploited the workforce. Their general bourgeois pre-revolution attitude appears as though they are superior to our ruling proletarian class and we recommend that proceedings be taken against them.

Salute to Our Work!
Long live the Soviet Union!
With comradely greetings
Comrade Bláhová, concierge
Comrade Novotná, cleaner
(Apologies for the handwritten report in pencil, as we haven't access to a typewriter)

From a Protocol dated 27 November 1951 by First Lieutenant Pavlíček, Director of Sector III Division 2 of the Ministry of State Security, Prague, as reported by the State Security agents placed in the Ministry of Foreign Trade.

A List of the anti-state activities of JUDr Rudolf Margolius, Deputy Minister of Foreign Trade:

Margolius organized the export of 5,000 tonnes of meat to capitalist countries despite shortages at home.

Margolius refused to import pyrites from the West despite the critical situation at home in relation to the manufacture of sulphuric acid, and now the West requires in exchange for the deliveries of the acid additional supplies of coke, coal and military supplies.

Margolius arranged the export of 1,000 tonnes of barbed wire to capitalist countries despite the fact that this material could be used for military purposes.

Margolius negotiated unnecessarily the import of 200,000 tonnes of grain from France despite an agreement with the Soviet Union for it to supply this to the Czechoslovak Republic.

The Czechoslovak customs seized a parcel containing US $14,165 sent to Margolius from Holland. This money was the profit of the Exico firm's trade with the Czechoslovak Republic and should have gone directly to the Czechoslovak State Bank.

Margolius failed to negotiate the successful sale of the Swedish mine Freja. Sweden decided to buy the mine and to pay Czechoslovakia 125,000,000 crowns in Swedish crowns but this amount, if not used up in time, could be forfeited and lost to the Czechoslovak economy.

Our secret agents found that Margolius keeps a large amount of dollars and diamonds in his Ministry safe.

Margolius signed some Ministry documents with the initial 'G' (as for his superior, Minister Dr Antonín Gregor) without Minister's knowledge.

Margolius spoke to an official in the Soviet Embassy on the phone in English and afterwards studied secret statistical documents.

Margolius offered 10,000 rifles and ammunition for sale to the USA and, out of that, 1,000 rifles have been passed to Israel.

Margolius invited foreign visitors to his office, including a Belgian newspaperwoman and an Italian businessman, without a third person present or without his superior's knowledge.

Margolius, together with Dr Karel Markus, Head of the Political Section of the Minister's Cabinet, obtained fabric for a suit from a certain Mr Elovič who later escaped from the Czechoslovak Republic.

Margolius proposed Dr Ctibor Brieger for the office of Commercial Attaché in Budapest. Recently this man was arrested.

During his stay in London, Margolius, as the leader of the commercial delegation, was in contact with Czechoslovak émigrés.

Margolius, together with his colleague Evžen Löbl, has been requesting entry visas for foreigners who were secret agents and needed legal commercial cover for their subversive activities.

Margolius passed important decisions to the First Secretary of the Ministry to disguise his own subversive activities and turn attention elsewhere.

A Part of a report and notes of State Security Captain Vladimír Kohoutek, the interrogator of prisoner Evžen Löbl, former Deputy Minister of Foreign Trade, in custody since 24 November 1949.

'During his interrogation in custody, Löbl freely volunteered information about subversive treasonable activity which had been carried out by his colleagues in the Ministry. Löbl drew up a confession on General Secretary Rudolf Slánský and other colleagues' crimes and their dealings with himself. Löbl confirmed that he acted on instructions from others in his foreign trade negotiations which were found to be acts of sabotage against the state. Löbl confessed among other things that Margolius was a close and trusted friend. They met frequently in Margolius's Veverkova apartment to discuss and share decisions on foreign trade directives and plans, especially with the capitalist countries. Löbl's confessions were obtained on advice and with the assistance of our Soviet teachers and advisors.'

Kohoutek made notes at the bottom of the page:

'Later Löbl confessed privately to me that he justified his accusations by thinking that when his protocols were seen by President Gottwald and the other members of the Central Committee of the Party they would realize that they could not be true. He suggested to me that they were all invented, especially as he would talk about conversations he had had with Gottwald but transpose Gottwald for Slánský or other people under suspicion and Gottwald would surely remember the conversations they really had shared. Then Löbl's confessions would be seen as false, he hoped. However, my opinion and belief as Löbl's main interrogator is that these excuses are nonsense and the original protocols must stand. I recommend that his protocols provide the true and correct information and are used to unmask further enemies of the Party.'

Based on the above information we propose to Comrade Minister to agree to have JUDr Rudolf Margolius, Deputy Minister of Foreign Trade, born on 31 August 1913 in Prague, living at 6 Veverkova, Prague 7 responsible for the Czechoslovak trade with the capitalist countries sector, arrested and interrogated.

Signed, Staff Sergeant Alois Šťastný, Sector III, Ministry of State Security

Approved by First Lieutenant Pavlíček, Director of Sector III, Ministry of State Security

Minister Kopřiva, supposedly a Gestapo agent during the Protectorate, having studied Šťastný's Report as well as hearing about Margolius's friendship with his colleague from the Ministry, Evžen Löbl, who had already been arrested for alleged anti-state activity, instructed the State Security agents to install listening devices in Rudolf Margolius's apartment. Margolius's attitude to the Party had to be carefully scrutinised.

Staff Sergeant Alois Šťastný ordered his men to engage in Action 'Rudolf'.

Marie Bednářová, a full-time nanny, hurried to the tram stop clutching her handbag on Saturday, 1 December 1951. Another girl waited for her and together they boarded the number 24, heading toward Charles Square. Their destination was the famous Prague brewery restaurant U Fleků in Křemencova Street. When they arrived, they joined a group of men sitting at the same table. One of them was the State Security Sergeant Jiří Sedmík.

After a while Marie's friend was asked to dance and Sedmík offered: 'Let's have a dance too, Marie, come on, and leave the handbag here, my friends will look after it!'

Sedmík took her round the waist before she could change her mind, although Marie loved dancing and did not really need to be persuaded. They whirled round the dance floor to the piano and violin music, accompanied by the loud clinking of half-litre glass tankards. In the meantime Sedmík's 'friends' borrowed the apartment keys from Marie's handbag and put a substitute set there so that the weight of the bag would not change. Agent Josef Zeman was sent outside and handed the keys to a colleague who took them to the mobile workshop installed in a van parked round the corner where copies were made within twenty-five minutes. By the time the keys were returned Marie was still on the dance floor. She enjoyed the entertainment and left with her friend after midnight; Sedmík arranged to meet her in a few days time. Marie wanted a trip to the countryside and Sedmík had promised to take her if she contributed money for petrol and if he managed to borrow a car. However, as they parted Marie remembered that the next week she had to stay in as the Margolius family expected Mrs Musilová to come and stay for several days. Sedmík reported to Šťastný that despite obtaining the keys they would not be able to use them.

Šťastný decided on another course of action.

On the evening of 6 December 1951, when the feast of St Nicholas was celebrated in Central Europe, St Nicholas, the Angel and the Devil were sniggering outside the door of our third floor apartment in Veverkova Street. They pushed elbows in each other's ribs to stop laughing. The Angel whispered to the Devil, who was the tallest: 'Stop it, this is serious!' and kicked him in the shins with his sharp boot; the Devil wobbled dangerously on his hooves.

6 Veverkova Street, Prague

St Nicholas pushed the doorbell, finally adjusting his halo. In his left hand he held a decorated bag with several toys and a small lump of coal at the bottom. Excited sounds were heard behind the door. It was me, jumping up and down in anticipation.

'Are you ready? Keep your eyes peeled!' ordered the Angel. The door burst open and I was waiting for them, extending my hands for the bag. Heda stood behind me, smiling.

'Not yet, son, recite us some poems you learned and let's go in the living room,' the Angel directed, taking charge. I could not see their faces behind their masks but their eyes were darting all over, taking stock of the apartment. I led them to the living room. They gave me the bag after I ran through a children's rhyme about a fox and a crow I had learned from a book by Josef Lada. Once I got the presents I paid no attention to the mismatched group. Gone was my initial fright when they had marched into the apartment almost like a group of soldiers, rather than dancing in like a fairy-tale fantasy. I should have been, or at least Heda should have been, a little bit suspicious then.

They got the presents from Heda, who left them with the concierge downstairs, as did the other parents in our block. The trio had to visit every apartment containing small children, bringing them their bags. I winked at Heda when I pulled out a piece of coal from mine. That was for being a bit naughty, and every child should have received one to keep them in check. It was worse if the bag was full of coal and nothing else; that message really meant something serious. In the meantime, St Nicholas, the Angel and the Devil separated and wandered around pretending to be lost. Heda forgot that she had to tip them and let them wait and look around even more until she found her purse.

'Gentlemen, thank you,' she shouted, waving the money above her head to summon them. They shuffled back reluctantly, flaying their arms and legs in the awkward costumes, the Angel bumping his frayed feathery wings on furniture and walls. Absentmindedly St Nicholas tapped the floor with the gilded curve-headed staff. On their way out, they turned their masked heads as if they had lost something. Strange behaviour, I would have thought had I observed them carefully.

After the door shut behind them, they let out sighs of relief and rushed down the stairs to the basement, throwing all caution to the wind, whispering: 'Who's got some paper, quick!'

'Don't forget we need to carry on with this, there are another three floors with the little brats waiting,' St Nicholas reminded them.

'Later, later,' muttered the Angel.

Down below they sat on the concrete floor with their backs against the wall spreading a piece of white paper on their knees. The Devil pushed his mask on top of his head and spat on the tip of the pencil. He started to draw while carefully turning the pencil in his fingers: 'All right, give me the hall dimensions.'

'It was a long one: five by twelve steps,' St Nicholas recalled. In fifteen minutes the plan of our apartment had been sketched and the trio returned upstairs to carry on with their charade.

Their State Security car and driver waited patiently round the corner to take them back, in their costumes, to the State Security Headquarters at Bartolomějská Street as soon as they had finished. It must have been a sight to see them clambering into the car, tripping over their costumes and swearing and pushing. 'I'll never do this farce again but we're great, especially you, Comrade "St Nicholas",' the Angel laughed.

To carry the St Nicholas action on to its successful conclusion, State Security agent Staff Sergeant Šťastný instructed Sedmík to prepare a report regarding the occupants of the 6 Veverkova Street apartment building. All occupiers, including their employment, daily activities and political background, had to be investigated to find a suitable Party sympathiser who would allow them to install the receiver for their listening devices. Sedmík's report concluded that none of the tenants was suitable but one occupier in the building next door, a member of the Party and a major in the Czechoslovak Army, signed the official secret document and agreed to keep silent about the planned action. He allowed them to use a spare bedroom. The wiring from the devices would be placed through the bathroom ventilation shaft, Sedmík recommended. The set-up would take three to four hours.

Now that Staff Sergeant Šťastný had the plan and the keys, unobstructed secure access to the apartment had to be arranged. Rudolf Margolius had to be detained at the Ministry by orchestrating a meeting with one of the State Security officers to discuss aspects of foreign trade with the capitalist countries. Second Lieutenant Jiří Rybín would go to the meeting, supported by Corporal Bartoš who would wait outside the Ministry should Margolius leave the building earlier than anticipated and send a warning from a public phone box. Heda Magoliusová's superior, Comrade editor Zajonec, in her place of employment – the publishing house Rovnost – would detain her by giving her urgent work which would have to be done by the end of the day. Sedmík took Marie, together with the Margolius' son, for a trip out of Prague in a car borrowed from Rybín. They were to return in the afternoon. The action was planned for the morning of Wednesday, 19 December 1951.

For the installation, Third Lieutenant Miroslav Čermák of Sector III had five security technicians at his disposal. He went up to the third floor first and shielded the view from the door of the other apartment on the same level while one by one the technicians arrived at one to two minute intervals. Čermák would be the last to enter the apartment. One security man would wait outside the building to give a warning should anything unforeseen happen by entering the building and knocking five times on the door. Sergeant Pokludová was present at Security headquarters in case any family members returned early and had telephone contact with all the comrades in the apartment. She was to phone the apartment telephone number – 751-18 – three times in succession and after the fourth ring of the last call the receiver would be picked up.

As the apartment walls, floors and ceiling were constructed in concrete the drilling for microphones and wires would be very noisy, so a gas and electrical repair in the building was staged by a State Security unit working from the early hours and masking any unwanted noises coming from Margolius's apartment.

A Bugging Surveillance Report
Action 'Rudolf'
Saturday, 27 December 1951

15.00 – Microphones are switched on, a conversation among several persons. There was a visit of a man with a woman and child. One man is called Rudolf, the other Grisha and one of the children is Ivánek. They are all in one room and it is difficult to understand because the children play and shout.
16.45 – Now the men remain alone and it is easy to follow. They talk about politics, about the Party, about the proletarian takeover, about the democratic centralism in the

Party. All these points were carefully politically scrutinized; they also referred to the teachings of Leninism. Rudolf leads the discussion, they are on friendly terms. At the beginning, they talk about Jews – that they are a convenient target – but it was not understood whose convenient target they meant. They also mentioned the Vatican.

17.00 – The visitors leave saying *au revoir* and Ivánek said *goodbye* [in English], and they all laughed.

17.15 – They have dinner and the sound of clinking dishes and glasses together with a wireless is heard.

17.30 – The surveillance is switched off.

Recorded in the apartment of Comrade Major Kokeš at 4 Veverkova, Prague 7, who has been sworn to secrecy.
Signed: Bohuslav Bartoš, Sergeant, Sector III

A Bugging Surveillance Report
Action 'Rudolf'
Friday, 28 December 1951

17.15 – The surveillance is switched on: children talking and reading fairy tales.

17.45 – Switched off: children talking. No relevant information received.

18.00 – Switched on: children talking. No relevant information received.

18.35 – When M. came home he immediately went to the phone and called his office and asked his secretary to give his chauffeur, who was on his way back, the invitations that he had left on his desk. M. with his wife is presumably invited somewhere.

19.00 – The wireless is on, talk is difficult to follow, they have a dinner.

19.15 – M. calls his wife to get dressed, Ivánek asks: 'Where?' – M. replies that they are going to visit the Soviet Ambassador, Ivánek asks again: 'Where?', M. replies: 'To see our Soviet friends.' M. calls: 'Heda, hurry up, we have to leave at 7.45.'

19.27 – A visitor arrives – a woman, after a short conversation with both M. and his wife she wishes them a happy New Year and leaves.

19.50 – They leave and say their goodbyes to Ivánek and the nanny.

19.55 – The surveillance is interrupted, because the object has left and his return could be expected late at night – they went to a reception as could have been presumed from the fragments of conversation and discussion with Ivánek.

Recorded in the apartment of Comrade Major Kokeš at 4 Veverkova, Prague 7, who has been sworn to secrecy.
Signed: Alois Šťastný, Staff Sergeant, Sector III

20 Ways into Detention

●

● *Život není peříčko!* – Life is never as light as a feather!

Heda Margolius Kovály

Noel Field, United States official of the Unitarian Service Committee, Office of Strategic Studies and possibly an agent of NKVD, Prague, 11 May 1949 (released in 1954):

> The Czechoslovak State Security agent Jiří Šindelář, code name Blue, who pretended to have arranged contact with Field's Soviet masters that Field was seeking, lured him to Prague from Switzerland. Field came in May 1949. Hungarian security originally requested Field's arrest in relation to the Rajk's Trial that was under preparation; they also arrived in Prague. On 11 May Field was enticed out of the Palace Hotel in Panská Street where he was staying. He was bundled into a car, chloroformed, handcuffed and handed over to the Hungarians who drove him to Budapest.

Béla Szász, Head of the Press Section of Ministry of Agriculture, Budapest, 24 May 1949 (released in 1954):

> We left the [State Security Headquarters] building. A powerful American Buick was waiting at the door. Only after we had taken our places in the car did I notice that all the windows, including the back window and that separating the driver from the passengers, were shrouded from the outside world by black curtains. They made me sit between the grey-haired man and the brutal-faced detective and when, with a sudden jerk, the car sprang into motion, the grey-haired one said: 'We shall now blindfold you.'
>
> 'Do we have to play cops and robbers?' I asked, vexed.

'You ought to be glad,' the detective replied, reaching for a folded napkin obviously prepared in advance, 'for if we blindfold you, there's at least a chance that you may come back ...'

We raced on for about half an hour but now none of us spoke. Finally, we must have turned into a side road because the motor slowed down, and soon afterwards we stopped ... They helped me out of the car and we started down a flight of stairs ... When we reached the bottom, the men let go of my arm. An iron door banged shut behind me and the bandage was ripped roughly from my eyes. Five or six savage-looking men surrounded me.

'Traitor!' a short, round-faced man hissed in my face.

'You rat!' another whispered almost inaudibly, baring his teeth.

Traicho Kostov, General Secretary of the Communist Party of Bulgaria, Sofia (executed 17 December 1949):

On 10 June 1949, the night of his arrest, Kostov was taken to the headquarters of the State Security police and placed inside a special, hermetically sealed cell with one window located at the top of a wall. A fire hose poured ice-cold water through this window. Kostov was threatened with drowning unless he agreed to confess to his spying activities.

László Rajk, Minister of Foreign Affairs, 16 June 1949, Budapest (executed 15 October 1949):

While the Hungarian State Security men were preparing to arrest Rajk, János Kádár, the Minister of the Interior, was instructed to keep Rajk company. In the morning they played chess and later they attended a meeting of the Party secretariat together. In the evening the Rajks hosted a dinner. The State Security agents waited for the guests to leave and burst into the house. The surprised Rajk was prevented from making a phone call and was forcibly dragged out and bundled into the waiting automobile.

György Hodos, Communist journalist, Budapest (released in 1954):

> I had been expecting them, more or less, when they finally came for me at one in the morning on 6 July 1949. For weeks my friends had been disappearing one by one – dragged from their beds at night ... Now it was my turn. But surely they sent for me only to ask for information, to help clear up the misunderstanding that was apparently taking place? I went with them feeling no fear. Good Communists need not worry about our State Security whose hard fist struck only at the enemies of our people's democracy. There were four of them. They showed me their identity cards and ordered me to dress. I was calm and sure of myself. There was a bowl filled with cherries in the living room.
>
> 'Comrades, help yourselves while I dress,' I told them. They looked at me in astonishment. My wife, Marta, white and shivering, told me to take a pullover with me. 'What for?' I answered. 'It is warm, and tomorrow I will be home.'
>
> I took 70 filler from my purse, the exact amount I would need for a return ticket on a streetcar, kissed my wife and daughter, and left, accompanied by two of the security men. It was a beautiful summer night under a sky full of stars. Their automobile, a large American model with drawn curtains [surely the same car used in Szasz's arrest], was parked at the next corner.
>
> Two security men remained in the apartment. Five and a half years later, when I next saw my wife and child, I learnt that the proceedings there were not so cheerful. They pulled down all the shutters, turned on the lights, and began tearing the apartment apart. Mattresses were thrown from the beds, letters and papers were stuffed into their suitcases, my two-year-old daughter was dragged from her room while they searched every corner of it ...

Hermann Field, American architect, member of the Czech Refugee Trust Fund, brother of Noel Field, Warsaw Airport, 25 August

1949 (released in 1954):

I turned from the window. At the counter, only my processed ticket was handed back to me. 'Your passport you will get on the plane.'

A porter picked up my checked-in baggage ... I followed the porter into the little adjoining departure room facing the flight apron. A man was standing inconspicuously over by the far wall ... He was staring intently at me. Without taking his eyes off me, he shifted toward the point where I had entered. My suitcase had been set down just inside the room. The man suddenly came to life. 'Passport.'

I was surprised. 'Haven't ... on plane.'

He had moved over to that door himself and beckoned me to follow ... I found myself in a small corner room and facing me, two men standing behind a large table.

'Quickly, quickly,' the man with the drooping cigarette broke in. 'Empty your pockets.'

Outside I heard airplane motors not far away ... Five, ten minutes went by in silence.

'Excuse me, but I think I should be going to the plane.'

The man with the cigarette nodded indulgently ... Another half hour must have passed by in silence. The man at the door pulled its window curtain a little to one side and peered out. He nodded to the man with the cigarette, who went over to the telephone. Some arrangements were made in a muted tone.

'Please, take your suitcase and follow this gentleman.'

I went through the door – and stopped abruptly. I found myself looking directly into the open rear-end of a small delivery van.

'Quickly, get on in.'

They lined up solidly between me and the building ... As if in a dream, I found myself clambering onto the floor of the van, the original stranger close behind me with my suitcase. The door swung shut.

Evžen Löbl, Deputy Minister of Foreign Trade, Prague (released in 1960):

On 24 November 1949, a man entered my flat and, having identified himself as a member of the Security Service, handed me a summons from the Minister of the Interior, Václav Nosek, requiring my presence. There was a car waiting outside. In the car sat two more men whom you could tell at a glance were 'plain-clothes men'. The car drove in the direction of the airfield at Ruzyně. When I objected that that was not the way to where Nosek lived, they told me reassuringly that he was waiting for me in another house. We stopped in front of a large building where uniformed members of the State Security awaited us.

One of them pronounced the 'formula of damnation': 'In the name of the law, you are arrested!' Straight away I was made to put on the dress prescribed for those under arrest for interrogation, consisting of little more than rags.

Jiří Hejda, economist, Government Central Planning Committee, Prague (released in 1961):

It was my daughter Šárka's twenty-fourth birthday on 21 December 1949. She invited a few guests to a little party in our villa. I was thinking about it in my study when I heard unusual sounds in the front room. There were some voices out of which I could only recognize the protests of my wife Louise: 'Do you mind! How dare you!'

I got up from my desk but at that moment the door opened and two men entered my study, pushing my wife to the side. 'We are from State Security,' announced the first one.

I was not that surprised because most of my friends had experienced similar visits and I wondered secretly why they were leaving me out. I had a clear conscience so nothing could happen to me. 'What do you want, gentlemen?'

They wanted some information, but did not express their wishes in detail. The Security men tried to get rid of Louise but she went only after my calm request to leave us alone.

Then they started searching my study. My study had over 6,000 books in many languages, including my memorandum for the five-year plan sent to President Gottwald and Zápotocký. They were rather helpless and kept leafing through it. The security men went over other volumes and appeared to look for something they could not find. After ten minutes they asked me to come with them to make a statement.

As it was already 7.30, I asked if I could have something to eat. They agreed and took me to the dining room where Louise gave me fried fish with potato salad and I ate it while they looked on. I was calm but could see Louise's fearful eyes and I was sorry for her. She kissed me briefly at the door and I assured her that I would be back soon and asked her not to be afraid. Downstairs there were two more security men waiting by their two cars. I was made to sit in the first car and we drove off. Their leader, who was sitting next to me, said while we were moving: 'You won't be home that soon. Is that clear? We did not contradict you to avoid scenes with your family. Do you know Milada Horáková, the former Member of Parliament for the Czechoslovak National Socialist Party?'

I concurred.

'So you know why we came for you,' he confirmed.

Erica Wallach, the foster daughter of Noel Field, East Berlin, 26 August 1950 (released in 1955):

It took a great deal of courage to make up my mind to go to the East. I washed my face, locked my papers and all my money, except a bit of change in the cupboard, and emerged east of the Brandenburg Gate. After carefully announcing myself at Party Headquarters, I talked my way through various security checks into the inner sanctum of a big Party congress. When I heard the footsteps behind me on my way out of the building, I did not even turn around. A hand on my shoulder stopped me. 'Criminal police. Please come around the corner!'

I had chosen well; I had walked right into the lion's den. They had been waiting for me, rubbing their hands. And when the heavy iron door of cell number seven of

Schumannstrasse Prison was locked and bolted behind me, I knew that all was lost.

Miriam Šlingová, the wife of Otto Šling, Spanish Civil War veteran, Regional Party Secretary, Brno, 6 October 1950 (released in 1953):

At about two o'clock in the morning the door bell rang and thinking my husband had forgotten his key, which he sometimes did, I went to open up for him. But instead of Otto three men were there, quite ordinary men in plain clothes. Taken aback, I tried to shut the door on them but one already had his foot there to stop me, and they forced their way in. I started to shout for help. At that one of them put a hand over my mouth and another meaningfully shifted the revolver on his hip. So then I asked them to show their credentials, although the next moment I said to myself that they might be forged. They also waved a bunch of keys in my face and asked me if I recognized them. They looked like my husband's. I was then curtly told to get dressed, and one of the men stood in the room as I did so. After that, I was told to wake the children and dress them. My suggestion that maybe I could ask the neighbour to look after them until I returned was waved aside.

I still had no idea of what it was all about, but when I was taken out and saw the usual official cars waiting round the corner from our house, and especially when I heard one of my escort address a driver as Comrade, I thought with relief that at any rate they were our people! Still telling me nothing, except to say that I was going somewhere to answer some questions, they packed the three of us in a car and drove off. Peering out into the dark, I saw that we were leaving the town. We drew up to rather grim-looking iron gates, which were opened by a man in uniform, and we pulled into a courtyard. As we got out of the car, the children excited and myself completely bewildered, two women who had evidently followed in another car came forward and spoke to the boys, saying: 'Mummy will be away for a while.'

Before I knew what was happening, I was being led away from them, and as soon as we were out of sight one of my escorts tied a black felt thing over my eyes.

Years later I heard how my husband had been arrested the same night and had evidently been taken straight to Prague, to the same prison building as that in which I was now held.

Artur London, Spanish Civil War veteran, Deputy Minister of Foreign Affairs, Prague, 28 January 1951 (released in 1955):

The security car drew up behind me; at the end of the street, another car of the same make was parked with three men inside it. I drove off without even realizing which road I was taking ... After three hundred yards, as I was entering the lane behind the Tuscan Palace, one of the cars overtook me and stopped dead in front of me. Six armed men rushed up, pulled me off my seat, handcuffed me and threw me into the first car, which drove off at full speed. I struggled, and demanded to know who they were, but they blindfolded me and shouted: 'Shut up! No point in asking questions! You'll know who we are soon enough!'

They were not arresting me, they were kidnapping me. The car drove through the town ... I heard trams and cars passing us ... On we drove. The noises diminished and then the tyres creaked on the gravel. Hands seized me, pulled me out of the car and pushed me down a passage ... After we had turned in every direction, my eyes were unbandaged, my handcuffs removed, and I found myself in a small bare room with no window. I was made to undress and put on some dungarees with no buttons and a pair of shapeless slippers. I asked to see a Party official immediately, but my demand was greeted with insults and threats.

Vladimír Clementis, Minister of Foreign Affairs, Prague, 28 January 1951:

Clementis used to go out regularly for a walk with his dog called Broček; most of the times his wife Lída also joined them.

181

One morning she was ill and Clementis and Broček went out alone. Clementis never came back. Two men seized and overcame him and shoved him into a car. He was driven westward, up to the Czechoslovak border and beyond until they arrived at the West German border station. The German and American officers welcomed him and inquired about the reasons for his defection. However, Clementis demanded to be taken back to Prague. Unknown to Clementis the border, the border control and the officials were all decoys arranged to test his reaction. Clementis was driven to Koloděje Castle near Prague and it was reported to Gottwald that Clementis had been arrested while trying to escape abroad. Gottwald's secretary noted in her diary: 'Gottwald laughed when he was told the details of this episode.' Broček was returned to Lída's parents nine months later. By then she was also under arrest.

Rudolf Slánský, General Secretary of the Communist Party, Prague, 24 November 1951:

The evening before his arrest the Slánskýs were invited to the party held at the house of Prime Minister Zápotocký. He was giving a farewell dinner for a group of Soviet economic advisors, who were returning to Moscow. Unusually Zápotocký was friendly and considerate and gave the Slánskýs a guided tour of his villa, stopping at every painting on the wall and giving their history. After midnight Slánský's wife, Josefa, urged Slánský to return home. When they left Zápotocký called the State Security commander waiting at Slánský's villa: 'They are on their way.' At home, the Slánskýs drove onto the garden drive. Unexpectedly, the garden and villa were in darkness. Josefa stumbled on the steps. Rudolf caught her but he was frightened that something might have happened to her. He asked their security man, who stood outside the villa and looked after it, to put the lights on and the guard walked off. They entered the hall which was still in darkness. Josefa was in front, Rudolf behind her. Suddenly the lights came on, and there was the rushing stampede of many heavy feet. In an instant, someone twisted Josefa's arms behind her back. Out of the other rooms sprang a number of men who all lined up along the wall, with automatic pistols levelled, ready to leap at them. Against the narrow section of wall between the entrance into the hall and the kitchen door other men were holding him. These included the uniformed Major Bohumil Doubek, Director of Sector VI A and the chief interrogator in Czechoslovak Security, and his colleague Captain Karel Košťál (in future to be promoted to Deputy Minister of the Interior!), who had been invited as a reward for helping to unmask Slánský in interrogations of Löbl, Šling and London.

Slánský stood erect, his eyes wide with astonishment. 'Gentlemen, what does this mean?'

He got no response. In the cry that Josefa uttered was the indescribable terror that filled her. Another man jumped forward and clamped a hand over her mouth.

Slánský asked to be allowed to sit down and repeated: 'Ježiš Maria, Jesus Maria.'

A man came out of the cloakroom and without a word handcuffed Slánský's wrists. Now there was absolute silence. They pushed Josefa into the kitchen.

'What's happened to the children?' she asked.

'Don't ask any questions,' replied the State Security man.

Then she heard the hum of engines and the sound of cars departing.

Hours before, Richard Slánský, Rudolf's younger brother and a diplomat, had been arrested in his apartment. The State Security men had their own keys and let themselves in.

Pavel Kavan, diplomat, Prague, 1 July 1952 (released in 1956), as told by his wife Rosemary:

The 5.00 a.m. ring at the doorbell came as a paralysing shock. We looked at each other dumbly. It could only be State Security. Somehow, I found my dressing gown and went to open the door. Five impassive, broad-shouldered young men in standard leather coats stepped into the hall. 'Your husband is wanted for questioning,' one of them explained, not discourteously.

'A routine procedure.'

Of course, entirely routine even at this early hour.

'I'll make a cup of tea.'

One of them followed me into the kitchen. Pavel, too, kept up appearances, chatting to one of them while he washed and shaved. It would have been impolite to interrupt the conversation; therefore it had to be continued in the bathroom. He left the bathroom door ajar. We both acted as normally as possible, as though we could ward off the abnormality of what had already happened that way. Pavel left with three of them. I slipped some lumps of sugar into his pocket, having heard of their reviving properties during long interrogations. We exchanged a brisk, leaving-for-the-office kiss. No significant utterances, no whispered protestations of innocence or declarations of faith. Just the quick dry brush of trembling lips on a cold cheek, the pressure of a hand that conveyed: 'Whatever happens, I am with you,' while aloud I said: 'Goodbye, darling, see you this afternoon.'

One of the remaining two security men said: 'We are obliged to search your flat.'

Rudolf Margolius, Deputy Minister of Foreign Trade, Prague, 10 January 1952:

The rear-engine Tatraplan cruised through the deserted streets of Prague on its way from the Ministry of Foreign Trade in the New Town to the Letná quarter on the left bank of the Vltava. Streetlights reflected on the wet cobblestones of the roads and pavements. Though it was eleven o'clock at night, here and there was a solitary figure walking the family pet.

Now the car sped along the embankment. The cold river carried broken pieces of ice which looked like torn fragments of white paper slowly floating downstream, underneath the numerous Prague bridges. Traffic was light as would be expected at this time of night but Rudolf had a feeling that another car was following closely behind. It was difficult to

Tatraplan

see from the rear seat as the view backwards could only be seen through the two small windows over the sloping back cover of the engine. Despite the uncertainty he was too tired to care, settled down and dozed off. The car stopped at the kerb and Rudolf's driver whispered quietly: 'We're home, Comrade Deputy Minister.'

Rudolf stirred, collected his hat and briefcase, thanked the driver for looking after him, arranged for him to pick him up at six in the morning and stepped out of the Tatraplan, closing the door behind him. With the sudden clunk of the door, powerful floodlights dazzled the whole street. The dark night was changed as if by magic into daylight. The lights were all directed at Rudolf who froze, blinded, on the pavement. Men in leather coats swarmed along the street making as much noise as possible to arouse citizens from their sleep and invite them to watch the spectacle they had arranged for them free of charge. Heads appeared cautiously out of apartment windows to observe what was being staged below. As intended, the scene was set for maximum impact on the neighbourhood. The Party's aim was to increase the citizens' fear and, at the same time, reward the Street Commune informants for their vigilance. Tactics had changed and now the arrests were made public.

Surrounded by the State Security agents like a trapped animal, the uncomprehending Rudolf was led without a protest to another Tatraplan parked further down the street. One of the agents grumbled: 'About time, we've been waiting since six o'clock.'

On the way Rudolf was silent, then asked if the Minister of Foreign Trade, Antonín Gregor, his superior, knew what had happened but got no answer.

In the meantime, three agents led by Corporal Beránek from Sector V, as instructed by the order of the Ministry of State Security, searched our apartment in the presence of the distressed Heda. Luckily, I slept through this; Heda begged the agents not to wake me. Rudolf's diaries, notes, photographs, various documents, his Leica, his ČZ 6.35 mm calibre pistol and holster, Škoda car keys, bank cheque and saving books were confiscated as, triumphantly, were the great pieces of evidence – two copies of Rudolf Slánský's book called *Towards the Victory of Socialism*.

Initially Rudolf thought that he had suddenly stepped into a film set but once he had been roughly pushed into the back seat between two silent State Security agents he woke up to the new reality. In May 1950, he had agreed to the Party's request – initiated by Slánský – that all members submit a detailed self-examination and autobiography of their life before the war and during the occupation in order to prevent the enemy infiltrating the Party. With all the arrests going on round him in his own Ministry as well as in other government departments, he was expecting his own investigation: but he knew that his past was clean and his work was important for the economic stability of the country. For that reason he thought that he would be spared, put it out of his mind and concentrated on his job. However, Heda kept worrying about him all the time.

Several days before this Rudolf had been sitting in an armchair, his profile illuminated by low light, in his typical evening posture. As usual, deeply concentrating, he was studying some Ministry documents. Heda began to discuss the current situation again when they heard of more arrests. She tried to point out the faults of the regime.

'If the system is fair and sound, it would provide ways of compensating for error. If it can only function when the leadership is made of geniuses and all the people are one hundred percent honest and infallible, then it's a bad system. It might work in heaven but it's a foolish and destructive illusion for this world. Look at all those idealists who wanted nothing more than to work for the wellbeing of others: half of them are in jail and the others start trembling every time the doorbell rings. It's all one big fraud – a trap for naive, trusting fools.'

After a while Rudolf replied, having stood up and looked through the window into the darkness of the Letná street. 'Heda, you know how much my work means to me. I've given it all that's good in me. And it's not only that. I thought that with this job, life had offered me a chance to do some good, to make up for our passivity in the past. I know I've been a bad husband and a bad father for the last two years. I've neglected you and Ivan for the sake of my work. I've denied myself everything I love. But there is one thing I cannot give up: I cannot give up my conviction that my ideal is essentially sound and good, just as I cannot explain why it has failed – as it apparently has. I believe this is a crisis that will pass. If you're right, if it really is a fraud, then I have been an accomplice in a terrible crime. And if I had to believe that, I could not go on living. I would not want to.'

This conversation ran through Rudolf's mind again as the car left Veverkova Street driving in the direction of Ruzyně, where the newly upgraded main State Security Prague prison was located.

21   To Nowhere

●

●   If I suffer it is because I cannot be without guilt. I am guilty
      because I am condemned. And I accept a punishment whose
      reason I do not know. I accept my neighbours' guilt by
      declaring myself guilty.

      Jiří Orten, quoted in Václav Černý, *Za Jiří Ortenem*, 1947

In the 1950s the Ministry of State Security had the following depart-
ments: Sector I – External Security; Sector II – Internal and Political
Security; Sector III – Combat of Economic Sabotage; Sector IV –
Police, Prison, Fire and Militia Services; Sector V – Surveillance,
Identification, Custody and House Search Services; Sector VI A –
Investigation of Party Enemies, Bourgeois Nationalists and Members
of the International Brigades in Spain; Sector VI B – Investigation of
Yugoslav Spies, Zionists and Economic Sabotage. Sector VI carried
out interrogations in preparation for the political trials.

        There were three main places of detention used by State
Security in Prague. They were the Koloděje Castle east of Prague, the
Ruzyně Prison close to Prague Airport and the Pankrác Prison.
President Masaryk had used the Koloděje Castle as a summer
residence in 1919 before the Lány Castle was made available for
him. After the war President Gottwald spent his holidays there.
Then the Castle was taken over by the Ministry of the Interior and
State Security and the political and professional training of their
staff took place there. Its primitive cellars, each measuring two by
two metres and without natural light, heating, any toilet provision
and with hard-packed earth floors, were used as prison cells. The
cells, nicknamed 'sanatorium', were so cold that the interrogators
had to wear coats and hats while the prisoners, barefoot, wore dirty
cotton trousers and light shirts. A popular method of breaking
prisoners was to dunk their head in a bucket of excrement and force
them to wash their face in it.

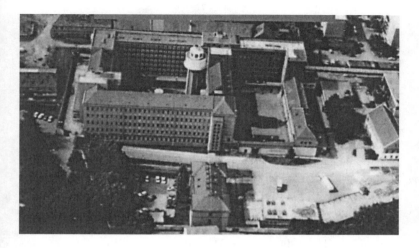

Ruzyně Prison

The Ruzyně Prison lies in the grounds of a former 1930s sugar refinery near the local cemetery. In 1935 the industrial buildings were turned into a prison labour camp and included the nearby farm. In the post-war period Ruzyně held petty criminals and collaborators. In 1950 a seven-storey main prison block was built to accommodate political detainees. Its cells were six square metres each: basically three steps forward and two steps across. A cell had two metal plates covered in thin mattresses folded against the wall, two seats that shut into the wall that were not allowed to be sat upon, a small desk, a Turkish closet with a water tap above, a concrete floor, a window with three panes covered in mesh – which made it impossible to see out – and a small radiator in the wall recess. Toothbrushes and spectacles were kept outside the cell on a shelf by the reinforced door. The light was on twenty-four hours a day and a prison guard was on continuous duty outside.

The Pankrác Prison, with the execution cells, was built on the green meadow between the Prague suburbs of Pankrác and Nusle in the 1880s and has been used by the Czech Prison Service ever since. It is adjacent to the High Court of Justice in Prague where all the major trials are held. Presently, it houses almost 900 prisoners.

In the 1950s the whole interrogation section of the Ruzyně Prison, located on the first floor where the questioning of political detainees took place, shook with the screams of the interrogators – 'Scoundrel, swine, bastard, traitor, spy, criminal, murderer, liar; confess, confess, confess' – mixed with the timid pleading of the accused. The physical and psychological tortures inflicted upon the prisoners by their own Party comrades, unlike those they suffered at the hands of their Fascist enemies, eventually destroyed not only their bodies and minds but also their entire lives, if they survived. Their moral resistance, their ideals, dreams and aims collapsed; many intended to commit suicide rather than continue living after their release. They felt guilty because their Party told them they were guilty, and in their eyes the Party was their ideal, their friend and guide and was always right. During Nazism, Gestapo interrogators forced the truth out of prisoners, while during Communism lies and inventions, the complete opposites, were sought from them. Both regimes aimed at destroying the human spirit to feed the political goals and ambitions of their respective Parties. The Nazis and the Communists created terror to achieve complete obedience.

Alex Weissberg, Kharkov NKVD Headquarters, 28 January 1937:

'Who recruited you?'
       'I was never recruited.'
       'Who recruited you, I said?'
       'No one.'
       'Who recruited you?'
       This time he almost shrieked the senseless question, and I made no answer.
       'You'll learn to talk in the end. We've dealt with tougher men than you. In a week you'll be soft enough, I can tell you.'
       'There is nothing I can say.'
       'Reveal the organization to us.'
       'What organization?'
       'The counter-revolutionary sabotage organization you built up in the interest of a foreign power.'

'I didn't build up any such organization.'
'Who recruited you?'
'No one.'
'Whom did you recruit?'

Evžen Löbl:

Prison is always associated with sitting, but in my case sitting was not allowed. I had to stand all the time I was being interrogated and was not even allowed to sit when in my cell ... I even had to eat standing up. You could not even sit on the toilet as what was provided was the so-called Turkish closet. The interrogations lasted an average of sixteen hours a day with breaks amounting to two hours, thus I had to stand or walk back and forth in my cell for a total of eighteen hours a day, which left six hours for sleep. You were not allowed to have your hands under the blanket. The cells were under constant watch and if a prisoner was seen to have his hands under the blanket, he was shouted at and cursed. This in itself was enough to keep me in a state of constant tension. Add to this the fact that you were scarcely able to sleep during the few hours available because every ten minutes the warder banged on the cell door, at which you had to jump to your feet, stand to attention, report your number and cell number, and that all was in order. For the first few nights, inevitably, I found it impossible to get to sleep again after being roused in this way but later I became so exhausted that I fell asleep again the moment I had made my report. Thus I was dragged out of deep sleep thirty or forty times a night. If I failed to hear the bang on the door, the warder would come in and kick me awake.

Another means of putting pressure on one was hunger. The food was inadequate, so that you had never had enough but were always aware of being hungry. Often the interrogations were deliberately continued beyond a mealtime and when you returned to your cell the warder told you that the food had already been round and he could not alter the prison rules. This combination of continual hunger, repeated interruption of sleep and of having to stand or walk in small, hard leather slippers throughout the day caused indescribable physical distress ... After about three weeks my feet were swollen and my skin had become tender to the slightest touch, so that washing had become torture and every step I took hurt. The interrogation was conducted by three men, who took the never-ending flood of insults, humiliation and threats in turns.

They organized fake executions. On six or seven occasions I was woken in the night, led blindfold to the chancery in the basement and there made to listen while the officer there spoke on the telephone. They were always threatening me that they could not go on feeding me at the expense of the state indefinitely, so I was, on each occasion, convinced that 'this was it', especially as they never tired of telling me that they did not need a court sentence before they did me in.

After resisting for several months, I was given drugs, though it was not until later that I realized that this is what it was ... I had a feeling as if a hand had thrust through my forehead into my brain. As long as I was in this state, I could not hold anything in my hands and if I happened to be walking, I had to stop. What was nasty was the fear I had lest I be going mad ... Fear of ending in a madhouse was worse than the fear of death. [The drug had been administered to prisoners in their soup.]

Artur London:

A border guard in field uniform, wearing a fur cap with a red star, stood in the doorway pointing a machine-gun at me. Another guard put a steaming bowl on the floor and took off my handcuffs ... But no sooner had he done so than my hands were again chained, this time in front of me. I was thirsty and terribly cold. I looked in perplexity at the bowls at my feet. A few minutes went by. I heard the sound of empty bowls being collected; I realized that I would have neither a spoon nor would my hands be freed to eat. I knelt down and raised the bowl to my lips with difficulty. But how could I eat it? At that moment, the door opened.

'Give me that,' said the warder, seizing my bowl, 'and start walking again.'

When I was allowed to sleep, the mattress had to be facing the spy-hole. The light was on all night and shone in my eyes. It was very cold. The dungarees I was wearing offered me no protection and in the evenings, before going to sleep, I had to fold them carefully and put them on the stool; if the warder decided they were badly folded he would wake me up any number of times to make me fold them again.

Every physical and moral torture was carried to an extreme. I had been forced to walk on continuously ... It went on for months, and was made all the worse by my having to keep my arms to my sides. My feet and legs became swollen. The skin round my toenails burst, and the blisters became suppurating wounds.

Erica Wallach:

'That depends on you, confess your crimes, co-operate with us, and we shall do anything in our power to help you. We might even consider letting you go free if we are satisfied that you have left the enemy camp and have honestly contributed to the cause of justice and progress. We are no man-eaters, and we are not interested in revenge. Besides you are not the real enemy; we are not interested in you but in the criminals behind you, the sinister forces of imperialism and war. You do not have to defend them; they will fight their own losing battle. People like you we want to help – and we do frequently – to find their way back to a normal life and a decent place in society.'

It all seemed clear to me now. It was make-believe, a farce. They knew as well as I that I never did any espionage. They meant it in a larger sense. I had been used by America as an instrument against Communism ... We were going to play a game ...

He spoke to me intently and convincingly: 'The Russians are known for their good hearts. I could cite many examples of it, and you know it is true. A Russian never harbours any grudge; he is only too happy to forget the past and start afresh. All the great Russian classics bear out this characteristic of our people. You have read them; you know I am right. Get rid of your past and we shall forget what was yesterday and help you as we would help any human being who is in trouble. Remember, we are your friends, the only ones who are in a position to help you.'

This was the first of many nights I spent standing up, without the support of a chair or the wall, and, although standing even for minutes had always been an extreme hardship for me, I became accomplished in the art and was able to go on for hours without once fainting or breaking down.

'You want to know what a capitalist snake looks like? Take a look at her, at that bag of filth standing over there. You will never see such a low and abominable creature ... Take that dirty smile off your face, you American stooge ... You are a prostitute! That's what you are. Worse than that; prostitutes sell only their bodies; you sold your soul. For American dollars, stinking American dollars ...'

Hermann Field:

'But what do you want of me? Look, it's not my fault if you are going after something that does not exist. I never did the smallest thing against your country.'

'Pan Field, you are obstinate. We will give you another chance. We are patient. Go down now to your cell and think it over and then start once more to write down for us what you really know about the activities of those friends that interest us ... I want you to start all over again, and this time tell the truth.'

Back in my cell, I was at a loss for what to do.

György Hodos:

'So you have not yet confessed? You are a swine, you stink, that you can still walk on two legs is a mistake that we shall correct immediately.' One of them took his rubber truncheon, made me lie down on my stomach, feet up in the air. I counted twenty blows on my soles. 'That is only the beginning. Tonight you will not be able to sleep from the pain, but it will pass. Next time, you will not be able to walk for weeks, only crawl and whimper, like swine do.'

The pain passed quickly, but I still did not know what they wanted of me, what crimes I was supposed to have committed. In the end, I knew they would have to let me free or beat me to death.

I spent weeks in the damp, cold basement cell with no blanket, my clothes in rags, the soles of my shoes worn out to a stinking, sticking, brownish-black mass covering my swollen feet. Every time I was escorted down to the eternal light of my cellar catacomb, I felt happy and relieved, but after a couple of hours, the deadly silence seemed to hurt more than all the fantastic accusations, all the beatings. I felt like I was buried alive, there would be no return, and I yearned to be led upstairs to my Lieutenant, to hear a human voice, to explain and to understand.

Rudolf Slánský:

Many attempted suicide to get out of the impossible situation they found themselves in after their arrests. In the Ruzyně Prison in the secure interview rooms, Doubek and Košťál conducted the afternoon and night interrogation sessions of 31 January 1952 with Rudolf Slánský. Late at night the exhausted Doubek took a break. Soon after he left, Slánský told Košťál he needed to go to the toilet. Košťál got up to escort him, opened the door, and carelessly started out first. Slánský shoved him out, then shut and bolted the reinforced door. Then he looked for the service pistol that the interrogators usually kept in the writing desk. It was not there or in Košťál's briefcase. The suicide plan collapsed, but not the idea. Slánský ripped out the telephone cord and hung himself on the window latch. Meanwhile the terrified Košťál mobilized his colleagues and maintenance workers who forced the door with an axe, just in time to save Slánský. He was immediately put in the care of the infamous prison physician, Dr Josef Sommer, who used all his skills and injections to save him, seemingly without any side effects.

Later Slánský had another nervous breakdown that escalated into an attack of frenzy. The attack was so powerful that he was straitjacketed and spent time in the prison hospital tied to his bed. He was taken to the following interrogations in handcuffs and was tied to a hook in the wall to stop him breaking his head by running up against the hard surface.

In the Name of the Party

22

●

●

Prosecutor Aleš: 'On your instructions certain goods were exported into capitalist countries whose lack jeopardized their supply to the Czechoslovak population.'

Defendant Margolius: 'Yes. In 1950 and at the beginning of 1951 in Czechoslovakia a critical situation developed in the meat supply. I knew about this difficult situation. In my harmful approach toward the people's democratic establishment, in order to arouse discontent of the public and to disrupt the food supply to the Czechoslovak population, I arranged for the export of most Czech meat produce to capitalist countries. I was keen to cover up the lack of local supply and organized meat imports from other countries of the people's democracies. When the government decided to stop the exports of meat altogether I took advantage of this situation deceitfully, as the ban did not include the export of tinned meat. Therefore I gave instructions to export tinned meat instead to the capitalist countries.'

Prosecutor Aleš: 'You helped the capitalist countries to increase their strategic reserves. Obviously your every single act of sabotage was a means of weakening our state and increasing the potential of the capitalist world.'

The Slánský Trial, November 1952, Prague

The Soviet advisors, through their Czech interrogator intermediaries, manipulated the minds of the accused by mixing the reality of their experiences with Party doctrines to pressure them into admitting guilt. They kept their distance to increase their authority and their power. They found weaknesses in the prisoners' activities and lives, and exploited those to highlight the inadequacies and anxiety of their

197

victims. The Party was always right, and Communists were taught that self-criticism led to perfection, and therefore did not suspect any wrongdoing in Stalinist practices. Their feeling of innocence was undermined by their arrest, which was ordered by the Party.

They were led to look into themselves for the responsibility for their mistakes.

Milan Kundera pointed out K.'s behaviour in *The Trial*: 'Without having done anything wrong, K. immediately begins to behave as though he is guilty. He feels guilty. He has been made to feel guilty. He has been culpabilized.' K. has been induced with feelings of guilt. This reaction was well used by the interrogators.

On one occasion early in December 1949 Löbl was taken to a large room on the first floor of the prison. Two men were seated behind a desk, one was bald and looked about forty-five and spoke Ukrainian; the other, about the same age, spoke Russian. The Ukrainian did the talking. Interrogators Doubek and Kohoutek were also present. At first they tried to persuade Löbl that sentence had already been passed on him and that, if he were to save his life, he must at least show positive repentance by revealing the identity of his accomplices and chiefs. When this attempt proved futile, they repeated their stereotyped accusations and threatened to have the hide off him. They had plenty of effective means of making him talk. Then they delivered a long tirade against the Jews which would have done honour to any Gestapo man.

The prisoners were always blindfolded or wore motorcycle goggles with black glass when taken from their cells to disorient them and prevent them seeing other prisoners in the corridors. They were beaten by truncheons and fed on bread and water.

Major Doubek confirmed how the Soviet advisors Likhachev and Makarov screamed, beat and shook the accused during interrogations. The main aims of the interrogations were to convince the prisoner of his guilt at all costs. During cross-examinations the Soviets stressed that the lack of actual subversive material evidence was easily explained on the grounds that experienced spies and enemies of the Party did not leave proof of their activities after them; therefore it was necessary to pressure them to confess. Because such people were usually especially obdurate it was necessary that they should be given no time to prepare for interrogation, as otherwise it would be advantageous for them if they came to the interrogation fresh – they would have the strength to resist the interrogator's arguments. It was necessary to exhaust them mentally and convince them that they had no hope of saving themselves and that only admission of the presented charges would secure them some small benefit.

To achieve the desired outcome of any interrogation it was established that it must be continued for at least fourteen to sixteen hours every day. In the remaining period the prisoner must not have time to rest, and the time for the interrogation was allocated in such a way that rest was impossible. That was why the Soviets established the hours of interrogation from 8.00 a.m. until 4.00 p.m., followed by a break and then resuming from 8.00 p.m. until midnight. Normally prisoners could sleep from 10.00 p.m. until 6.00 a.m. During the day, even if a prisoner was in the cell, no rest was possible because the prisoners could not sit and had to walk all the time. Time to sleep was reduced because the prisoner was taken back to the cell at midnight, could not generally go to sleep straight away being upset by the interrogation, and was then regularly disturbed by the wardens. Because prisoners had to stand even during their interrogation, they were physically and mentally exhausted, so the interrogators did not need to do much work to persuade them to 'confess'; they became acquiescent. On the other hand the interrogators, as opposed to the prisoners, had an advantage with these working hours. In the morning they could sleep longer and had four hours free in the afternoon which could be spent sleeping or resting – and their proper food and normal living conditions were additionally favourable for them in their confrontation with the prisoners.

The result of this method was that the prisoners were physically exhausted, were in a completely apathetic state and nothing mattered to some as long as they could sleep. In the end they accepted every possible formulation of confession the interrogator offered. Some of them hardly perceived what they were signing.

This was not the only forcible method employed. To exhaust the prisoners further physical force was used. They were placed in solitary confinement and normal prison allowances were suspended. To keep the Czech interrogators' spirits up the Soviets convinced them that they were the 'fist of the proletariat'. Pravoslav Janoušek was one of the Czech interrogators, and his preferred way of working was to place a metal bucket over a prisoner's head and beat it with a heavy stick. He liked to wear a red jacket and a Lenin-like cap with a large five-pointed star. It was said that he could make an Egyptian mummy confess to espionage.

On 2 November 1950, a month after Otto Šling's arrest, he was questioned non-stop for twenty-two hours in order to make him admit his 'crimes'. Major Doubek later confirmed that 'during his entire interrogation career he had never seen a suspect treated as badly as Šling was in the early interrogation sessions'. Doubek instructed his subordinates 'to turn the Regional Party Secretary into cow dung'. However, after this session Šling retracted the state-ment that had been forced out of him. On 11 and 12 November, and involving five interrogators in a continuous rota in order to exhaust Šling completely and break him morally, they launched an interrogation that lasted over thirty hours. Even after this session an interrogator reported that the prisoner 'still refused to expand his statements'. It took interrogators months to achieve Šling's eventual submission.

All the confessions were first translated into Russian and approved and corrected by the Moscow Centre before they were forwarded to the higher Czechoslovak authorities. The Soviets had full control of the proceedings down to the last detail. The forced confessions they achieved were passed on to presidential and ministerial departments, as well as those confessions reached and gained under normal interrogation conditions. On such a basis the Czechoslovak Communist Party made its decisions about the fate of the accused, although Stalin and his men knew what happened in the proceedings and interrogations long before the Czechs did. The Soviet advisors established and imposed their own methods and set up their leading roles in the major security decision making. The idea of stationing Soviet advisors in all the Eastern Block countries was to subordinate their own State Security departments fully and keep them under the tight control of Moscow.

Gottwald's deputy Zápotocký had been a young political detainee in the 1920s, when Communist Party members campaigned against the oppression of the proletariat by the capitalist system, and he confirmed that the treatment of political prisoners in the 1950s was pure hell in comparison with his own experience.

23 Making Trade

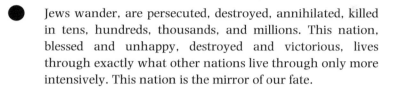

Jews wander, are persecuted, destroyed, annihilated, killed
in tens, hundreds, thousands, and millions. This nation,
blessed and unhappy, destroyed and victorious, lives
through exactly what other nations live through only more
intensively. This nation is the mirror of our fate.

Jiří Kovtun, *Tajuplná vražda – Případ Leopolda Hilsnera/*
A Mysterious Murder – The Case of Leopold Hilsner, 1994

Surprisingly the Soviet Union encouraged the establishment of Israel
during the United Nations negotiations in May 1947. The Soviet
Union wanted to have a foothold in the Middle East, and her position
was opposite to that of the West and Great Britain. British and
Western policies favoured the Arab states and safeguarding oil
supplies. After the war, Czechoslovakia supported the founding of
Israel with the help of her Minister of Foreign Affairs Jan Masaryk,
and was one of the first countries to recognize the new state in May
1948.

Even Czechoslovakia's internal policies propped up the
minority population, those who were left after the war, and the
government suppressed the unrest against the Jews in Slovakia in
August 1945. The next year the government allowed thousands of
Jews to make unhindered journeys to the West through Czechoslovak
territories and helped in the resettlement of uprooted Jewish children
from Poland. In the summer of 1947 David Ben Gurion, the leader
of Haganah in Palestine, asked sympathetic countries to supply
them with weapons for their struggle for independence. In January
1948 a secret document of cooperation between Haganah and
Czechoslovakia was signed with the agreement of the Soviet Union.
The weapons were delivered to Palestine via Hungary, Yugoslavia
and, clandestinely, through Italy, eventually reaching Tel Aviv.
In March 1948 more weapons were requested and a Czechoslovak

DC3 was sent to fly to Palestine with another consignment, which aided the defence of Jewish positions in the conflict with Arab states. Czechoslovakia wanted to help more, but did not have enough hard currency to finance further supplies and therefore offered hardware from her own surplus. Similarly, the young state of Israel had no money to buy the weapons needed to defend the country. In March 1948 Deputy Prime Minister Zápotocký discussed additional weapons supply with the politicians and diplomats Mordechei Oren and Ehud Avriel, who represented the Haganah. Zápotocký also promised to train Israeli pilots and parachutists in Czechoslovakia. In April and May, the Czechoslovak government agreed to supply Haganah with eighty-five aircraft.

However, in January 1949, the first Israeli elections were won by the pro-Western David Ben Gurion's Mapai Party, which formed a coalition with the religious parties rather than with the leftists' parties which were supported by the Soviet Union, and Soviet hope of influence in the region collapsed. Moscow had also become isolated from the Arab world. In a complete turnaround, the Soviets began anti-Zionist political campaigns resulting in rabid anti-Semitism. Jews were attacked both at home and abroad as the enemies of Communism, the Soviet peoples and policies. The Soviet objective of self-interest was to push Britain out of the Middle East by creating a vacuum in the region. Britain was losing her hold on Egypt, and Iraq and Syria were in discontent. The Soviet intention was to appease the Arab world by indulging in anti-Semitic, anti-Zionist policies and provocations as part of their reorientation.

At the time of Czechoslovakia's support for permanent Jewish settlement in Palestine, Rudolf had a meeting with Avriel at his office in the Federation of Czechoslovak Industry. Avriel requested help with finance to buy more weapons for the Haganah units and Rudolf made him a proposal that would benefit both parties. A Czech drinks company would export kosher slivovitz to the United States in large quantities. Each bottle would be decorated with a chain and the Star of David. All bottles would be individually packed in well-designed packaging, and religious and rich Jewish customers would buy the slivovitz. The profits made from sales would partly be invested in the Czechoslovak economy and partly go into the Haganah fund to finance weapons supply from Czechoslovakia.

Prosecutor Aleš: 'Testify about Action Überall.'

Defendant Margolius: 'The Action Überall came about at the beginning of 1948 initiated by the former Israeli Ambassador to Czechoslovakia, Avriel. Avriel, then under the name Überall, had already arrived in Prague in 1947. In reality he organized a Zionist organisation and its activities here. With Avriel-Überall both I and Löbl had developed continuous contact during which I did not try to conceal my hostile relationship toward the people's democratic regime.'

Procurator Aleš: 'What was the purpose and aim of Action Überall? Who would profit from it?'

Defendant Margolius: 'The American Zionists, Jewish capitalists in the United States and other emigrants especially from the ranks of Czechoslovak emigration. In the framework of Action Überall those were to become the main buyers, suppliers and coordinators of business dealings with Czechoslovakia. With this arrangement we wanted to facilitate enormous profits and cause further losses to the Czechoslovak economy.'

Prosecutor Aleš: 'And you knew that then?'

Defendant Margolius: 'Yes.'

Prosecutor Aleš: 'And did you actively participate in this Action?'

Defendant Margolius: 'Yes.'

Prosecutor Aleš: 'Why did you do it?'

Defendant Margolius: 'To harm the Czechoslovak economy.'

Shimon Orenstein, Commercial Attaché at the Israeli Embassy in Prague, was arrested on 13 November 1951 at the Czechoslovak–Austrian border post while driving to Vienna. The pretext was that the stamp on his exit permit was rectangular instead of round as required by regulations. Later he was called as a witness in the Slánský Trial. Then he was accused of espionage, treason and sabotage, tried in a public court in August 1953, sentenced to life imprisonment and released on 28 October 1954. After his return to Israel, Orenstein wrote that he met and knew

Rudolf Margolius: 'Margolius did his best to absent himself from meetings between the Israeli representatives and staff members of his Ministry, even on matters in which he was involved as Deputy Minister of Foreign Trade. He was a cautious man, and saw to it that all trade agreements with foreign countries were solely to Czechoslovakia's benefit.'

Late in the 1940s, Luossavaara-Kiirunavaara Aktiebolag, the international ore-processing company located in Koskullskulle near Malmberget in Lappland and owned by the Swedish state, started the acquisition procedure for the Freja open-pit mine with its high-quality, rich magnesium ore deposits by way of negotiations between Sweden and Czechoslovakia.

In the mid 1880s the Rothschild family had bought the Swedish mine through their Vítkovice Mining and Iron Corporation in Ostrava in Moravia. After the Second World War the Czechoslovak Republic confiscated the Vítkovice steelworks – as a foreign-owned property – and in that way became a major shareholder in the Freja mine. In 1948 the Communists took over, trade links with the West were cut and forced co-operation with other Communist states and

Rudolf Margolius (third from left) signing a treaty with Indian government officials (ČTK)

the Soviet Union was demanded by Moscow. The Soviets insisted on transferring the lesser-grade ore supply from their own mines at Krivny Rog to Vítkovice. An outlet for the Russian ore had to be found in order to keep their miners employed, and the supply of the Freja's exceptional ore was sidelined.

A group of Czech diplomats arranged to see Rudolf to obtain instructions for the negotiation strategy prior to the Freja sale. To debate tactics, Rudolf decided to meet his colleagues in the Letná apartment. In an informal setting, more open debate could take place. 'Look, guys,' he said, when they settled down around the low table sipping the strong Turkish coffee provided by Heda, 'I've realized that it would be stupid to resist the Freja mine's repatriation. I've an idea. When we start negotiating, we'll not ask for Swedish crowns in return but for materials that are currently not obtainable on the open market. We'll make a list of the items our industry desperately needs totalling the sale price of 125 million crowns. As the Swedes are keen to close this deal and get their mine back I'm sure we'll succeed. And that will be used as the basis for negotiations. Let's overestimate our demands and then we can downgrade under any Swedish pressure – that way we do not lose anything and appear to give away concessions. We should ask for aluminium, copper, ferrosilicon, pyrites, ferrochrome, atypical ball bearings ... '

To have these rare materials and products in those days of embargo and post-war shortages would be an enormous boost for the Czechoslovak Republic. Without them, the five-year economic plan would have collapsed. The difficult discussions with the Swedish government took several months. The Swedes wanted their mine on their territory back, and in the end agreed to supply the materials in exchange although in slightly amended quantities. Even materials which were not available in Sweden were supplied; pyrite came from Chile and copper from Spain. The resulting source of raw materials saved a number of Czechoslovak industries from total production closure.

Prosecutor Aleš: 'Defendant Margolius, your interrogation ascertained that you were engaged in your subversive anti-state activities also in the interests of the Swedish capitalists. Testify what happened.'

Defendant Margolius: 'In this subversive activity I was engaged through the office of the late Swedish ambassador to the Czechoslovak Democratic Republic, Otto Wilhelm Winter. I knew that Winter was in touch with Löbl, Geminder and Slánský, my co-defendants. Löbl acquainted me with Winter in 1948. From 1949 during our contact I passed on to Winter various spy data about Czechoslovak foreign trade and primarily about the state of our preparations for political and economic discussions with Sweden. Winter was particularly interested in the Czechoslovak discussions with Rothschild regarding the Swedish iron-ore mine, Freja. This mine was owned by the Vítkovice Iron Corporation, which before the war belonged to the Jewish magnates Rothschild. Because I was not interested that the mine continue to belong to Czechoslovakia I betrayed the state of our negotiations to Winter. I told him that the fate of Freja was in the hands of Sweden and if Sweden would not take any action then the mine would remain the property of the Czechoslovak state.'

Prosecutor Aleš: 'In which way did Winter use this information?'

Defendant Margolius: 'Not long afterwards the Swedish government passed new laws regarding the nationalisation of mines belonging to the foreign companies. In fact, the only such mine in Sweden was the Freja. That is why they passed a new law specifically concerning this mine. Czechoslovakia was thus forced to sell the Freja to Sweden for very disadvantageous conditions resulting in enormous losses for the economy of the Czechoslovak Democratic Republic ...'

24 Ruzyně Interlude

●

● Take pity on the hangman,
go straight to the gallows and sing,
sing to the end!

Jiří Orten, *Scestí/Off the Path*, 1941

When Rudolf was driven to the Ruzyně Prison, they did not bother to blindfold him. The State Security agents forgot to bring the blindfold. They had waited for him for over five hours and by the time he arrived home at 11.10 p.m. they were impatient.

As soon as Rudolf was ushered into the prison building, they put a wastepaper basket over his head and he was cursed at: 'You traitor, the cage has fallen, you won't get out of here.'

During the initial interrogation, physical and psychological pressure was exerted on him. Rudolf was punched in the face until his nose and mouth bled. He was not given adequate rations of food and his foot was roped to a nail in the wall. Later, on a number of occasions, he was injected by the prison doctor while being held down by two guards. The injected drug had the effect of making prisoners give positive answers to all the questions, as well as volunteering further evidence under their own initiative during the long and exhausting interrogations.

His case officer, Third Lieutenant Miloslav Kukla, frequently pricked his body with a sharp pencil to show how much fat he had, even though he had not – he was quite trim. Kukla, a younger man of modest background and a former trainee pharmacist, felt inferior to Rudolf, a doctor of law and a highly placed official, and had to learn to overcome his insecurities in a similar way to Sergeant Major Rouček – by force. Kukla's cruel, brutal behaviour arose from his sudden sense of power and domination. He and his interrogator colleagues realized that they held in their hands the fates of important people, members of the government and the Party elite, and now they were able to humiliate and threaten them and treat them in any way they liked.

'You criminal, you're tied like a pig by your foot, pigs are taken to slaughter tied by their feet,' shouted Kukla. Rudolf was placed in a cold, dark, solitary confinement cell with a small open window and did not have adequate clothing. Kukla called him a spy, traitor, saboteur; when he refused to admit anything illegal he was not allowed to go to sleep and when he did, he was awoken every ten minutes. Kukla screamed and swore at him: 'You Jewish swine, we'll teach you how to behave! We respect killers and murderers, they've only done in a person or two but you plotted to kill the whole nation!'

This treatment went on for days. Rudolf was so tired he was falling over – and then they came to put him under a cold shower. They would not let him sit or lie down; he had to walk, day and night.

My Dearest Heda,

Thank you many times for your lovely letter. I am glad that both you and Ivánek are well. Do not trouble yourself about me and do not send any parcels because I do not need anything. I have enough food. You do not need to send my tobacco and pipe, I have enough cigarettes, which I bought from the money I had on me. If it is at all possible, send some money for cigarettes, about 500 to 1,000 crowns. I think of you and Ivánek daily and I kiss you both.

Yours Rudolf

P.S. You can write once a month.

Prague, 30 January 1952

Soon Kukla was sent by his immediate superior, Captain Kohoutek, to see the Sector Director Major Doubek: 'Comrade Director, Margolius refuses to cooperate. I can't get anything out of him. He's all despondent and keeps asking to see Gregor, his superior, or Gottwald, who apparently congratulated him personally on getting some foreign deal together only last month. He wants them to confirm his innocence. Even when I told him the Party would expel him if he didn't confess, that made no difference. What shall I do? I pushed him several times already, called him dirty names, shouted, bloodied my fist but he won't budge.'

'Yes, I don't want to know that,' interrupted Doubek.

Doubek was puzzled as to why Margolius was included in the conspiracy. Slánský had been surprised that Margolius was sharing the same prison accommodation when Doubek told him. They did not know each other and they never communicated with each other, even professionally, yet they were accused of having collaborated in the conspiracy, and Margolius was the only recent Communist among the veteran Party members.

Kukla offered his thoughts to Doubek: that the 'teachers' needed people from Foreign Trade to take the blame for the current economic crisis. The Soviet Union kept complaining that the Czechs were trading more with the imperialists and were not producing enough goods for them. Czechoslovak agriculture was in poor shape and they had to keep supplying the Czechs with foodstuffs. Kukla was convinced that Margolius together with Löbl, both being Jewish, fitted the bill perfectly. Galkin had told him that Margolius

Rudolf and Heda, Krkonoše Mountains, 1950

dealt with large sums of money and that affected public feeling the most.

Doubek carried on. 'Back to your original question, Margolius has a wife and a five-year-old kid, hasn't he? His parents kicked the bucket in the camps or were shot in Latvia, something like that, so that won't help. Tell him we'll arrest the wife and send her off to hard labour in the uranium mines. Auschwitz was a piece of cake in comparison with Jáchymov. That will show him,' laughed Doubek. 'And his brat will be packed off into some municipal orphanage in Slovakia, as far away and as primitive as possible. Over there they hate Jews more than we do. You'll see, he'll change colour after that. The same trick worked with the others. We'll do it anyway to get them out of our sight. Psychology, comrade, that's the best approach, as our comrade teachers tell us,' and Doubek patted Kukla on the back.

'I was remembering you even more than usual on the anniversaries of our birthdays. Sometimes I have images of Ivan together with you, other times my thoughts concentrate on him, other days on you. These days I was only with you, I saw only you. The same as you, I remembered our evening trip uphill under the singing telegraph wires near Příbram, and all our rendezvous and discussions; our roaming in the Prague streets; our first unforgettable glance of a boy at a girl in Chodská Street, twenty years ago; our discoveries of Prague with lovers' eyes at Petřín, Nebozízek or the summer evenings at Hradčany, at Hradiště Hill near Nová Huť with owls hooting, the mushroom picking and playing with kittens (do you remember how a kitten cured my flu in Huť?); our listening to Beethoven or Brahms together, our common joy over your first dust jacket and bookbinding designs and drawings with repaired makeshift glasses; our trips to Žamberk, Písek, Chlum, Podsedice, Babice, Krkonoše, Nouzov and all the rooms where we spent our days and nights, and the windows through which we looked into the green- or snow-covered countryside, or on to the street, or the grey walls of a courtyard; all our lovely, happy, painful and sad moments, precious because they were spent together and blessed by our mutual feeling, up to last year's holiday at Lišno and up to our embrace at the beginning of this year ... '

At one time Rudolf thought he heard a woman cry and shout in a nearby cell. Then Kukla came in: 'You shyster, did you know that just now your whore who was arrested a few days ago tried to commit suicide? And your delinquent brat is in a Slovak orphanage, where he belonged right from day one. And it's your fault, because you haven't confessed.'

Rudolf was so tired that in the end he could not even sign the confession they extorted out of him. The interrogator had to grab him by the shoulder and guide Rudolf's hand with his right hand in order to get him to sign the protocol.

Long before their arrests the persecuted detainees had done everything possible to assimilate and at the same time negate their Jewish background. Most of them had discarded typically Jewish names in favour of more common ones: Schlesinger for Šling, Freund for Frejka, Reisman for Reicin, Katz for Simone. Rudolf had also considered changing his name but abandoned the idea. He wanted to honour the memory of his father and mother and their tragic death by excelling in his work and being remembered for it. The accused remained faithful Communists, fully committed to Socialist causes, even after it had become obvious that their Party had betrayed them.

> Prosecutor Aleš: 'What intelligence reports did you hand over to Koni Zilliacus?'
> Defendant Margolius: 'In summer 1949, when I was in London as the leader of the Czechoslovak delegation which negotiated with Great Britain about trade treaties, financial compensation and debt settlements, I was in touch with British Intelligence. I handed over to Zilliacus via Pavel Kavan secret information about Czechoslovak foreign trade. I knew that Zilliacus was a British Intelligence agent.'
> Prosecutor Aleš: 'No one would suspect that in this way you could so audaciously carry out your spying activity. Is that true?'
> Defendant Margolius: 'That is true.'

In 1957 Koni Zilliacus, the left-wing Labour Party member, recalled: 'It was queer to read in the reports of the Trial

Ivan and Rudolf, 1950

detailed confessions by people I had known in London and Prague to things that neither they nor I had ever done. What I found significant was that all of this was mixed with some of the things that actually happened, but in strangely distorted forms.'

Your memories of our lives and our wishes and hopes for the future, all that brings me closer to you; I lose the feeling of loneliness, your words and memories interleave with all those pictures, images and remembrances which resound within my inner self and transform them into an almost tangible reality. When I close my eyes, I imagine that I can just extend my hand and touch your face or Ivan's little hand; my being is as if I were walking with you again, hand in hand, on a field road shining with daisies, behind the pond at the statue of the Saint, as if I felt the strong air saturated with tree sap on the edge of a forest where we lay, as if I saw again the sun's reflection and shimmer of small fish in the clear water of the stream and heard the muffled and happy screams of the playing Ivan. And immediately I am taken somewhere else, to some other past, or even into your present time, attached to you more deeply than I could ever imagine, as if I permeated, breathed and thought through your body and soul ...

Rudolf felt and thought in prison the same way as many others. His time was spent in interrogations about his activities at the Ministry and exploring past contacts with his colleagues who might have been spies or traitors.

Primarily he learned by heart his falsely constructed evidence protocol, based on the forced confessions prepared by the Soviet advisors and Czechoslovak State Security, and was tested in its delivery twice a day. The whole trial was scripted beforehand, including all the questions to be asked by the judges and the prosecutors. Rudolf had to sign each page, endorsing its content.

Apart from that, in the little spare time left, he read books by Russian authors from the prison library, contemplated, remembered, paraphrased music and relived his life.

My dearest Heda, you wrote correctly last time that we have inside ourselves a bottomless well of life-impressions in common, from the books we have read and the musical scores we have listened to. Now I live on these memories, some of which seemingly have disappeared from our remembrance, and presently these almost dry streams of our cohabitation come alive in their full strength and freshness ...

The American Erica Wallach, who was imprisoned by the East Germans in the early 1950s, had exactly the same experiences: 'Whatever reality could not supply I filled in with memories. I relived my whole life, every detail of it ... and I got a great deal of pleasure out of it. How lucky I was to have had such a happy childhood, such a wealth of interesting experiences, such an abundance of all the beauty life can provide. The lack of beauty in prison – music, a good smell, something pretty to look at – was sometimes harder to bear than loneliness and loss of love and freedom ... The re-creation of music I knew was one of the hardest but most satisfactory of my occupations, although I never did get all the pieces of the various symphonies, concertos, and suites together. Sometimes I worked systematically on symphony after symphony ... on everything I had ever heard and loved ... When a whole passage of *Eine Kleine Nachtmusik* suddenly sang in my ears, I was overjoyed.'

After their confessions were forced out of them and they had learned their evidence the prisoners were better fed and drugs were no longer administered by injection or in the soup they were getting. They were taken out of solitary confinement, had one hour of exercise a day and shared cells. Rudolf was allowed to be with Vladimír Clementis for a short time. They recreated Dvořák's Cello Concerto in B minor, Op. 104, whistling the whole score – all three movements, *Allegro, Adagio ma non troppo* and *Allegro moderato* – with one replicating the solo instrument and the other filling in the orchestral support, for its full extent of over forty minutes.

Dr Josef Sommer kept them under strict medical supervision in order to eliminate any signs of hardship they may have suffered in preparation for the 'show'. He gave them tranquillisers during the Trial itself – though as soon as the sentences were passed all their 'privileges' ceased.

The sun that visits me (now less frequently with the grey autumn sky) and with which I am intimately acquainted, sits at the same place when I arrived here and counts with me the days that I have spent here with it. We talk together about both of you. What you are doing, how you are feeling; we recite the contents and words of the letters that I received from you and in this way we shorten our time leading to the beginning of the new month, when your new letter usually arrives, reviving the memories of my 'two little mice'. In the last few days I lived through a period of strong longing for you and Ivánek, maybe because of the overcast days and the sun that was neglecting me. I overcame the sadness; I urged on the sun and it appeared again to speed up the arrival of November and your new letter to let me know how things are with you. I look forward immensely to your news, I want it in front of me, including your photographs.

A week before the commencement of the Trial of the fourteen defendants – eleven described as being of Jewish origin, two Czechs (Frank and Šváb) and a Slovak (Clementis) – President Gottwald sat in his private office, drunk, staring at the list of the accused who were selected for execution. Beschasnov had dropped it on his desk only some minutes earlier. They had not spoken since they had clashed several weeks previously. The Soviets demanded that the indicted Jews should be labelled as being of Jewish nationality. Gottwald resisted, arguing that this could be done in Moscow but not in Central Europe while the whole world was watching.

Then Gottwald relented: 'Yes, call them Jews.' He had changed his mind since his trip to Moscow on Stalin's invitation in the late October of 1952. He was fearful for himself. They had been discussing the Trial in Stalin's dacha. Stalin was well informed of its details, as well as having intimate knowledge of the running of the Czechoslovak government. He had even criticised Gottwald's deputy Zápotocký for spending more time writing books than running the country. In July 1951 Stalin had invited Gottwald to discuss the further need for show trials following Horáková's case but Gottwald was frightened and sent his son-in-law and close confidant, Alexej Čepička, Minister of Defence, instead.

And now this list. 'Why eleven, that's too many surely; can't we cross some out? In Horáková's case there were only four!'

General Beschasnov stood firm: 'In fact we wanted all the fourteen but thought you would never consent. Now, this is what we require: the maximum impact in all the sectors of government, otherwise we lose the whole effect. Enemies of the Party have to be eliminated.'

'Is that what they are after? How is it possible that suddenly old Communists, hardened revolutionaries, my old friends, should raise their hands against their own country, against the revolution, against the working class and against Socialism?' thought Gottwald, still unsure even after seeing the reported confessions.

Beschasnov lectured him as if reading his mind: 'You know Stalin's directive: the class struggle continues and escalates even after Socialism is achieved. The revolution uses up men like an acid eats away softness. The least conflict with the Party, the least deviation, necessarily leads to crime. The class enemy pushes his way into the space that opens up between our Party and the man who deviates from the general line. A man is either for us or against us. There's no middle or any other way.'

'If I don't agree it'll be me next, Slánský may not be high enough for them ...' Gottwald remembered Security telling him that he was being watched by the Soviets. He had his private apartment checked for surveillance and, sure enough, they found hidden microphones of Russian manufacture, but left them so as not to arouse any suspicion that he knew. He had to play along. He had not had the chance to discuss this with Stalin privately and was extremely worried.

Beschasnov advised Gottwald to send a high official to talk to the defendants to make sure they would 'perform' without a hitch as the Trial – as usual – would be broadcast in full over the national radio network. They could not have a repetition of the Triacho Kostov Trial fiasco of December 1949 in Sofia when Kostov refused to recite his statements during his trial as agreed in his preliminary investigation. The judges panicked and Kostov's agreed deposition had to be read by the judges while he was not allowed to speak.

This time they arranged a safe scenario should a defendant fail to recite his prepared script. A general rehearsal was arranged. In a special room with a hidden microphone Doubek asked questions and the defendant replied, thinking that he was being tested. In the next room a State Security agent recorded the statements. In case of mishap, should the defendant refuse to answer, the tape would be switched on in the court. The tapes were played for Gottwald and the Party Political Secretariat to give them a preview of the coming 'show'.

Gottwald swallowed another gulp of wine and picked up the phone with trembling hands; he had difficulty in dialling. He summoned his Minister of State Security Karol Bacílek, who had replaced Kopřiva in January 1952, and the rest of the Secretariat of the Party Central Committee. Later the Czechoslovak Party political commission argued with Beschasnov and amended the defendants' designation to 'of Jewish origin'.

At that time, the aftermath of the Korean War that lasted from June 1950 to July 1951, US Senator Joseph McCarthy's anti-Communist witch-hunt and the 1952 American presidential election all distracted world politicians from perceiving the continual increase of Soviet repression. The elimination of German military power at the end of the Second World War created a political vacuum in Europe. No long-term strategy was established by the victorious Western nations for the post-war years in Central and Eastern Europe, apart from the agreements reached at Yalta. The Western governments and their ageing leaders were too weak to resist expansionist pressure from Moscow. They had enough problems to solve in their own countries and unrest in the Far and Middle East was taking priority. The USA stood back from European affairs.

The Russian Revolution of 1917 had replaced a decadent, feudal and authoritarian Tsarist dynasty with the new, vigorous and ruthlessly single-minded dynasty of Lenin and Stalin. The prime driving force in Russian politics had been the distrust of other peoples. The Russians have experienced ten centuries of constant fear, as they have had to defend their territory against armed hordes of hostile nations. Their country lacks natural defensive frontiers and mortal danger could appear from all sides. Russia, throughout history, had always made an effort to create a large, safeguarded buffer zone around herself for protection. This was confirmed in Georgy Malenkov's report to the 19th Soviet Party Congress in October 1952: 'The Soviet state is no longer a lone oasis surrounded by capitalist countries. We are moving forward together with the great Chinese people, together with the many millions of the people's democracies and the German Democratic Republic. We have the sympathy and support of all progressive mankind.' (Prolonged applause.)

The Theatre of Absurdity

> Suddenly into the world on all sides
> wireless news and telegrams have flown
> and tomorrow they will read in the newspapers
> that in Prague dummies in the shop windows
> raised the red flag above the town.

Jaroslav Seifert, *Revoluce/Revolution*, 1921

The Communists had played an outstanding part in the wartime resistance movements, their discipline was exemplary, their reputation was high and their political cohesion, obedience and strength was massive. All these factors, as well as sympathy for them, created the contemporary atmosphere of giving the Soviets the upper hand without interference from outside.

In the summer of 1952 the eye of the world focused on the 15th Olympic Games in Helsinki. The Czech runner Emil Zátopek won three gold medals in the 5,000 and 10,000 metres and the marathon, the first athlete to achieve this feat, and lifted the Czech spirit which was wading in the gloom of arrests, trials, food shortages and continuous rationing.

While Zátopek competed against the clock, Rudolf was learning his closely typed deposition protocol of over fifty pages by heart, rehearsing it with a stopwatch so he would speak at a normal conversational rate. He had very bad recall and it was agony for him to memorize anything. 'Slow down!' shouted Kukla when Rudolf reeled his lines off too quickly so that he could get it over.

My dearest Heda, you write about your longing and you call to me to return. I also feel the same, I long terribly for you both and on top of that, my conscience worries me that all this happened through my guilt, that I caused you all this pain. My dear Heda, you must not submit yourself to sadness. Longing is an expression of our mutual feeling, which at least for me, with separation from you, is greatly enhanced. This feeling must give us strength and courage.

A day before the Trial all the accused, except Slánský, were taken blindfolded from their cells to talk to Bacílek, who sat in his General's uniform in Major Doubek's office in the Ruzyně Prison.

'Who's next?' he asked Doubek.

'Margolius from the Foreign Trade, Comrade Minister,' answered Doubek politely.

'Yes, this one is something, Gottwald tried to cross him off the death sentence list, but the Soviets insisted it had to be at least eleven men, Beschasnov was very adamant on this. And I suppose Löbl deserves a lighter sentence as he was the first in custody and helped to unmask the rest of the gang.'

When Rudolf entered and his blindfold was removed Bacílek told him that the Party relied on his good performance. This was a political trial and his testimony had to correspond to the agreed protocol which he had memorized. He must adhere to that, there must be no deviations and his sentence would depend on his presentation and behaviour. This would be his greatest contribution to the victory of Socialism. He did not need to worry: the Party would look after his family while he was in custody.

'I won't do any damage to the Party or the country,' Rudolf nodded. Kukla had already threatened him that if he tried to alter his testimony it would be the death of him – and his family would be 'destroyed'.

Rudolf recalled reading Søren Kierkegaard's *The Concept of Anxiety*, written in 1844, where the great philosopher stated: 'The individual becomes guilty not because he is guilty but because of his anxiety about being thought guilty.' Rudolf felt it was his duty to perform as demanded; he was not guilty but the Party asked him to support it in its hour of need. After his arrest and realization of the true situation Rudolf had great doubts about whether the people he envisaged taking the country to its ultimate goal – a true socialist society – actually had the intellectual capacity and moral integrity to lead it and whether they were fully responsible and in charge of their actions. Ironically it was exactly like Koestler's *Darkness at Noon* which Tigrid had lent him. Bacílek sounded like Gletkin who told Rubashov: 'Your testimony at the trial will be the last service you can do to the Party.' The Party denied the free will of the individual – and, at the same time, exacted his willing sacrifice. Except all that had been fiction: Rudolf was in the real world.

In the 1950s' political trials the main figure in courtroom proceedings was the public prosecutor, not the judges, as laid down by the Czechoslovak laws and regulations based on the Soviet system: 'In principle, the judges are to regard as binding proposals presented by the prosecutor in the course of a public trial. If the judge does not intend to do so, he must first consult the court presidium. The court must inform the prosecutor in advance of the judgement it is about to hand down and get his opinion whether the judgement is correct and appropriate to the situation, for the information available to the prosecutor is generally more complete. The prosecutor's opinion is binding on the court.' The court does not decide on the basis of the evidence it has heard and observed, but functions according to the instructions of the prosecution, which has gathered its information outside the courtroom. In turn the material for the prosecutor has been prepared word for word by the State Security interrogators and Soviet advisors.

The Trial was held at the High Court in Pankrác between 20 and 27 November, was presided over by five judges and attended by a selected audience from the ranks of the proletariat that changed daily. At the opening, Dr Josef Urválek, the chief public prosecutor later elevated for his outstanding effort to the post of Chief Justice of the Supreme Court, read out passionately the indictment stating that 'the accused as Trotskyite, Titoite, Zionist and bourgeois nationalist traitors created, in the service of the US imperialists and under the direction of Western espionage agencies, an Anti-State Conspiratorial Centre, undermined the people's democratic regime, frustrated the building of Socialism, damaged the national economy, carried out espionage activities, weakened the unity of the Czechoslovak people and the Republic's defensive capacity in order to tear the country away from its close alliance and friendship with the Soviet Union, to liquidate the people's regime in Czechoslovakia, to restore capitalism and destroy the Republic's national sovereignty and independence . . . The conspirators did all they could to prevent the supply of our goods to the Soviet Union and the other people's democratic states, neglecting contracts and asking for higher prices for these goods than the current prices on the world market. In the capitalist states, on the other hand, they sold the same goods at considerably reduced rates in comparison with the prices for the USSR, and far below the level of the prices on the world market . . . '

On the second day of the Trial Bedřich Geminder, Chief of the International Section of the Party Secretariat, was interrogated and humiliated.

> Judge Novák: 'What nationality are you?
> Defendant Geminder: 'Czech.'
> Judge Novák: 'Can you speak Czech well?'
> Defendant Geminder: 'Yes.'
> Judge Novák: 'Do you want an interpreter?'
> Defendant Geminder: 'No.'
> Judge Novák: 'Can you understand the questions and will you be able to reply in Czech?'
> Defendant Geminder: 'Yes.'
> Prosecutor Urválek: 'What school did you go to?'
> Defendant Geminder: 'I went to the German school in Ostrava.'
> Prosecutor Urválek: ' . . . you never really learned to speak Czech well, not even in 1946 when you came back to Czechoslovakia and occupied important posts in the Communist Party?'
> Defendant Geminder: 'No, I didn't learn to speak Czech properly.'
> Prosecutor Urválek: 'What language can you speak perfectly?'
> Defendant Geminder: 'German.'
> Prosecutor Urválek: 'Can you really speak German properly?'
> Defendant Geminder: 'I haven't spoken it for a long time, but I know it well.'
> Prosecutor Urválek: 'Can you speak German as well as Czech?'

Defendant Geminder: 'Yes.'
Prosecutor Urválek: 'You cannot really speak any language properly, can you? You are a typical cosmopolitan. As such you sneaked into the Communist Party.'

André Simone, one of the defendants who lived abroad before the war, the editor of the Czech Communist daily, *Rudé právo*, was accused of having intelligence contacts with Noël Coward and Paul Willert in Paris restaurants and cafés, specifically to recruit him as a British agent in 1939. Apparently Coward and Willert had requested information about German propaganda in France, the French Army and the activities of the proletarian movement and the Communist Party of France.

Simone concluded his testimony on November 22: 'There is a beautiful saying that the writer is an engineer of human souls. What kind of engineer was I who poisoned these souls? Such an engineer belongs on the gallows. The only service I can still render is to serve as a warning to those who, because of their origin, their character and qualities are in danger of going the same diabolical way as I did. The more severe my punishment, the more effective will be the warning.' Simone used Stalin's description of writers as 'engineers of human souls', which he had stated in a talk in Maxim Gorky's apartment on 26 October 1932.

On the fifth day of the Trial, on 24 November, Rudolf Margolius testified.

Defendant Margolius: 'Not only have I agreed to the trade agreement to supply television tubes to Great Britain, but in the following years I supported and actively enforced the fulfilment of this export despite a warning from the Ministry of National Defence that it was possible to use these tubes for military purposes. By this action, I weakened the defence of the Czechoslovak Republic consciously and strengthened the military potential of Great Britain.'
Prosecutor Aleš: 'In this case, it is specifically obvious that you tried to drag the Czechoslovak Republic into a war conflict. Is that so?'

Defendant Margolius: 'Yes.'
Prosecutor Aleš: 'Therefore your conspiracy was a part of a greater conspiracy that the imperialists plotted against the Soviet Union and against the whole democratic peace movement for years.'
Defendant Margolius: 'Yes.'
Prosecutor Aleš: 'By doing this, did you infringe world peace?'
Defendant Margolius: 'Yes.'
Prosecutor Aleš: 'Did you place yourself among the collaborators of warmongers?'
Defendant Margolius: 'Yes.'

The Trial proceeded without any major difficulties for its instigators. However, one of the public prosecutors was sharply rebuked by his colleagues for twice skipping a scripted question so the defendant ended up giving answers that did not match. Then there was one light moment when Otto Šling, having lost weight in two years of custody, dropped his trousers, which had become far too big for him, while gesticulating during his evidence. He bent down to pick them up and exposed his behind to the court. Everybody laughed till tears ran down their faces. Clementis was one of the ones to laugh most. He tried to calm himself by squeezing his pipe to breaking point between his teeth. Slánský laughed so much that his whole body shook. The audience roared and the judges and prosecutors hid their faces behind their papers. Above all the defendants saw in this event the whole absurdity of the occasion.

The absurdity continued with the public prosecutor's summing up, but by then the laughter was long forgotten: 'They hid behind their Communist Party cards, behind that red booklet sung by one of our poets ... They hid in vain. The Party, with President Gottwald at its head, crushed this gang of traitors in time. Our people will never know the gratitude it owes to Comrade Gottwald for having systematically thwarted the criminal efforts of the conspirators plotting against the Republic ... Citizen judges! In the name of our people, whose liberty and happiness have been endangered by these criminals, in the name of the peace against which they have conspired so infamously, I demand the death penalty for all the accused. May your judgement be pitiless, like a fist of steel. May it be the flame that burns out the roots of this tree sapped by treason! May it be a bell ringing across our beautiful country, calling it to the new conquests in her march toward the sun of Socialism.'

The defence lawyers, mostly members of State Security who were there for show, made weak speeches supporting the public prosecutor's view rather than defending their clients' position. The defendants were each asked to say a last word.

Defendant Margolius: 'I am conscious of all the terrible crimes which I caused. I served the Anglo-American imperialists; I served those who were the followers of Nazism. I helped them to disrupt and hamper the achievements of millions of honest hard-working people. I know that I am not able to offer anything to apologize for my crimes. At least during my detention I tried to reconcile myself with the crimes I committed and that was why I confessed. I cannot ask for less than the severest punishment.'

On Thursday, 27 November – the eighth day of the Trial – at 9.30 in the morning, as the final act, the sentences were passed. The defendants, the audience as well as the rest of the courtroom were

The Accused, Slánský Trial, Rudolf Margolius (second from the left)

225

stunned; most of the interrogators were astonished by their severity. There was hushed silence. Eleven death sentences and three life imprisonments! The defendants were led out in a line with warders between each of them and placed in the plywood boxes along the corridor at the rear of the courtroom. They were looking for their interrogators to find out what would happen; the interrogators who had been reassuring, telling them before the Trial that they would get a maximum of twenty-five years. Rudolf was predicted to get only ten.

Now, though, Rudolf was calm and dignified and watched others seeking their interrogators and defence lawyers. But the interrogators who were there with them to support them and lead them during the Trial had disappeared; the ones who made them promises, their only link to the Party, to Gottwald, to the world outside, the little hope they had, had gone. Surely that meant the end; the show was over.

When the defence lawyers came, they advised them against appeals. There were mountains of resolutions arriving, the international situation was very difficult, the Americans were becoming more aggressive and, inevitably, a new world war was imminent. In the end the defendants accepted the harsh sentences imposed on them, as they had been persuaded that their punishment would hasten the triumph of the Communist cause throughout the world.

They were taken back into the court and one by one accepted their sentences and renounced their right to appeal. They were then escorted back to their cells in the basement of Pankrác Prison. After two hours, the three with the life sentences were driven to Ruzyně, leaving their eleven comrades behind. The lawyers acting on behalf of all the eleven condemned to death sent clemency pleas to Gottwald. Heda also wrote a personal letter to the President requesting clemency for Rudolf. The requests were rejected on 2 December. Heda never received a reply.

The *New York Post* of 24 November 1952 wrote: 'One explanation advanced [for the Trial] may be called the 'theory of domestic consumption' – that the Communists are putting on a big show for the restless Czechoslovak people – thus when Ludvík

Frejka, who headed the economic Ministry, says that as a result of his conspiracy the Czech economy was wrecked, hence the food and electricity rationing now in Czechoslovakia, the purpose is clear. It is to explain the wretched living standards of the Czech people, turn their wrath away from the Russians who have looted their economy, and turn it against the Jews.'

During and at the end of the Trial over 8,500 resolutions and telegrams addressed to the Central Committee of the Party and the High Court arrived calling for strict punishment or death for the accused. They came from Party members, Peoples' Street Communes, factories, mines, schools, trade unions, workers' committees and even non-Party members. Anti-Semitic feeling prevailed in most of them. Thousands of resolutions even conveyed a lack of confidence in the judges because they gave three defendants reduced sentences. Delegations from factories arrived at the court communicating their mistrust and demanded an investigation as to whether the judges were not deliberately covering up for the enemy.

Publicly, the majority of the population believed in the Trial but privately many expressed real doubts. To survive and preserve their families and livelihoods the Czechoslovaks had to act and think as the Party demanded.

Václav Kopecký, Minister of Information and a member of the Political Secretariat of the Party, voiced his opinion at the December 1952 National Congress of the Party: 'During the Trial we saw how the sympathies with people of Jewish origin that our working people had after the time of Hitler's racial purges were criminally misused. This situation was taken advantage of so the Jewish bourgeois nationalists in the service of American imperialism could plot their criminal activities against our Republic; the capitalist elements of Jewish origin shamelessly pilfered from our state; the sons of rich Jewish men have wormed themselves into important economic positions under the auspices of Socialism to make money to supplant profits for the Western racketeers and to slow down the building of Socialism in our country, to sabotage, to injure and to try to sell off the achievements of our working people and the freedom and independence of our country for American dollars.'

Workers sending a resolution (Kaplan Productions Archive)

The Times of 25 November 1952 mentioned that a gruesome letter written to President Gottwald by Lisa Londonová [née Ricol, born in France], wife of Artur London, had been read in court. Mrs Londonová wrote that hitherto she had believed her husband to be a victim of Slánský's machinations, but now she recognized that he was a traitor. 'I and my family are all Communists,' the letter continued, 'and I now have the difficult task of telling the two older children (there is a third who is still very young) the truth about their father. I am happy to be living with my family in a Communist country – a country that is fighting in the peace camp. I am happy that the Slánský gang has been rendered harmless, and I ask the court to pass a severe sentence on my husband.'

Three days later, on 28 November, *The Times* reported that a Czechoslovak Radio commentator had brought two miners and an electrical worker to the microphone. The miners said they and their comrades had already decided to work harder to repair the damage done by the dastardly saboteurs. The other man, who was from Armaturka factory in Ústí nad Labem, said that while listening to the sentences this morning he and his factory had decided to work an extra voluntary shift and give their earnings to the children of Korea as an expression of gratitude to the judges.

The Slovak poet Milan Lajčiak wrote on the same day: 'Farmhands looking after the sows committed to wean at least thirteen [!] piglets each. We announce with pride that to celebrate the birthday of Comrade Gottwald we fulfilled the pork meat contract to 107.38 per cent and completed the autumn deep ploughing at the same time. That is the response of the Nový Dvůr Cooperative to the imperialist spies.'

Even serious local newspapers such as the *Literární noviny* (Literature News) of the Czechoslovak Writers Union published an anonymous poem illustrating the feeling of the common man, brainwashed by the current events of the time:

'Traitors'

A traitor lurks behind the border
To destroy us is his order
He is training all his spies
And they cross the borderlines!

You are liars, you promised us
Heaven right by our door
But your lies could not chain us
We are not slaves any more!

Listen you fascists and all traitors
Your plans lie now in shambles here
Our guards have done a good job
Be prepared, the end is near!

The verdict is just and fair
Signed by every citizen

We all know well how to get rid
Of treachery and fascism!

Since we are free of landowners
Our life is happy too
And all spies and troublemakers
We shall beat as we now do!

An infamous article – 'Three Benches' – by writer and poet Ivan Skála published in *Rudé právo* on Friday, 28 November described Rudolf Margolius:

'At the time when the critical grain supply situation developed and flour coupons had to be introduced the accused Margolius, in his criminal effort to institute hunger and discontent, contrabanded 20,000 tonnes of grain to Holland, Switzerland and Belgium. During the 1950–51 period Margolius with his treacherous collaborators fraudulently dispatched 1,000 tonnes of tinned meat to Great Britain, Switzerland and France. This vermin, under the pretext of lies, sabotaged our trade with the people's democracies and instead exported our products to capitalist countries for a price that was lower than the price of the basic ingredient, and did so often with the knowledge that the price of our goods would not be honoured. When you turn this villain, reeking of treason, inside out you find a disgusting procreation of capitalism – a millionaire's son whose father was a Freemason and mother a Zionist. These people hindered our journey of progress. Such reptiles!

'And today, today we can say: the dirty vipers' nest is crushed. It squirms here in the last spasm in front of the anger of the nation. We shall eradicate this race to the last snake. We shall search for them in all the crevices and we shall look in each at least twice.

'Three simple oak benches sag under the weight of the crimes committed by the treacherous conspirators. But all this terrible heaviness after years of compilation of sabotage, ghoulish treachery, colossal clumps of leaches, all this enormous weight has fallen from our people. We breathed with difficulty under this pressure but the legionnaires of imperialism did not succeed in throttling us. Now without them we shall work and sing, rock children on our laps with clear conscience. Now under this burden they will suffocate themselves.

'For their services, they got just rewards. The dog's death to the dog!'

The report on the sentences in *The Times* of 28 November 1952 read: 'The only surprising aspect of the presiding judge Dr Jaroslav Novák's statement pronouncing the sentences is that Margolius, who was one of Löbl's colleagues at the Ministry of Foreign Trade, is not among those who have been given the reduced penalty.'

The Party's travesty had to go on to keep satisfying the anger aroused in the public, and the men remaining in power had to protect themselves from the awful deeds they committed in the name of the Party and the Soviet Union. However, sensible observers could see through the veils of the false accusations. It must have seemed unbelievable that the accused would readily confess to the long lists of political crimes. There were no credible reasons for the offences of long-standing Communists and no plausible proofs offered by the prosecution. Unbelievably, the defendants voluntarily requested the harshest punishment. Shame, that any sensible onlookers were afraid to act or protest against the outcome of the Trial. However, incredibly, some naive observers and even some from abroad swallowed the propaganda and believed the Trial word for word. One such opinion was voiced by Louis Harap in *Jewish Life*, New York, in January 1953. 'It is hard to believe that fourteen men, who possessed considerable ability and were noted public figures, would all confess to something for which they knew the penalty was death unless they were guilty of what they confessed. The only sane conclusion at which one can arrive is that these men confessed because they were confronted with irrefutable evidence of their guilt.'

An article published in the *New Statesman* on 6 December 1952 mentioned: 'Motives of personal gain were never alleged: the "crimes", the "economic" sabotage, were always "political". But public credulity, even in Prague, must surely have been strained by some of the allegations. Dr Margolius, Löbl and others, were "guilty" of negotiating with the West limited trade agreements of which the government had fully approved. In consequence, they had "increased British war potential" by exporting to the UK, for use in television sets, certain component parts produced by the large and at present under-employed Czech glass industry.'

On the same day *The Economist* summed up the feeling of people living in the free societies: 'Sometimes history imitates art in a grotesque and terrifying manner. In that wistful city of Prague where Kafka wrote *The Trial*, there ended last week a travesty of justice more bestial and absurd than any ever conjured up by a novelist. Revolutionary leaders and Czech Communists whose lives had passed between underground and barricade, men who had survived Nazi torture camps, rose before the judges of the people's courts to plead for their own death ... As one, the eleven doomed men rose and demanded that no appeal be allowed and that the sentence of hanging be carried out at once ... The story is more appalling than that of Rajk or Kostov because it took place in a cultured modern city, within short range of Western Europe and amid a population familiar with democratic processes and ways of thinking.'

The outgoing American President Harry S. Truman issued a statement on 21 December 1952. It said: 'Decent men everywhere are disturbed by the revelations of the Prague Trials. We Americans cannot condemn these procedures too forcefully. The persecution of political, racial or religious minority groups is contrary to everything we stand for and believe in.' The new President elect, Dwight D. Eisenhower, confirmed on the same day: 'The Communists, like Russian Tsars and the German Nazis, are using the Jews as scapegoats for the failure of their regime.'

The Czechoslovak government ignored all the protests and none of these free-world views were accessible to the Czechoslovak people; foreign radio broadcasts were jammed and Western newspapers were unobtainable. Only the Communist press from other people's democracies was available on Prague's news-stands, and it followed Moscow directives.

The sound of broken furniture and shattered glass was heard over the fields and small gathering of houses. The beer glasses, full, half-full and empty, were thrown into the air, going right through the windows and landing in pieces on the muddy porch followed by a shower of window glass. The few customers that were there, now wet from the spilled beer and bewildered, scattered into the countryside. A cousin, Otto Margolius, was the only close relative of Rudolf who lived in Czechoslovakia; he survived the war because he was married to a Christian which saved him from deportation to a concentration camp. He was running a public house in the tiny hamlet of Píšť that he inherited from his father Alois. As soon as the Slánský Trial verdict was announced, Otto, already strengthened by beer, stood up from his seat by the radio, his muscles all tensed, anger twisting his clouded face, stormed off down the stairs into the bar and smashed it up in protest.

26 A Trip to the Land of No Return

●

●

Never in my life have I heard or recognised the nightingale's song. Now under the window, outside, I hear every day, mainly in the morning when the sun rises and in the evening at sunset, a beautiful solo song of the nightingale ...

Rudolf Margolius, letter from prison, 1952

On the evening of Tuesday, 2 December they shaved Rudolf and changed him into the suit that Kukla had fetched from Heda before the Trial. Heda did not know why Kukla wanted the suit then – he would not say. Rudolf was blindfolded and taken to the prison visiting room. They locked him into a cage, one side of which was enclosed with a wire mesh so dense that not even a finger could be poked through. In front of this cage was about a metre-long corridor down which the guard walked and behind it was another grille where the visitors stood. There were about ten cages, one in each separate room; you could hear the visitors through the thin walls separating the cages. The visitors were always surprised on seeing the cages, so reminiscent of the ones in the zoological gardens. But this was the time of the last visit. The sentences were to be carried out in the next few hours. Rudolf only had eyes for Heda. He was worried she would not come.

Heda was very ill and lying in bed that evening in the Veverkova apartment. She had peritonitis and had been in hospital the previous week, but the hospital director had been ordered to send her home before she was fully recovered after Rudolf's testimony and a resolution by the hospital staff in support of the death sentences for all the accused. Heda was aware of the Trial for the first time while being treated in the hospital. She saw the headlines announcing it in *Rudé právo* and was utterly traumatized on finding Rudolf's name among the accused. A nurse let the frantic Heda listen to the radio broadcast in her private office.

Now Jan Hanuš was comforting Heda and persuading her that the sentences would not be carried out, saying that it was impossible that Gottwald would let his old friend Slánský die as well as the others. Perhaps they would be sent to Siberia for some time and allowed to return when things quietened down. Suddenly the doorbell rang and Heda asked Jan to hide in the bathroom. 'And when they are in my room, you leave,' she added; she had a premonition about who it was. The State Security men had arrived to take her to see Rudolf for the first time since his arrest – and for the last time. One of them was Kukla. They heard the door click and asked who it was and Heda said it was the doctor; he was washing his hands. Heda begged them to wait while she dressed. They took her to the car standing outside and drove her to Pankrác Prison.

While waiting to see Rudolf, Heda heard Mrs Frejková, the wife of one of the accused, being persuaded to see her husband. She did not want to see him, she believed in the Trial; Frejka never lied to her during the whole of his life so his confession must be true, she believed he was a traitor, spy and saboteur; he had confessed as such. When she finally agreed to see her husband for the last time, they shouted at each other, with loud recriminations and condemnations. Both had to be taken away without reconciliation by the prison guards. A few days earlier Frejka's son Tomáš wrote a letter asking that his father, '... this creature, who no longer deserves to be called a man because he did not have the slightest feeling of human dignity, my greatest and vilest enemy,' should be executed. 'Hatred toward my father will always strengthen me in my struggle for the Communist future of our people. I ask that this letter be shown to my father and that if possible, I may be given an opportunity to tell him personally what I have written in it.'

Heda thought it unbelievable that even the defendants' families had been so affected by these events that they had sunk so low: 'How fortunate that Ivan is not old enough to understand what is happening; anyway, I know he would never have done anything dreadful like this.' Ludvík Frejka's last letter was addressed to President Gottwald, so in the remaining hours of his life he was abandoned by his closest family. Tragically, when the truth came out, Tomáš Frejka committed suicide.

Clementis told his wife: 'Be composed, I don't feel bitter toward anyone, and even if Broček would not take a crust of bread from me, one day the archives will open . . . '

Others on the death cells saw their wives and there were indescribably heart-rending scenes.

However, Heda was calm and promised herself not to break down under any circumstances. They told her only to talk about personal matters; nothing else was to be discussed otherwise the interview would be stopped. Heda threw herself onto the wire mesh and hooked her fingers through the loops. She saw Rudolf's face, crisscrossed by the wire pattern as though by a tissue of scars. But then, in a moment, the black web began to dissolve. She looked straight into his eyes and saw no despair, no fear, only a strange, distant calm. It was the calm a man finds only at the very bottom of suffering.

He looked at her for a long time before he spoke. Then he said: 'I was so afraid you wouldn't come!'

At first Heda could not utter a word. 'Are you already so far away from me, Rudolf, that you could imagine that I would not come?' she answered.

He kept looking at her silently. Heda wondered what she looked like to him, probably skin and bones, worn out by illness and pain. 'You're so beautiful,' he said. 'Tell me about Ivan,' he then asked, and Heda started to talk. She told him everything she could think of, all about their son who sang and played all day long. After a while, they were both smiling. 'Now listen, this is important: I want you to have the boy's name changed. He must not be made to suffer on my account. Don't argue with me. Just do it. It's my last wish.'

They were silent again. Then he said: 'Come, let's have a cigarette together.' A State Security agent leaped to Heda's side with a cigarette and a lighter. They smoked for a while without saying anything, looking at each other.

'Don't question the Trial. Believe it!' Rudolf said suddenly. 'Please. Think of Ivan, not of me.'

'Don't say anything. I understand it all. Don't worry about me or the boy. I'll raise him well, I promise you. I'll bring him up to be a good man,' Heda assured him.

'And forget me, Heda. Find him a new father. Don't stay alone.'

'I know I have to take care of the child but, believe me, I'd rather go with you. It would be easier than living ... I'm with you anyway. You know that, don't you?' Heda pleaded.

'Have you noticed that all the important events of my life have taken place either on the third or thirteenth of the month?' asked Rudolf. 'Tomorrow is the third and I'm three times thirteen years old.'

'Three times thirteen hard years,' Heda said. 'But you had at least one good thing: a woman who always loved you and believed in you.' She paused, then turned to the agent who was standing

Heda and Rudolf, 1951

beside her and said 'I've brought my husband photographs of our child. Can you give them to him?'

'That's prohibited.'

'Won't you even allow us to shake hands?'

'That's prohibited.'

Heda stretched a finger through the wire barrier as far as she could, trying to touch Rudolf's hand, but could not reach it. Rudolf smiled. They spoke a while longer, with a growing awareness of each passing minute. One of the uniformed guards on Rudolf's side looked at his watch. Rudolf nodded.

'I just wanted to tell you one more thing,' he said hurriedly. 'I read a good book while I was here. It was called *Men of Clear Conscience.*'

Heda did not know whether he said anything after that. All she could understand was that these were their last moments, the very last. Rudolf backed away toward the door and, as he stepped through it, the expression in his eyes changed suddenly, and what appeared in them for that brief moment Heda would carry within her as long as she lived.

'My dearest, most beloved Heda,
A few hours ago, I saw you for the last time; I spoke with you and saw a picture of our little darling Ivan. My thoughts have been with both of you almost all the time throughout this separation. I retraced my life many times, step by step, from my first childhood memories up to our last days together ...'

Highly Classified
3 December 1952
Dear Comrade President Gottwald

Hereby I report that the sentences of the State Court in Prague passed on 27 November of this year regarding the Anti-State Conspiratorial Centre who were namely: Rudolf Slánský, Bedřich Geminder, Ludvík Frejka, Josef Frank, Vladimír Clementis, Bedřich Reicin, Karel Šváb, Rudolf Margolius, Otto Fischl, Otto Šling and André Simone – of the deaths by hanging were carried out early this morning.

The executions were completed without any problems. I enclose a copy of the official report regarding the process of execution of each condemned individual and their last words.

Further arrangements regarding the cremation and burial of corpses of the condemned are placed under the competence of the Ministry of State Security.

With Comradely Greetings,
Štefan Rais
Minister of Justice

Enclosure:
Highly Classified
Subject: Rudolf Slánský and the Collective – The Execution of the Death Penalty
3 December 1952, Prague

Today early in the morning in the County Prison of Prague death sentences of the condemned prisoners in the 'Case of Rudolf Slánský and the Collective' were completed.

The executions took place in the following order:

1. At 3.06: Bedřich Geminder – death declared at 3.10 – he did not pronounce any last word.
2. At 3.18: Otto Šling – death declared at 3.25. – After the sentence was announced he exclaimed: 'Mr Chairman, I wish the Communist Party, the Czechoslovak people and President of the Republic the best.' Under the gallows he shouted: 'I have never been a spy.'
3. At 3.34: André Simone – death declared at 3.40 – he did not pronounce any last words.
4. At 3.49: Karel Šváb – death declared at 3.55 – he did not pronounce any last words; after the sentence was announced he shouted: 'Long live the Soviet Union, long live the Communist Party of Czechoslovakia.'
5. At 4.00: Otto Fischl – death declared at 4.05 – he did not pronounce any last words.

6. At 4.20: Rudolf Margolius – death declared at 4.25 – he did not pronounce any last words.
7. At 4.31: Josef Frank – death declared at 4.40 – he did not pronounce any last words.
8. At 4.55: Vladimír Clementis – death declared at 5.00 – he did not pronounce any last words.
9. At 5.05: Ludvík Frejka – death declared at 5.10 – he did not pronounce any last words.
10. At 5.25: Bedřich Reicin – death declared at 5.30 – he did not pronounce any last words.
11. At 5.37: Rudolf Slánský – death declared at 5.45 – he did not pronounce any last words; after the sentence was announced he said quietly: 'I have what I deserve.'

Signed, Dr Milan Cícha

There were two adjacent execution cells in the Pankrác Prison. Two hangmen, each with two assistants, carried out their long assignment alternately using these cells. Following the executions the prison cleaners also removed the paper wrappings the hangmen left behind after having eaten their morning snacks there.

The Last Journey 27

Learn to wear a small bitter smile in the corner of
   your mouth.

Jiří Orten, letter to Věra Fingerová, 1937

On the cold December day, the vague silhouette of Prague Castle
loomed behind the car which was pointing in a southerly direction.
It was snowing heavily and the reality of the horizon melted away.
By the time the car reached the edge of the city the white sky
was tightly merged with the snow-covered landscape. Through
this formless concentration, a grey Tatraplan forced its way to an
unknown destination. The driver belched loudly, observing his
passengers' reactions from the corner of his eye. Two of his
companions stared fixedly ahead, unmoved by such a common
provocation, preoccupied with their thoughts. All three crowded
the bench seat in the front. The heavy car's rear air-cooled engine
roared at the countryside, disturbing the outward calmness of the
untouched white blanket. Snowflakes were beating against the
windscreen and the driver swore at the weather. Hot air from the
heater rose against the glass and the flakes dissolved quickly, sliding
down, leaving a wet trail behind them before being swept away by
the half circling motion of the wipers. A plastic butterfly charm
dangled from one of the switches on the dashboard, swinging into
the rhythm of the moving car.

      The three men, all wearing heavy winter coats, were
squeezed together making it difficult to move. Their hats, pushed
down hard, partly hid their faces. Perspiration appeared on their
foreheads, glistening in the rising heat in contrast to the snow
beating against the smooth, streamlined body of the car.

      Now that they had left the city behind them there was
little to talk about. On the back seat was a large and full canvas bag
shaking every time the car went over a bump in the road surface. The

241

contents were settling, mixing together, rustling against the inner paper liner. 'Step on it, Franta,' shouted the man nearer the door, 'I can't stand it any more. There're too many of us here.'

'Yeah, this is the first time I've driven that many passengers all together in the Tatraplan,' the driver confirmed, trying to cheer them up. He changed down, wrestling with the gear lever on the steering wheel column. The road was getting worse and

242

more slippery. The bag's movements with every change in the car's direction made the men squirm. They kept sitting tighter together, trying to find comfort from each other's company, fear clearly showing in their drawn faces.

'Are we being followed? If so, it would be Galkin or one of his men,' the middle one enquired, thinking of the black Moskvich with a Russian number plate that had stuck to their fin-tailed back through the town.

'No. The coward turned back as soon as the weather deteriorated,' Franta commented with relief, and increased his speed on a more levelled road. He pressed the Bakelite button on the radio and the illuminated oblong of the station dial came to life.

From the little loudspeaker on the dashboard the shouting voice of the public prosecutor invaded the car's interior. 'Our people's democratic court has never before dealt with a case concerning such criminals as those who are in the dock today . . .'

'This must be a repeat of the show a fortnight ago. I'd have thought they wouldn't bother to broadcast it again so soon', one of the passengers explained.

'Comrade, these are excerpts and congratulatory telegrams as part of the past month's events review. The pressure is on to make sure that comrade citizens have swallowed the point,' said Franta and stepped on the accelerator.

' . . . all this was done with the sole aim of introducing a Tito fascist regime in our country with all its consequences, to restore capitalism, to hand our homeland once more to the imperialists as a colony, and transform it into a base for the war against the Soviet Union and the people's democratic countries . . . The Workers' Collective at the Klement Gottwald Factory unanimously signed their declaration demanding just punishment for those capitalist spies, saboteurs and traitors! The People's Militia declare: they all have to get a rope or we'll march in the streets! We'll take our machine guns and get them ourselves!' The loudspeaker droned on in other voices while Red Army band music increased in the background.

'This country is no longer ours,' muttered Franta under his moustache. He thought to himself: 'Most people must have found it peculiar that if they were such hardened criminals they did it for no personal gain, no money ... no real villain would ever do that ...'

'Oh, God, come on, change the station, Franta, once was enough for a lifetime!' exploded the one by the door.

'It was your theatre anyway so why do you complain!? What about them eleven on the back seat?' Franta retaliated abruptly without thinking of the consequences.

The white road went into a sudden sharp bend, which was indicated indistinctly by poles stacked in at intervals along its edge, now half their normal length; the rest was buried in a deep drift. The rear wheels of the Tatraplan caught the snow, swept the white mass partly away and slid on the hidden ice underneath. The tyres, unable to grip the road surface, spun helplessly and the weight of the car pushed it into the ditch on the side of the road. The wind increased, lifting the snow, covering the tracks. The heavy car stopped moving.

The three men looked at each other and Franta punched the radio button to stop the prosecutor's screeching tones underlined by the familiar melody. The sudden silence was interrupted only by the cold wind thrusting against the car body.

Franta, heavily cranking on the lever, lowered the window and then partly opened the door to survey the situation. As he turned back to his passengers his gesticulating hand swept the butterfly off the dashboard and it fell without a clatter through the open door into the snow. 'Come on, you have to get out and try to push me,' he pleaded with his companions, slammed his door shut and reached over to open the passenger-side door. Wrapped in their coats, grumbling, the others staggered out and leant against the stuck Tatraplan.

At that moment it stopped snowing. The weather seemed to have calmed down as if to wait for the next course of events.

'We won't move her without help from the eleven in the back,' the driver barked, suddenly inspired, out of the open window at the two State Security interrogators who were already red in the face from their physical effort which was not getting anywhere.

They laughed quietly. 'Perhaps that is the best solution to our problems. Go and fetch the bag, Jarda,' ordered the fat one.

Jarda opened the rear door and picked the large bag, considering its weight in his hands. 'Eleven people, imagine . . . here, have a go.'

The fat one squatted by the car and spilled the ashes under the wheels. At the same time, as if by command, a gust of strong wind lifted the light fragments into the eyes and open mouths of the interrogators. Blinded and choking, they groped round the car trying to get inside. Franta, without waiting for his colleagues, brought the engine into life. The wheels gripped the remnants of the ashes and freed the streamlined machine from its entombment. The Tatraplan surged forward. The cold air, laced with white flakes and the grey ashes of the burnt bodies of the executed defendants, danced and mingled, enveloping the two interrogators left behind standing on the Benešov road.

My dearest, in each of your letters there is always something new and precious and it would still be so, even if you only wrote the same, because your every kiss, your every touch with your hand, glance or word even if repeated a thousand times a day have, and will always have for me, new magic. And all this is realized for me in your letters, always with our common past, as well as your and Ivan's presence today, which I live through with you, together with hopes of our shared life in the future when I shall be able to return to you . . .

28 Sinking Deeper

> The evil is already present in the beautiful, hell is already contained in the dream of paradise and if we wish to understand the essence of hell we must examine the essence of the paradise from which it originated.

Milan Kundera, in an interview with Philip Roth, 1980

It took two years, over seven hundred and thirty days, for Heda to receive Rudolf's official death certificate stating the cause of death as suffocation by hanging. The place of his burial was left blank.

With the death of Stalin and his paranoid obsession with seeking enemies, and the new struggle for the Kremlin leadership, the show trials backed by Soviet Security lost their reason to continue. This break clearly indicated Soviet complicity. However, at the same time, contemporary regimes in Central and Eastern European countries beyond the Iron Curtain, including Czechoslovakia, were still headed by local politicians deeply involved in the murders and torture carried out in the name of the Party. Long after 1953, it was in their interest to continue suppressing the freedom of their populations, and maintaining silence about their crimes. In fact the demise of Stalin became a call for the Communist Party of Czechoslovakia to carry on rigorously along the path set out by him, to complete the unfinished work of the dead 'leader of the world proletariat'. Additional trials were staged and continued in the following years, and all sent innocent people to their death or to prison with long sentences.

      The Czechoslovak President and Chairman of the Party, Klement Gottwald, was the one political figure mostly involved in staging the trials. He was too weak to resist Moscow and feared the Soviets would choose him as another scapegoat. He thought that the only way to survive was to collude with the construction of the monstrous crimes against selected Party members. Because of the mass hysteria created by the Party to justify the murders, the Trial's outcome had to be the most severe possible in order not to undermine its desired political effect and credibility. Any clemency offered by the President would have been perceived by Moscow as protecting the accused. Gottwald opted to participate actively in the murders and sacrificed others, even his closest colleagues, to save his own skin.

Gottwald went to Moscow to Stalin's funeral on 9 March 1953. On his return journey he was depressed and worried about what would happen in the Soviet Union with Stalin out of the way. How would Malenkov, his successor, continue? Suddenly he felt very exposed, isolated and left to his own devices. On 14 March 1953, just after his arrival in Prague, he suffered an aneurism of the aorta and died.

In April 1953 the Czechoslovak Communist Party Central Committee, rather than helping the close families of the executed 'criminals' as they had been promised, passed a resolution to:

Remove the next of kin into remote countryside districts with only essential furnishings and clothing, and employ them there in local agriculture or heavy industries.
Arrange for them to be constantly supervised by State Security.
Strip them of their Party membership.

Regardless of Bacílek's promise, Heda's Party membership was revoked in May 1953.

The State Security interrogators and public prosecutors acted as if they believed in the indictments and testimonies, though several years later they admitted that in their heart they had real doubts. Some tried to resign in January 1953; they remembered that their Soviet colleagues and teachers never collected their pensions.

Despite the allegations of conspiracy and economic sabotage heaped onto the heads of the accused at the Trial, the Czechoslovak economy did not improve after the liquidation of the 'state enemies'. It needed an immediate boost as total collapse was imminent. For months, leading up to June 1953, the Communist government – now led by President Antonín Zápotocký who replaced Gottwald – secretly planned a harsh monetary reform which would usurp people's savings to the order of 14 billion Czechoslovak crowns and bolster the country's failing economic structure. Rumours of the extremely unpopular reform were denied even up to the day before its announcement when Zápotocký, to squash any discontent and further rumours, categorically stated in a radio broadcast that no such measure was forthcoming. 'Do not be concerned, our currency remains firm!' he stated.

The monetary reform downgraded the Czechoslovak crowns in a ratio of 50:1 for wages and allowances, with bank deposits calculated in the ratio of five old crowns to one new crown. A day after the devaluation was announced, workers at an armaments factory in Pilsen began a protest march. The demonstration soon spread to other factories in the city. The workers waved British and American flags, destroyed factory machinery and looted a government office. Troops called in to end the demonstrations fired on the protestors, killing six people. Similar demonstrations were reported in other Czech cities. The Czechoslovak government at first denied reports of riots and later confirmed that demonstrations against the currency reform had ended.

Another shadowy figure was the forthcoming First Secretary and President Antonín Novotný. In mid-December 1952, during the Czechoslovak Communist Party National Congress meeting, Gottwald praised the Trial as the great victory for Socialism. One of the other main architects of the Trial, Karol Bacílek, now considered a Soviet agent, boasted that the material against the accused was acquired with the great help of Comrades Gottwald, Zápotocký and, most of all, Comrade Novotný. This statement was a continual reminder of Novotný's own guilt and a danger to his future career in the Party. Two years later, at the June 1954 10th Congress of the Czechoslovak Communist Party, Novotný reminded his audience: 'With the liquidation of Slánský's terrorist band we squashed the head of the dangerous fifth column of the imperialists.' The Communists expressed extreme emotions. Their hatred of capitalism was the driving force of the proletariat, and they rejoiced in the removal and putting to death of their foes.

But the state and its political system taking citizens' lives away, even the lives of assumed enemies, should not be a cause for celebration and the expression of joy. The shameful shallowness of the men in charge of the country, who assisted in sending their comrades to the gallows, was exposed when high-ranking Party members were given the opportunity to buy the confiscated property of the victims after the Trial at give-away prices. Božena Novotná, Antonín Novotný's wife, remembered a lunch visit to Vladimír and Lída Clementis's house when their special Chinese porcelain service had caught her eye. With the help of her husband, she bought the service as well as a set of their bedding.

Following Khrushchev's second denunciation of Stalin's crimes at the 22nd Congress of the Soviet Communist Party in October 1961, Novotný, by then the First Secretary of the Czechoslovak Communist Party and President, was urged by the Soviets to reassess the personality cult within the Czechoslovak Party. Novotný was unwilling to do so because any punishment of those who were responsible for the 1950s purges would have included him. He was anxious to suppress the real investigation as long as possible. This hard-line political climate continued until Alexander Dubček replaced Novotný early in January 1968 and a general thaw, at least for some months, occurred.

Immediately after the Trial the State Security agent Miloslav Kukla, Rudolf's interrogator, was promoted to first lieutenant and was awarded a 'For Courage' medal by the President for exceptional bravery and self-sacrifice in the course of his duty. He also received a 10,000 crowns reward for helping to unmask the enemies of the Party and the country. By 1960, he was a captain and was further decorated 'For Service to the Country' and 'For the Defence of the Country' because of his fending off class enemies successfully. Following the 1963 rehabilitations of the Trial victims, his Courage medal and diploma were quietly taken away from him.

Bohuslav Doubek was decorated with the Orders of the Republic and Victorious February, promoted to lieutenant colonel and received a 30,000 crowns reward. On July 12, 1955, Doubek was arrested in his apartment with his collection of chrome steel handcuffs, knuckledusters, transcripts of Rajk and Slánský Trials and pornographic cards. He was stripped of his decorations, held in custody and tried between 13 and 17 May 1957. Doubek was sentenced to a nine-year imprisonment for the use of illegal interrogation methods but by Christmas 1957 he had been released on Novotný's order; his innocent victims were still in prison and had to wait many more years for their own release and rehabilitation. No other people, apart from Vladimír Kohoutek who was tried with Doubek (Kohoutek's original sentence of seven years was reduced to four and he was released in 1958), were ever prosecuted for their part in the trials. They were requested to return their decorations, some lost their posts in the Security Service, were moved elsewhere and had their Party membership revoked.

During the Dubček thaw, in April 1968, when censorship was lifted and the Party crimes of the 1950s were being revealed in the newspapers, Dr Josef Sommer, the specialist in medical torture in the Ruzyně Prison hanged himself in his Prague apartment. Belatedly, in May 1968, Dubček's Party Central Committee decided to suspend the Party membership of Antonín Novotný, Karol Bacílek, Štefan Rais and Josef Urválek for their part in the preparation of the Trial.

Heda kept sending letters to the President, the Party Central Committee and the Public Prosecutor's Office in 1956, 1963, 1968 and 1999 asking for the persons responsible to be charged, as they must have known that they were sending an innocent man to his death and had therefore committed a crime of premeditated murder. On none of these occasions was anything done: unsurprising, although the last letter was sent during Václav Havel's democratic reign and while one of the prosecutors was still alive. The Czech authorities, still employing the old Party officials, dragged their feet for so long that the individual died. Heda and I did not want revenge, only a full public and thorough examination of the people and processes involved, an explanation of the events that happened in 1952 and an apology.

These are the sad statistics of Czechoslovak people affected by the Communist regime from 1948 to 1989: executed, 248; died in custody, 4,500; killed crossing the country's borders, 327; imprisoned, 205,486; emigrated, 170,938.

In 1958, two years after his release, Pavel Kavan drove his Hillman Minx – a car that State Security used while he was in prison but now miraculously returned to him – round Prague and up Wenceslas Square. He saw Vladimír Kohoutek, his former interrogator, walking along and was about to swerve onto the pavement and run him down. His English-born wife Rosemary grabbed his arm just in time.

Ota Pavel's *A Race through Prague* concluded with an anguished expression of betrayal: 'Father was sitting in his drawers at the table, and he was crying. His hair had fallen over his forehead, and his tears were dripping onto the newspaper in front of him. It was *Rudé právo*, the Communist Party daily to which he subscribed and without which he could not have made it through the day. I leaned over him and brushed the hair from his forehead. For the first and last time in his life he slipped into my arms, the way children do. By that time, I was already a man. I held him and looked over his head at the newspaper, where he had underlined with a red pen:

Rudolf Slánský, of Jewish origin,
Bedřich Geminder, of Jewish origin,
Ludvík Frejka, of Jewish origin,
Bedřich Reicin, of Jewish origin,
Rudolf Margolius, of Jewish origin.

The list of Jews went on and it was blurred with tears. When he had calmed down, he looked absently at me, as if he did not know who I was, and said: 'They're killing Jews again. They're looking for someone to blame it on all over again.'

'Then he stood up and punched the newspaper and shouted: 'I can forgive murder – even judicial murder, even political murder. But a Communist newspaper should never print 'of Jewish origin.' The Communists are dividing people up all over again, into Jews and non-Jews.' And then he punched *Rudé právo* again, and it fell apart as though it had been made of rotten winter leaves. The antique table with its inlaid deer collapsed. He sat down and sighed deeply. We all knew he was thinking about how useless all those demonstrations and flags had been, those speeches about truth and justice ... My father stood up and went into the woodshed. There he picked up the biggest axe, the one used for splitting logs. I was afraid and I went after him. Mother begged me to leave him alone; she had never seen him like this before. After a while I pulled myself loose and ran out after him. I ran up to the gate on which he always painted a five-pointed star every May Day. Today he had carved two large stars into the wood. I stood there and counted the points: one-two-three-four-five-six . . .

'I moved closer, as though I could not believe my own eyes. Father thought I was going to efface those Jewish stars, and he raised his axe. But I had no intention of doing that, for I understood him very well. At that gate, he had ceased to be a Communist and had become a Jew once more. We looked at each other. He had something in his eyes that I had never seen there before, the terrible disappointment and despair of a man who thought he was crossing a river on a solid bridge only to discover that the bridge was not there at all. In those eyes too were Slánský and Margolius, swinging at the end of their ropes. All around in the dusk birds were singing, and it was like the old Jewish Psalms.'

Towards Beauty 29

We need beauty as we need love, water, bread.

Jaroslav Seifert

'People need beauty, especially today. A century ago, art was meant to be revolutionary and produce social change. Today I'd like to think we're left with a more modest task: for art to be beautiful,' said the art critic Robert Hughes in 2004. Nowadays this is true; in the world full of hunger, extreme natural disasters, epidemics, the wrath of minor wars and terrorist groups trying to influence and destabilize civilisation, in such a world there is little of beauty to spare. Any real beauty we can find or contribute will make living more worthwhile. However, beauty cannot exist without reference to its opposite, otherwise it could not be defined.

When I came to join Heda in Veverkova on my return from Bratislava I was still in ignorance about Rudolf's fate, but soon my heartbreaking premonition was confirmed. On a cold winter day Heda sat me down after I had enquired yet again why she looked sad and kept wearing black clothes and told me that my father had died while on a trip abroad. It was a long time before I found out what had really happened; Heda protected me from the truth until I was sixteen. She decided that I would have to grow up and acquire mental strength before facing the events that had affected our lives so radically. Immediately after the sentence was carried out Heda wore black in public, bravely, in defiance of the Trial's outcome, challenging the Party to indicate that she was absolutely sure of Rudolf's innocence. Later many people learned to respect her courageous stance.

In a way Heda was fortunate. They did not take me away from her; she was not arrested. However, we had no furniture, clothes, books, money or any possessions – everything was confiscated. State Security used our Škoda and we never saw 'Ferda'

Rudolf and 'Ferda'

again. The Musils, our guardian angels second time around, concealed some of our precious items – Persian carpets and a couple of paintings – in their apartment before State Security carried out the full inventory of our goods. Heda had to argue with the officials to keep the Tesla Largo radio. She had to prove that she, rather than Rudolf, bought the radio in order to hold on to it.

We were forcefully moved out of the Veverkova apartment soon after the end of the Trial and the executions in the winter of 1952–53. Heda was threatened with relocation to the village of Únětice near Horoměřice north of Prague, into an abandoned falling-down cottage with a rotten floor, no heating, water, electricity or sanitary accommodation; it was even unsuitable as an animal shelter. In those days, every family had to have a permit for accommodation from the local council, which controlled all allocations as directed by the Party Central Committee. Officials had to be bribed to exchange the permit for something better. In the end, Heda found a room on the second floor of a ghastly dilapidated apartment building in one of the most depressing and run-down quarters of Prague – Žižkov. The empty room had grubby floorboards, a cracked plastered ceiling and draughty windows with broken glass. The one toilet – for the whole building – was in the dirty, dark corridor as well as the only water tap, which was shared among twelve families. There was no heating so Pavel Koválý, who befriended Heda while she worked for Rovnost and who was in the Czechoslovak Army at the time, obtained a small cast iron stove and installed it during one of his visits, along with a long convoluted chimney to generate maximum heat.

The Žižkov building's one redemption was a small green park outside with a dirty sandpit and creaky swings with peeling seats. I had no toys either until Heda scraped ten crowns together to get me a paper-mache military bunker and some pottery soldiers. I saw this in the local tobacconist's window and begged for it continuously despite knowing we had no money. After I received good marks at school Heda bought it for me and amazingly bought another set for a school friend with whom I used to play, so we could stage war games together.

On a sunny day, I sat outside kicking about in the sandpit observing other children and their toys. There was a snotty little kid, about three years old, playing with the most beautiful thing in the whole world, a big chrome ball bearing. He was throwing it in the air and watching it get buried every time he dropped it. I could not take my eyes off this wonderful object. I had not seen anything like it before and was hoping the kid would lose it in the sand; however, he always found it. Every time it flew in the air, it shone like a precious stone.

The kid's mother was sitting on the park bench absorbed in conversation with other mums. I lost all hope of getting the ball and adding this gem to my measly toy collection. Suddenly his mother looked at her watch and exclaimed, startled, that her hubby was already at home and she would be in trouble; she grabbed the kid who had just thrown the ball into the air and did not have time to retrieve it. The poor thing was screaming, extending his hands for it, but his mum was on the run and did not pay attention. It was my time to claim the prize. To this day I see this sphere as the perfect object and was greatly influenced by it in my interest in design and choice of profession.

Down the street from our apartment was a big murky school building that had an inner courtyard used for assembly and games. On my very first day our new class gathered there. Just a week before, the approval had come to have my surname changed to Marek, as Rudolf had wished in his last conversation with Heda so that I would not suffer as a child of 'a traitor and spy' – although at that time I did not know the real reason for the alteration of my identity. We stood in line and our teacher, a kind, pretty and small woman, Věra Smrčková, held a large bouquet of autumn asters in her arms and was giving one to each child. They were all white or purplish blue with yellow centres and there was one of maroon colour. As I stood in the line I wished so much to get the maroon one; I did not like the others. It was still in the bunch when it was my turn and she must have read it in my eyes when she pulled it out, specially selecting it, and pushed it in my hand, smiled and said: 'Welcome to the school.'

When I got home, I gave the aster to Heda to cheer her up, the only bit of bright colour in our room that Heda had named appropriately *Myší díra* – Mousehole. After the flower passed its prime, I pressed it in a book and had it for years to remind me of the first happy day at school.

To get out of the gloomy room we used to go for walks through Prague pretending we lived in a nicer part; it made us feel better. From the same tobacconist I obtained another 'toy': this was an old-fashioned pipe with a long stem and carved head, and I pretended to be puffing it as I walked along. In fact, I was impersonating Rudolf who smoked a pipe instead of a cigarette when he was relaxing at home. I, as Rudolf, was taking Heda for a stroll. I walked proudly beside her offering my arm for support in spite of my small stature. We were crossing the Čech Bridge, with the pipe dangling out of my lips. Something caught my eye in the river, it may have been a fish jumping out for a fly, and I lent over the balustrade – and in the excitement the pipe fell out of my mouth. It splashed into the water below and disappeared. A fish jumped out again very close by. I was upset and when we got home Heda took an old cookery book we had by a famous Czech cook called Marie Sandtnerová. There were pictures of various fish inside. She

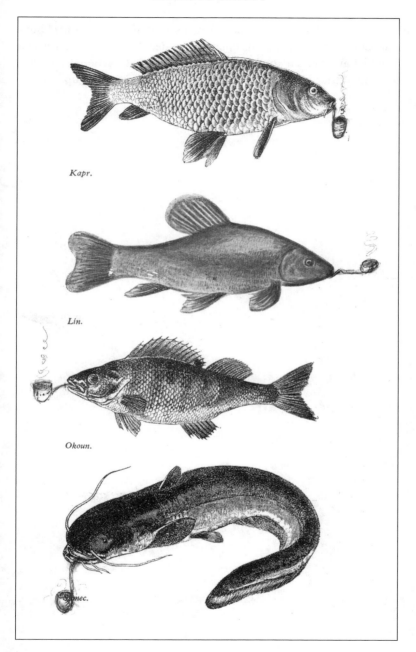

Kapr.

Lín.

Okoun.

Sumec.

drew a smoking pipe for each fish, as that was what must have happened when the pipe disappeared under the water, otherwise it would have floated to the surface, wouldn't it? When I felt low, looking at the 'doctored' illustrations always cheered me up.

A Walk from School 30

●
●

Do you hear?
From the depth of my night I speak to you
and I want to melt my words into a river
so they would be like a bridge from me to you
when our hands cannot hold together.

Hanuš Bonn, *Volání/Calling*, 1934

It was a spring day in Prague. Down in the heart of the town by the
river, the Petřín Hill provided the luscious green background to that
extraordinarily theatrical scenery of ancient, classical and modern
architecture. In the Baroque gardens under the Castle clipped box
hedges infused the air with their fragrance. On the quays and river
islands, the trees, already in blossom, slowly shed their petals into
Vltava and the sun's reflections bounced off the rippled water.
The light fluffy seeds from poplars floated all around, forming white
drifts on the pavements that were now and then pushed around
by the slight breeze. From the open window of the Kampa
apartment the sounds of a sonata that a student was practising on
the piano invaded the charmed atmosphere. The countless sharp
church spires penetrated the blue canopy arching over the city. The
kaleidoscope of Prague's life, culture and people was imprinted on
the city's every surface. All this unity of forms, colours and history
brightened up and lifted the spirits of the passers-by, locals and
visitors alike. However, Prague is not only famous for its harmony
but also for its contrasts, paradox and absurd. It is these extra layers
which give the city that special appeal. To discover them one has to
explore deep within.

We lived in another sad, soot-ridden industrial suburb
called Vysočany tucked far away from the medieval and picturesque
centre having moved there from Žižkov after Heda and Pavel Kovály
married.

Prague in the spring (Václav Jírů)

As usual before school, pupils gathered outside waiting for the gates to open. 'You're a Jew today,' shouted Milan, my best mate, a long way off, before I reached him.

'Why?' I asked when I got there.

'This morning you turned up the seventh,' he confirmed counting in the new arrivals.

'But what's wrong with being Jewish?'

'They are peculiar, different people and nobody likes them,' he explained.

Now it was after school and I sucked my bleeding finger, breathing heavily after running up the three storeys to our miniature apartment in a grimy block in a narrow side street. Its windows overlooked a ramshackle factory with a threateningly tall chimney. As I walked up to our storey a certain aroma brought memories from the past. This happened quite easily. Smell is a very evocative sense and helped to take me back to Rudolf again. The forest smelled of summer, with a little breeze clearing the hot air shimmering over the sandy paths turning in between the trees. Rudolf and I sat down on the moss in the shade to cool down, looking at a stream which ran at our feet and carried on further to supply the Lišno pond. Rudolf folded a sheet of paper to make a small boat and dropped it in the stream. We followed the boat all the way, freeing it at times with sticks when it stuck behind stones. Eventually it bobbed down to the pond. Rudolf stripped off, waded in, grabbed me and dipped me in and I hated the sudden coldness; I shuddered, feeling there was no escape. I begged him: 'Not the whole body, táto, please nooo!' And he pulled me up and dipped me in again, laughing.

Would I ever see Rudolf again? Perhaps he did not die after all?

I opened the apartment door. There was a tiny hall, a kitchen – where I had my sleeping corner – with two or three reproductions of Raul Dufy French Riviera seascapes on the wall, a living room-cum-bedroom with a tall ceramic stove and a bathroom.

Heda and Pavel were out. Heda was delivering her book jacket design, created on the kitchen table, in amongst the remnants of a modest evening meal; a bit of illegal work done against all the rules. When the graphic work ceased Heda constructed a simple weaving frame and made small carpets for a home-craft cooperative to sell in their shops. The Party prevented her from getting a proper job and consequently earning any money, although normally not working was a punishable offence in our proletarian society. Later she turned to her language skills and translated the works of eminent authors such as Zweig, Böll, Ferber, Roth, Wells, Miller, Bennett, Steinbeck, Chandler, Amis, Golding, Spark and Bellow from German and English into Czech, eventually becoming one of the most respected translators in the country. She also met Saul Bellow and Muriel Spark, while living abroad from 1968. Initially she could not be identified and the translations were published under Pavel's name.

PhD Kovály, philosophy professor, mucked in as plumber's mate, having been thrown out of the Czechoslovak Academy of Sciences for marrying my mother. I do not know how he managed since he could not even change a washer on a leaking tap. I knew that Pavel's colleagues had also lost their academic jobs for not conforming to Party doctrines, or not having the right proletarian background going back generations. They had to support themselves by becoming cleaners, stokers, toilet attendants, dishwashers. At that time, the Party positively discriminated against the well-educated and fired over 77,000 intellectuals who were moved to work in industry or in menial jobs about which they knew nothing. The proletarian Party members substituted for them, but had no qualifications to work in their place. No wonder the country was in trouble.

Somehow, I never questioned why we had these difficulties especially when I saw that our acquaintances were in the same boat.

I had cut myself, and it hurt, with that typical Czech pocket-knife carried by every boy; its handle was shaped in the form of a fish. It served me right for fiddling with it on the way from school. It took a few steps to reach the bureau; I was looking for a plaster or some bandage that I knew should have been there. All the upper drawers were full of junk. There was nothing there that I needed right now. But when I opened the bottom drawer, my life changed forever and the sky, despite the beautiful day outside, darkened.

In the deepest corner lay a thick book with limp brown covers, printed on cheap flimsy paper. The title was *The Trial of the Leadership of the Anti-State Conspiratorial Centre led by Rudolf Slánský*. Out of natural curiosity, and because of my love of books, I opened it at random and read:

> Prosecutor Aleš: 'Accused Rudolf Margolius, which way did you deceive the Communist Party of Czechoslovakia?'
> Defendant Margolius: 'I come from a Jewish capitalist family, I have been educated in truly Jewish and Zionistic spirit ... I gave false facts in my cadre report when I stated that my father was a left-leaning social democrat who taught me about

Marxist principles and that my experiences in the concentration camps were the ideological reasons for my entering the Party. I made this up in order to deceive the leadership of the Party ...'

Involuntarily I glanced up on the wall above me where there hung a life-size reproduction of Van Gogh's *Reaper*, a vision of death painted in St Remy in the last days of his life. I grew up with the predominantly acidic, sulphur-yellow picture, but did not know its significance until I read about the unhappy genius who painted it.

I forgot to suck my finger and the blood dripped on the lino floor, missing the Persian carpet, the last of our treasured possessions. There was much more in the book but I turned to the end page. 'Accused Rudolf Slánský, Vladimír Clementis, Ludvík Frejka, Rudolf Margolius ... are sentenced to death by hanging.'

As I took this in, I heard my dear mother again, as she gently and protectively announced nine years ago: 'Ivan, your father died while on a trip abroad. He won't be coming back. When you're older you can travel there and put a flower on his grave.' And I had nodded after a minute: 'Don't worry mother, I'll take care of you,' with the naive courage of a five-year-old.

My sense of strong foreboding that there was much more to Rudolf's disappearance, which I had secretly harboured, was transformed into a painful ache that remained permanently inside me.

After my discovery in the bureau, I did not try to find out more. Occasionally I visited the book trying to read it, but could not understand it. What mattered most was the concluding passage on the last page. Was I son of a criminal and was this the reason for our troubles? I had my surname changed before I started my primary school. Now Heda and Pavel were considering whether I should be adopted, then Pavel would become my father and I would have his name – Kovály, my third surname in my short fourteen years of life.

I had to wait another two years before my mother told me. She did not want to worry me but thought, quite wisely, that any attempt to surprise or upset me by a third party, especially a school bully, should be forestalled. Over the Easter weekend, we were staying in the house at Nižbor. This villa, with a large garden, was confiscated during the war as Jewish property and the house was turned into a village police station after the Communists took over. Two police officers' families were living in the house. Heda and Pavel started proceedings to have the house returned but the dealings were prolonged and bureaucratic; initially we got the attic room and much later the first floor apartment. One police officer's family still lived downstairs and the police station office remained below. It was not easy living with dedicated Communist police officers on our doorstep, especially with our politically tainted past.

In the evening my mother called me to come up from the garden and sit in the attic room. It was getting dark. As Heda later noted, this was her most difficult moment: to communicate to her only child the fate of her first husband, my father. I did not let on that I already knew the bare facts. For the facts to mean anything, the details were essential. She uncovered the events as they unfolded, as orchestrated by the dastardly political regime committing a vicious murder, compounded by Rudolf's abominable fate. The evening was getting longer and darker. There was much to be learned and much to be read but the material was not available and rehabilitations were being discussed only at the Party level. Even in those days one was acting against the state, and everything I was being told should stay within our four walls. There was no freedom of expression; this was still a one-party state and what the Party decided was the law.

Inwardly I was very angry but what can a sixteen-year old do in a totalitarian state? My parents would pay heavily for any deviation from the road set by Communist-led Socialism. After all I was a pioneer, with a red kerchief round my neck.

Once I understood we kept looking back, recounting the staged Trial, the circumstances and the sentences passed on the fourteen people, eleven of them 'of Jewish origin', as the court's public prosecutor shamelessly pointed out; most of the fabricated cases ruthlessly exploited this fact. This was the largest group ever sentenced to death outside the Soviet Union in a single trial. We could not believe that the government, even a Communist one, could commit such a publicly acclaimed crime in front of the whole world, a crime taking place in a comparatively civilized Central European country with strong democratic traditions in the second half of the 20th century. We almost assumed that this was a set-up pretence for political reasons, not a harsh reality. We still hoped, rather naively, that all the defendants would quietly reappear after a period of absence and continue their lives.

Heda had a useful philosophy. 'You must never take pity on yourself, and to hate is senseless; if you hate, it is you who suffers for it. Hate drowns your mind like dirty water. When you harbour hate in your heart there is no space left for other feelings. You must not hate because it keeps feeding the evil that has been perpetrated on you. However, that does not mean you have to forgive. My parents were murdered by the Nazis and that I cannot forgive, I believe that it's not within human power to do so.'

It was Tuesday, 3 December 1963, the eleventh anniversary of my father's death. I decided spontaneously, rather than by intent, to commemorate the day. At mid-morning at the high school, I asked the teacher to leave the classroom for ten minutes, stressing that I had to announce something special to the class. I was so threatening in my determination, appearance and posture that he became frightened and left without a word. I did not consider any come-back, I did not care – and the consequences could have been serious. I could have been expelled from school with a negative cadre report barring me entry to university, banning me from travelling abroad and meaning my parents losing their jobs and livelihood. Especially if any of the pupils reported on me. I stood in front of the class and I did not mind what happened. The class was bewildered, but they were old enough to understand.

I told them: 'Sit and listen. Eleven years ago on this day early in the morning after the so-called Slánský Trial the Party murdered eleven innocent men. They never committed the crimes they were accused of and yet they have never been publicly rehabilitated. One of them was my father. Stand up! We'll commemorate their deaths by three-minute silence.'

They all stood to attention without a question or single word for the full three minutes. I thanked them and went to sit down. After a while, the teacher came back and nobody commented on the special event of the day. Thirty-seven years later, at the class reunion, someone mentioned it and they all remembered and congratulated me on my 'brave' stand. Better late than never. The pity was that in the 1950s, at the time of the Trial, people did not realize what fools they had been.

I came home from school and said: 'Mother, comrade teacher said that if my red pioneer kerchief ever fell into a well that I would have to jump after it and retrieve it. But I think why should I jump for it, it's only a scrap of cloth, isn't it?'

Jan Hanuš, Rudolf's best friend, dedicated his 3rd Symphony of four movements in D minor (*Pravda Světa – Truth of the World*), opus 38, composed in 1956–57, to Rudolf. Hanuš thought of him primarily in the second movement, which expressed in heart-aching sound man's situation in the world and wonder at how much hate there was among people. In 1960, when the score was published in Prague, Hanuš could not openly proclaim to whom the work was dedicated and, poignantly, only the English resume said: 'It was dedicated to a friend of the composer who had met a tragic death.' Neither the original Czech text nor the French, German and Russian translations in the rear of the score included this veiled dedication. The Czech Philharmonic under the direction of Karel Ančerl first performed the symphony at the concert of the Union of Czechoslovak Composers in March 1958.

In this work, Hanuš deals with the shattering personal experiences of tragic contradictions among people of our times. All humanity throughout the world is concentrated in these horrifying events. We hear a song of pain, tones of fear and anguish, but also the sounds of strong opposition, of a faith in life and courage. There is a sharp expression of the dangers of our era and we hear an anguished cry. Why should man – and must man – kill his fellow man again? Humanity's tragic question stands out like a pillar of fire. We cannot ignore or underestimate it, nor is it possible to answer it. The final chorale crowns the symphony. Tragedy once more shows its sharp teeth; however, life has been saved, understood and liberated. Traces of cloud are driven from the horizon and soon the rising sun will greet us.

Youthful Dreams 31

Vltava touches the river banks with flows
veils over drowned women the night throws
and I uncover them like extended sounds of musical notes.

Vítězslav Nezval, *Pražský chodec/A Prague Walker*, 1948

In the house in Nižbor, the stair's top landing, with a small sink and a paraffin Primus stove, was just big enough to prepare simple meals. In the summer, we used this accommodation for weekends and school holidays. I was a loner, inevitably influenced by the experiences of my early childhood. I loved the local countryside, riding my bicycle over forest paths, picking mushrooms early in the morning, climbing rocks overlooking the valley or paddling in a canoe up and down the Berounka river. A funfair visited the village once a year and I saved enough money to stand for hours at the shooting gallery aiming at the artificial paper roses scented with cheap perfume, displayed on thin wooden sticks which had to be broken with an airgun pellet to claim them. The dance hall in the local hotel was used as a cinema once a week where I watched favourite films, Jacques Tati's modernist *Mon Oncle* topping my list. I was entranced by its show of stunning cars, avant-garde architecture, advanced design and elegant humour.

In Prague Rudolf and Heda had some very good friends, Pavel and Jean Eisler, who used to live in a smart villa in the suburb of Smíchov. Pavel was an economist and diplomat, who worked for the Presidential Office in the 1950s advising on economic planning; he was frequently in contact with Rudolf at the Ministry.

His wife, Jean, was English. They had known each other during the war in Britain where Pavel had stayed as a Czech refugee and joined the Czechoslovak Army unit fighting within the British forces. The Eislers had two boys, the older one was Johnny and the younger Ivan. I often visited the boys and played Monopoly, which was how I came to know London so early in my life. While there I was looked after well, eating bowls of cornflakes and peanut butter sandwiches and, of course, drinking English tea – all new stuff for a five-year-old Czech. Jean got her supplies sent by her relatives from Britain. I also practiced some essential English words; no wonder I love Britain and her people, having had such close connection from childhood. And of course I was born in Prague in a sanatorium located on London Street ...

I remember one particular get-together in the early 1960s when Johnny took me to his bookcase and showed me a second-hand copy of Sir Bannister Fletcher's *History of Architecture* with its exquisite collection of drawings. From then on we were hooked, dreamed about designing buildings and decided to study architecture.

To me Prague was not only beautiful, but on many occasions it also felt threatening and hateful. Kafka had already expressed the same feelings in 1923: 'Prague that I not only love but also fear.' My native city and Czechoslovakia became a prison; a ghetto ran by people who murdered my father, populated by many I could not trust. The Western borders were heavily guarded with barbed wire and an exclusion zone several kilometres wide. Getting a special exit permit to travel abroad was impossible for those with a tainted past. The country had a suffocating atmosphere and Prague was giving out ambiguous messages; I loved the city one day and was afraid the next.

Since the age of five I had suffered from frequent nightmares and always woke up terrified, covered in sweat. It took me hours to get back to sleep. I had many unpleasant experiences and visions.

A drunkard staggered from the tram, hesitated uncertainly on his wobbly legs and collapsed on the narrow island pavement. A passing car made an avoiding arc at the last second. The man got up, slowly pulling himself on the bollard, and swayed, trying to overcome the inevitable force of gravity. Traffic increased in the streets.

The red-and-cream-coloured tram was passing by, empty and slowly, and in the end carriage a paramedic in orange overalls pumped rhythmically on the chest of a collapsed person lying on the

Vodičkova Street, Prague (Václav Jírů)

floor; only the paramedic's head bobbing up and down was visible. Was this the direct line to a hospital, would the sad cargo have to change trams on the way or make a detour out of the normal route?

A pickpocket gang gathered in a group whenever a crowd of Praguers developed, to ensnare them by the simple strategy of encircling their victims, who were blinded by the beauty of the city and formed into a sudden, tight mass; in the distracted confusion the gang rifled their bulging pockets.

Under the infrequently used quayside staircase the smell of piss and spilled beer dominated the air. 'In Prague each street has a different smell; in this respect there is no place to beat Prague,' wrote Karel Čapek. Albert Camus had noted an unpleasant smell permeating empty and hot Prague which he had visited during the summer of 1936 with Simone Camus and Yves Bourgeois. In his novel *La Mort heureuse (The Happy Death)* he writes: 'A strange odour reached him out of the darkness. Pungent, sour, it awakened all his associations with suffering. He tasted it on his tongue, deep in his nose, even his eyes, somehow, tasted it. It was far away, then it was at the next street corner, between the now-opaque sky and the sticky pavement it was there, the evil spell of the nights of Prague. He advanced to meet it, and as he did so it became more real, filling him entirely, stinging his eyes until the tears came, leaving him helpless. Turning a corner, he understood: an old woman was selling cucumbers soaked in vinegar, and it was their fragrance ...'

The Old Town Square, Prague (Václav Jírů)

As always, death was also present. 'He came closer: the dead man's head was lying in a pool of blood. The head was turned so that it rested on the wound. In this remote corner of Prague, between the faint light on the moist pavement, the long wet hiss of passing cars a few steps away, the distant screech of occasional trams, death seemed insipid yet insistent too, and it was death's summons, its damp breath ... '

A thin scraggy girl stepped out from the shadows of a medieval street, her dirty hands nervously playing with her unnecessary handbag, urgently leaning forward and speaking enticingly: 'Sex, sex, want sex?'

And then ... In the queue outside the state grocery store two women gossiped. 'Comrade, did you see Margoliusová, in her fur coat, all hoity toity, and did she acknowledge us like a true equal? No, just 'Good morning ladies!' can you imagine – ladies! And

Reflections of Prague (Václav Jírů)

271

when I replied 'Salute to Our Work, Comrade,' she smiled at me. We've got to report this to the Street Commune Committee and discuss her twisted attitude to the hard-working proletariat.'

A pair of shoes stood on the pavement, carefully aligned as if someone had been snatched from Prague's busy road and left them behind as a warning to others. The one thing left was the pair of shoes. How I wished I had Rudolf's shoes left to me.

The State Security's Tatraplan cars cruised the city; watchful eyes within scanned the hard urbanity; flashed headlight signals alerted their pedestrian counterparts.

The drunkard vomited noisily into the gutter, stupidly staring into the mess. The thin girl pushed her first eager client into the doorway. The beggar relieved himself under the stone staircase while his dog used the nearest lamp post. Two women whispered in each other's ears giggling: 'We'll nominate 'er to clear the dog shit

Charles Bridge and a Tatraplan (Václav Jírů)

from the playground next week, Comrade! I'll offer to lend 'er my factory dungarees. I didn't bother to go back to my lathe after lunch, Květa promised to cover for me. By the way, got a lovely piece of knuckle under the counter from the butcher for a bottle of Becherovka my daughter 'borrowed' from the shop where she cleans, you'd try the same.'

The chief pickpocket nonchalantly passed the booty to his companions and started selecting the next victim. A black Tatraplan stopped by the apartment block entrance and three men in leather coats entered, looking over their shoulders. In minutes, they were back leading a pale elderly man with trembling hands to the car. Before he disappeared inside the sun caught the gleam of the Communist Party badge in the lapel of his jacket.

A heavy truck drove at breakneck speed along the street leading out of Prague while I walked along the pavement. I heard a swishing sound and a heavy steel joist about a metre long left the truck and luckily only landed at my feet. Was someone trying to kill me? The truck picked up even more speed as if its mission had been completed.

A very real-looking leg, up to half-thigh, was suddenly lying in the middle of the road with the shoe and sock still on, appearing as if from nowhere. People gathered on the pavement stupefied, puzzled as to where this bizarre object came from. A cyclist was hiding in between two parked cars further up the street, looking embarrassed. One of the onlookers picked up the leg and carried it under his arm to the cyclist. The cyclist's artificial leg had dropped off as he was passing by.

The paramedic, perspiration marking his overalls with a large stain, kept pumping – up and down – the man's chest in the tram that was still on the move, its wheels screeching on the rails as it was on the way toward the hospital quarter at Charles Square.

I lived in a dream and at most times could not distinguish reality from what I might have imagined.

32 ● ●   The Emergence of Truth

> It would have been better if you did not care for the Party
> and had with your fellow beings more sympathy.
> It is a mistake that you respect the Party,
> in reality it is your adversary.

Jan Zábrana, *Deníky/Diaries*, 1976

3 December 1952

My dear Ivan

Many years will have passed before you receive this, my first and last letter to you. By now, you are an adult and you will correctly understand the life and the end of your father. Your mother will have explained my fate to you, and you will have learned about it from the press and from literature. You surely do not remember me any more; your mind will have erased all memories of us playing, jumping about and cuddling, at home and outside in nature, by the Lišno pond, in the mountain snows. You do not remember, and that is as it should be. You can evaluate my life and draw your own conclusions soberly.

I have grievously offended society and was justly condemned for it. There are no excuses, not even for you; you, too, should condemn me harshly. Blame is not hereditary, though, and a son cannot be reproached for the offences of his father. On the contrary, the socialist order in which you are living will help you become a proper citizen and to develop differently than did your father, who grew up in a capitalist world.

I would wish that knowing my fate will give you strength in life, that it will help you become better than others, that you will always act in the interests of society and progress and devote all your energies to the construction of a Communist world.

Study, continue expanding your knowledge, become a master of your vocation. Enjoy nature, music, poetry and creative arts. And love people!

Help them to be better, to eradicate whatever bad is in them. The world is beautiful, Ivan, and you have a chance to make it even much more beautiful for yourself and for your fellow citizens.

Ivan, cherish your dear mother. She is a lovely and wonderful person. She is a woman who has suffered a lot and lives for you alone. Make her happy with your love, devotion, and your successes.

Best wishes, Ivan!
Your father

In May 1963 Heda was given Rudolf's last letters. It took the Party eleven years to release them.

In the same year, under pressure from Moscow to investigate the crimes of the 1950s, the Czechoslovak Communist Party Central Committee – after secret sessions and a special sitting of a Commission led by Secretary of the Central Committee Drahomír Kolder – issued a Communication of the Central Committee on the Slánský Trial. The Communication fully rehabilitated all the defendants, admitting that mistakes had been made and that Czechoslovak laws had been broken in obtaining forced confessions. It annulled the verdicts. The cancellation of the original judgement was signed by the High Court of Justice of the Republic but was only distributed to top Party officials and the affected families, who were under strict orders not to pass it any further. Heda was invited to the Ministry of Justice to receive her private copy. The general public knew nothing.

Previously there had been a government commission led by Minister of the Interior Rudolf Barák that started to investigate the trials in 1955. However, too many old comrades were still in power at that time and its ultimate outcome was the suppression of all the findings and the eventual jailing of Barák, who had used the acquired evidence to try to dislodge the Party leadership and take over.

In March 1965 Heda had a chance to travel abroad as a tourist for a week on the invitation of a family friend who lived in Belgium. Such an invitation secured permission to obtain an exit visa. The main purpose of the trip was to go to Paris to see Pavel Tigrid, her old friend, who edited the highly influential émigré magazine *Svědectví*, and deliver the Communication in order to have it published. Heda reserved a couchette in a sleeper train; a train journey would offer more opportunities to conceal the document than would flying. When she was shown into the compartment by the train guard, she was happy to find that she was to be on her own. She stripped a lino square from the floor, hid the document under it and settled down to read her detective story. At the border the guards and custom officials searched the compartment but did not find anything even though they stood on top of it all the time.

When the train crossed into Germany, the same Czech train guard came to tell Heda that he had arranged another, more comfortable, compartment for her. He stood in the doorway carefully watching her gather her things.

'What can I do now?' she thought frantically, and then remembered the solution suggested in the detective story she was reading. When they reached the new compartment, and while the guard helped her with the luggage, Heda exclaimed that she had left a glove behind and without waiting for the guard to react, rushed back. She pulled the lino off, slid the report under her thick pullover and walked back waving her gloves high in the air. Tigrid published the Communication as a supplement with the next issue of *Svědectví*.

Publication abroad created a furore at the top of the Party. Eventually, Novotný, a hardliner, lost the post of the powerful First Secretary to Alexander Dubček on 5 January 1968. A couple of months later the new President was named as Ludvík Svoboda and Novotný retired. Dubček's rise to power and his subsequent democratic reforms brought a great relief to the country with the introduction of 'Socialism with a Human Face'.

His agenda included the abolition of censorship, the right of citizens to criticize the government, the improvement of the relationship between the government and the churches, the creation of works councils in industry and increased rights for trade unions to bargain on behalf of their members. Czechoslovakia planned to welcome Western capital investments and the full convertibility of the Czechoslovak crown into foreign currencies would be implemented. A central economic policy-making body would preside over a completely decentralized industry. Free enterprise would be permitted in the service industries where private individuals could set up businesses. The Action Programme of the Party, called 'The Czechoslovak Road to Socialism', confirmed that 'Our democracy must provide more room for the activity of every individual, every collective ... People must have more opportunity to think for themselves and to express their opinions ... Every citizen ... must know with certainty that his political convictions and opinions, his personal beliefs and activities, cannot be the object of attention of the bodies of State Security. The Party declares clearly that this apparatus should not be directed and used to solve internal political questions and controversies in socialist society.'

'Let us eliminate all defamations, arbitrariness and illegalities; let us develop Socialist-Democracy and give Socialism in this country the human face which is appropriate to it. This and nothing else is the essence of our policy,' said Dubček.

Regretfully, this deviation from the Communist path survived only for the short period of two hundred days. The relaxed attitude, without political Party doctrines and uncompromising ideology, was the vision of a country Rudolf had worked for, anticipated and dreamed about, but was prevented from seeing.

At last, at that year's May Day celebrations, a number of Slánský Trial defendants, including Rudolf, received posthumous honours after the determination of the third government commission of Jan Piller. The commission re-examined the 1950s trials and confirmed the defendants' full rehabilitations. Again its report was kept secret as Piller informed the Party leadership that it contained such alarming facts that publication might touch off an explosion likely to undermine the authority of the Party and some of its top men. When Gustav Husák became First Secretary, the documents were marked top secret and deposited in the archives in the hope that they would never see the light of day.

CZECH 'MARTYR' HONOURED

Executed in 1952

Czechoslovak President Ludvik Svoboda has awarded the Order of the Republic posthumously to Rudolf Margolius, former Deputy Foreign Minister executed in 1952 after the Stalinist Slansky trial.

Margolius was accused of being a member of the "anti-party conspiratoral centre," and was sentenced to death along with former Party Secretary Rudolf Slansky and nine others on November 27, 1952.

Slansky and the others were juridically rehabilitated by the Supreme Court in 1963. All had been accused of high treason, espionage, sabotage and organising a Jewish plot to bring down the régime.—Reuter.

The *Scotsman*, 16 May 1968

On 14 May 1968, Oldřich Černík, the acting Prime Minister, as President Svoboda's representative, handed Heda a small red box at home with the Order of the Republic marked 'in memoriam', together with a diploma. This order was normally given for the high appreciation of personal merit achieved in contribution of the country's economic, political, social and cultural advancement. The honours were decided on at the Party Central Committee meeting on 24 April. The ones who received sentences of life imprisonment were given their orders at the Castle by Dubček but, amazingly, even this 'liberated' comrade was too embarrassed to invite and face the surviving families of the murdered victims there.

In my eyes this gesture was devalued as fifteen years earlier Doubek, the chief interrogator, had received the same honour even though Rudolf's award was given under the changed circumstances.

In August 1968 I was camping in St Ives in Cornwall in a farmer's field high above the seaside town. Two years before, in the summer, we had arrived in Britain on holiday. We loaded our small white Fiat 600D, called Plašmuška ('Fly-Scarer'), with our possessions and drove across the Charles Bridge to bid goodbye to Prague. For a long time I had been uneasy living in Czechoslovakia where the leading politicians and the Party governing the country were guilty of my father's murder and had got away with it. I was determined to leave at the first opportunity. The Czech official who issued my new passport and exit visa remarked, sounding slightly underhand, 'Mr Ková́ly, this is the last time you are getting a passport.'

With this veiled threat hanging over me, I had no choice. I felt they were trying to get rid of me. I must have been an embarrassment, still classed as the son of a traitor and reminding them of their past crimes despite being disguised with Pavel's surname. I had managed to get a place at the Czech Institute of Technology to study architecture but was told that on completion there would not be any work for me because of my bad cadre report. Pavel had a philosophy lectureship promised at Sussex University, and that would have set us up quite comfortably. Having driven across Europe, spending a night at a French campsite, we got to London the next day – 27 July 1966.

We rented a room with a coin gas meter, a hissing gas fireplace, and a single gas ring placed on the floor to cook on, in a house owned by a Yugoslav émigré in Belsize Park. I was quite thrown by the primitive nature of our accommodation – the draughty single-glazed sash windows, the exposed external drain-pipes, the lack of central heating – but overwhelmed by the freedom of swinging London at the time. The Beatles, Carnaby Street, Flower Power, Twiggy and miniskirts, as well as discovering the sculptures of Henry Moore and Barbara Hepworth, the paintings of J. M. W. Turner, classic English literature, the poems of Philip Larkin and John Betjeman and the variety of daily newspapers ... The mysterious film *Blow-Up* by Michelangelo Antonioni was released that year and exemplified the contemporary London scene. I loved the photographer Thomas's drives through London in the Rolls-Royce drop-head coupe, his involvement with skinny girls, the dark

London streets, parks and dusty corner shops and his enigmatic murder investigation. What he perceived might not have been reality but what the camera saw might have been the truth. The concluding tennis-match scene confirmed that underlining theme. The film was similar to my disorientated life and its connection with dark secrets of the powers in charge. I was not sure what was reality and what I imagined, recalling my past continuously – and the father I missed.

One distant family friend and active Labour Party member knew Harold Wilson, then the Prime Minister, and contacted him when we applied to extend our stay. Wilson remembered Rudolf from the 1949 trade negotiations and we had no problems continuing our visit. In fact we were astonished, after our interview at the Home Office, how much detail was known about our affairs. However, there were problems with getting work. Pavel's offer of a lectureship fell through and Heda's employment as a shop assistant in the Medici art shop off New Bond Street did not produce enough money to support us all. This was a disappointing result despite our well-planned departure from Prague.

In addition, an English friend of Ervín, who had kept some emergency money for him since the 1930s, died a week before our arrival. Pavel was upset with the failure of our move. Heda was very proud, learned to fend for herself and refused any financial help from friends who tried to persuade us to stay. After a lot of heart-searching, she and Pavel decided to return to Prague. The visa was running out and the Czechoslovak authorities had to be prevented from finding out that we had wanted to leave the country permanently without their permission. However, I refused to return and insisted on staying on my own at all costs. Heda was worried; I was nineteen and had no means of supporting myself, but she saw my point of view. In Czechoslovakia I had no future.

Rudolf had two cousins in London who had emigrated from Czechoslovakia before the war. Josef let me stay for several months in his house in Ealing and his brother Karel gave me work in his import business in Soho, helping with packing cases of Hungarian gherkins and Romanian jam as well as doing some bookkeeping. For lunch, he used to take me to the local Italian and

Jewish cafés or to his modest rented apartment in Paddington. This was a good way to get to know the people of London, the English language and British culture. Karel was a likeable, heavily set man with a circle of baldness crowning his head: a loud, jolly, wheeler-dealer character. Everywhere he went he used to boast about his business exploits, proudly announcing that he supplied Prince Charles with the Hungarian chocolate-covered plums that Charles ordered from the firm. He was also a fanatic football fan.

Since the days when he did not have much money after arriving in Britain, Karel had devised a trick to get to see football matches. He came with a pencil and pad and manufactured a false press pass from some obscure provincial magazine to gain entry into the press boxes of the London clubs. While Karel watched the match he pretended to scribble notes into his notebook and in this way saw the match for free. After a time he became a permanent fixture in the press galleries and was always warmly welcomed by his colleagues as a 'fellow journalist'. Later, when Karel was better off, the stadium stewards used to get little parcels of tins and jars as presents for letting him slip in to the box once it transpired that he was not a sports reporter after all.

With his vast contacts, only three days after my arrival Karel got me a standing ticket for the World Cup final played at Wembley on 30 July. It was a great feeling being there as part of the almost 97,000-strong crowd and witnessing the legendary match, now etched for ever in the sporting minds of the country as one of its greatest successes. I was swept away by the enthusiasm of the English football fans. So, early after my arrival I had embraced my new setting. Sporting occasions break down barriers between people if you support the same side, and I joined in the celebrations.

Prague and her shadows were pushed out of my mind and new horizons opened. I was learning all over again. The British countryside with its rolling hills was similar to the Bohemian lands, though the towns were much prettier. They had attractive houses and gardens, clipped green hedges, stone walls, welcoming and cosy public houses, churches with turrets or spires in the centre and majestic trees. As Karel Čapek observed in his *Letters from England*: 'The trees are perhaps the most beautiful things in England.' The villages were well-groomed and tidy in comparison to their Czech counterparts which consisted of scattered, half-dilapidated houses, falling-down stables and working farms with reeking piles of manure in their courtyards, and with poultry, cows and sheep running where they pleased. Seeing the elegant figures of horses and riders galloping through the English landscape brought the George Stubbs paintings I remembered from books in Prague suddenly to life.

The immaculate, evergreen English lawn was another surprise. Everywhere I visited I begged to mow the lawn. I could not get enough satisfaction unless I could smell the cut grass and see the green velvety texture expanding under my feet.

London was so different from Prague: bigger, more progressive, open and less mysterious, busy with activities of all kinds, many nationalities and cultures brimming with freedom, all sharing the same ground. The seaside was a revelation, the vastness of water constantly lapping at the rocky, shingle or sandy shores, conveniently isolating Britain from her neighbours and providing security all around.

Jan Masaryk, the son of the Czechoslovak President, whom Queen Elizabeth always preferred to sit next to at wartime royal receptions so she could be entertained by his sharp wit, observed: 'I love this country of England because my charwoman keeps her hat on when she's scrubbing the floor, and because the plumber who comes to mend the plug in the bathroom offers me a Player's cigarette. He would offer the King one. That's democracy.'

You could express what ever you wanted, including criticism of the government and monarchy, and no one minded. People had no political pressure imposed on them, they were free to go, travel or say what they pleased and they had a great sense of humour. They were not morally corrupt; their thoughts matched their actions. They did not separate their public thoughts and their private minds, having a split personality, something which almost every Czech had to develop in order to survive. They did not harbour the constant resentment and fear of authorities and government. The Brits expressed their beliefs without being afraid of the consequences; they trusted their siblings, colleagues and friends. If they were betrayed, it was not to bend their minds to conform to the rules of the Party and the so-called Communist 'Socialism'. There were no secret policemen in Tatraplans roaming the London streets hunting spies and saboteurs. It felt very safe and I could breathe deeply again. I made more discoveries of information normally inaccessible in heavily censored Prague, such as Le Corbusier's designs and paintings, Norman Bel Geddes's *Horizons*, the broad range of Penguin books, *Encounter* magazine, Franz Kafka's and Adolf Loos's writings, Ludwig Wittgenstein's philosophy, Karel Reisz's and Jean Luc Goddard's films.

In London, I visited the places Rudolf saw when he came in 1949. St Martin's Theatre, seat C50 in the upper stalls. It did not matter what the play was, I wanted to sit in the same seat, stretch my legs and observe the theatrical scenery as Rudolf would have done seventeen years ago.

I closed my eyes and imagined that *The Young and Fair* was being staged and I could hear clearly Sara Cantry, the owner and head of Junior College, saying: 'Patricia, I've done you a terrible wrong. If I can ever make it up to you ...' and Patty Morritt, a sixteen-year-old student, reply coldly: 'You can't make anything up to me!'

Cantry pleaded with her: 'Please bear with me! I'm not equal to my burden any more – what will I say to the school ...'

Frances Morritt, Patty's elder sister and teacher in the College intervened: 'Might I suggest the truth, Miss Cantry?'

'The truth will treat me cruelly, Frances! And you, too!'

Frances agreed: 'We've done cruel things.'

Cantry cried out: 'From fear – can't you understand it – from fear.'

'Is that supposed to excuse us?'

'If there's no excuse for us, Frances – then the whole frightened world is guilty!'

I visited Museum Street where Rudolf had bought an etching of a woman's head by Wenceslaus Hollar, a Czech artist who worked in the British Isles in the 17th century, for Heda. It is mounted on a piece of velvet in a gilded frame and mysteriously keeps turning on its axis clockwise, very slowly ...

On the corner of the same street was a shop selling woollen blankets. Rudolf acquired one, which had a tartan pattern and tassels along the short edges. Wherever I travel, I carry the blanket with me. It is still pretty good, though it has some moth holes and it has lost the tassels.

In the autumn, I found a little room above and over-looking Finchley Road underground station, which was big enough for a bed, table, chair, sink, a two-ring stove and a half-size fridge. In the winter the walls, which had no insulation, copiously sweated with water. The bath and toilet were one floor up, shared with all. The rent was five pounds a week and another five pounds sufficed for food, travel – the underground was four pennies a ride – and one weekly visit to the local cinema, or more likely to the Hampstead Everyman. The rattle of tube trains and presence of fellow, like-minded young tenants kept me company.

A friend took me out in his Jaguar 3.8 Mark II. We cruised around the Buckinghamshire countryside through narrow lanes marked with hedges. We came to a junction while another car turned up on the right at the same time. Both cars stopped waiting for each other to go, both drivers politely bidding each other to drive off first. 'This is Britain, this could not take place anywhere else,' I thought with satisfaction. Yes, that was the 1960s.

On Wednesday, 21 August 1968 I woke up early in the morning, rolled up my sleeping bag, left the tent and went downhill to St Ives to have some breakfast. It was a beautiful sunny day and I was enjoying my holiday in Cornwall, exploring the surrounding countryside and seascape. When I entered the main street there was a large crowd of people gathered around the window of the Radio Rental outlet. This was unusual so early in the morning, so I pushed through the throng to find out what was going on. In the middle of the window was a small black and white television set and on its screen white letters announced 'CZECH INVASION'.

For a long time I was not able to see anything else on the screen. The crowd was fascinated but not as frightened, as I had been. Then a Russian tank rolled into view and someone tried to fight it with a bloodied Czechoslovak flag. Now I understood what was happening. The invading Red and Warsaw Pact Armies were crushing Dubček's courageous reforms.

I went to buy a paper from a newsagent. There was a long queue as people were getting four or five papers each, including the Communist *Daily Worker*, to find out what the various political parties had to say. 'RUSSIANS MARCH INTO CZECHOSLOVAKIA, PEOPLE TOLD NOT TO RESIST, TANKS BLOCK BRIDGE ON AUSTRIAN BORDER' shouted the headlines. In Prague Heda was alone; by then Pavel had got his long-sought philosophy lectureship at Northeastern University and had relocated to Boston a year before. I gathered a handful of pennies and tried to phone Prague from a red phone box by the harbour while the screeching seagulls dive-bombed the local fishing boats returning with the early morning catch. I could not get through and kept pressing buttons A and B, but the line must have been cut.

Here people watched the boats, read their papers sitting on the sea wall, with the blue sky hanging comfortingly and

A Russian tank in Prague, 21 August 1968 (B. Hajný)

securely over them while Russian tanks roared through the Prague streets and Czechs tried to stop them with their bare hands. Knowing Heda, she would have been resourceful enough to get out of Prague in time. I realized that I was in the wrong place, I packed my tent and got a coach back to London so I could be there and help as much as I could by campaigning, collecting money and giving blood. On the door of my room, I pasted an angry note: 'Bloody Russians'.

A few days after the occupation, while the Musils stored some of our things for the third time, Heda left Czechoslovakia and joined Pavel in Boston where they remained until 1996.

Living Anew 33

Life taught me long ago
that music and poetry
are the most beautiful things on earth
that life can give us.
Except for love, of course.

Jaroslav Seifert, *Býti básníkem/To be a Poet*, 1983 (translated by Ewald Osers)

My first marriage was not a happy one. It was with a Czech girl I got to know in secondary school and our relationship had continued on and off since we were sixteen. We broke up before I left Prague but Olga persistently followed me to London when I was half way through my studies. We stayed together for twenty years, and had two super children, but the union did not last longer. Olga became withdrawn and distant, eventually living in a world of her own that could not be shared with anyone.

It helps to get to know someone at work. Being in contact every day over a long stretch of time gives the opportunity to find out another person's make-up, quirks, interests and attitudes. I admired Mandy's common sense, her practical approach to life and the ease with which she unravelled problems that at the time seemed irresolvable. I was drawn by her uncomplicated view. She always manoeuvred through situations without creating waves, getting her way and satisfying all the other parties at the same time. She was pretty and dark-haired, with round glasses over her green eyes, like a wise little owl. I had fallen in love. We worked together on architectural projects, had lunches and went out in the evenings. Mandy came along at the right time to pull me back into the true way of living, into a faster-moving stream.

In the summer of 1989, I packed the car with my essential possessions and moved out of London into the countryside.

I always wanted to live a rural life, perhaps spurred on by the life forced on my ancestors who lived simply in small villages in Bohemia. Cities were suffocating my sense of freedom and Mandy, who lived in a village north of London, allowed me to fulfil my dream.

I felt at home there when I discovered that the nearby country house's gardens, designed by Capability Brown, contained an unusual eighteenth-century summer pavilion. Nikolaus Pevsner described it as an exceptional building, an essay in the Borrominesque in its plan with interlocking triangles, one expressed in apsidal ends and the other in oblong ends, like chapels round a perfectly circular domed room. For me this was a beautiful building of its time, with trompe l'oeil decoration by Handuroy which had been inspired by the Baroque architecture of Prague – of all the places on earth. Deep in the English countryside, I found a fragment of my native city.

As a book lover, on arrival to Britain, I went to Foyles Bookshop in Charing Cross Road to rummage on their shelves for all the forbidden books I could not get in Prague. The surprising discovery was that there was very little about Czechoslovak culture and technology available. There were books by Kafka and Hašek, and some on Dvořák, Smetana and Janáček. There was nothing on the unique Czech Cubist movement, Czech design or about Škoda or Tatra cars. I decided that it was my mission to improve the knowledge of my former country in the West. During the following years, I wrote on these subjects, despite not being able to travel back to Prague to carry out research and obtain illustrations. Foolishly, when asking the Czech archives and museums for images for a book on Czech Cubism, I wrote under my original name. I had decided to have this back as soon as my paperwork was in order and my permanent permission to stay had been granted. The Czech institutions refused to send anything. Later I was told that the picture curators were specifically instructed not to reply to my letters. Here I was trying to promote Czech culture, and in return being given no encouragement from the Czechs. In the end, my sister-in-law borrowed some photographs under a different pretext and sent them secretly to a friend's address.

For the book on Tatra, I had to get together with a fellow architect and car enthusiast who travelled to Czechoslovakia to obtain the research material and pictures we needed while I wrote at home. In the United Kingdom at that time there was one Tatra T87 car, the best known and most admired Tatra streamlined design. This car was designed by Hans Ledwinka, an Austrian who worked for the Tatra Company based in a small Moravian town of Kopřivnice. As a motoring genius, Ledwinka had a troublesome life. Hitler admired his designs and Ferdinand Porsche, on his master's orders, copied Ledwinka's ideas for his Volkswagen proposal. After the war, on the strength of the Hitler connection, the Czechs gaoled Ledwinka for five years for alleged collaboration with the Nazis; he was later rehabilitated.

We borrowed the T87 from her owner to take the car to the book launch that had been arranged in the RAC Club in Pall Mall. The car was not roadworthy so she was trailered from the Midlands down the M1 motorway to London. It was memorable to see passing cars overtaking and then stopping on the hard shoulder to have another look at the futuristic car, designed in 1936, on her way south. In Pall Mall there was near pandemonium; buses were stopping and passengers were craning out to see what was happening, and a large crowd gathered round the Tatra. Some people recognized her and praised Czechoslovakia for both the country's democracy and Czech engineering, remembering the highly skilled workforce, quality of craftsmanship and inventiveness between the two wars. Later, for a month, we arranged for the same Tatra – which originally belonged to the Romanian Embassy in Dublin – to be exhibited at the London Design Museum alongside a Volkswagen. Our book inspired an interest in Tatra and a British club was formed with an ever-increasing number of members keeping this extraordinary marque alive.

Throughout my architectural career, I had the opportunity to work with and write about Eugene Rosenberg, Norman Foster, Tony Hunt and especially my fellow countryman, Jan Kaplický, and treasured the experience that enabled me to participate in their design processes and ideas. I learned enormously by talking to them, watching them create buildings and describing their projects. Jan and I even wrote a very enjoyable book together.

Villa Müller in Prague is my favourite building. Adolf Loos, a Czech German-speaking architect born in Brno who spent most of his life in Vienna, designed it. Loos proposed this family house for a building contractor, František Müller, and his family in 1928. The building's complexity and the intricacy of the interior reflects the labyrinth of life. There is an erotic symbol in the narrow entrance and the string of spaces beyond. The visitor penetrates the building at the centre bottom of its mass; its recessed entrance door is safeguarded by wisps of geranium flowers. The journey follows, leading us through the restricting corridor and suddenly opening into the colourful rooms. When visitors enter, they have a feeling of physical and mental elation comparable to sexual arousal, are thoroughly excited within and totally exhausted on leaving, almost as if fully spent of their strength and senses after experiencing an artistic orgasm. The entwined volumes of spaces interlock and close or open up to more vistas, depending from which point one observes the architecture. There is nothing on the outside; there is everything on the inside. It is an architectural jack-in-a-box. This villa is not a lifeless building or architecture, it is a complex living organism able to adapt and communicate with and respond fully to human behaviour. As in any family saga, the villa reacted in its own way, leaving a wake of tragedy in the history of the people who created it. Müller's mother-in-law, who lived in the top floor bedroom, was run over by a Prague tram. In 1951, its owner, František Müller, died from the inhalation of carbon monoxide while stoking the villa's Strebel boilers and his only daughter left the country.

Even more inspiring was the Baťa Department Store on Wenceslas Square, the 1927 creation of Ludvík Kysela, which was conceived as a shining advertisement for the progressive shoe manufacturer. The opaque spandrel panels of the elegant glass façade, suspended on a slim reinforced concrete frame, are brilliant white during the day and are illuminated from behind at night. This transformation makes this building stand out from its dark neighbours like a sparkling diamond placed among worthless pebbles. It is still as fresh today as it was seventy-five years ago.

Another discovery was the Slovenian architect Jože Plečnik who worked in Prague in the 1920s. My admiration was not necessarily for the architectural quality of his buildings but for his design philosophy, meticulous detailing, use of materials, his spatial compositions and alignments of building elements within urban context on a ley-line principle, which enhanced the perception and appreciation of space and beauty.

The experience of the engineering of glass block vaulting always overwhelms me. It can be found in the many Prague passageways that have innovative, elegantly slender, translucent roofs designed by René Wiesner in collaboration with a number of Czech avant-garde architects in the 1930s.

While practising the art of building I revered my heroes: Le Corbusier, his astonishing and varied output from paintings, sculpture to writing, town planning and unique building and furniture designs; and the pure simplicity – so difficult to achieve – of Mies van der Rohe's architecture. I maintained that architecture had to look forward and never turn back, as Lewis Mumford had said: 'Everything we take over from the past must disappear in the act of digestion and assimilation, to be transformed into our own flesh and bones. Each age must live its own life.'

I persevered to maintain the principle Henry Wadsworth Longfellow wrote about in 1849 in his poem called 'The Builders':

In the elder days of art,
Builders wrought with greatest care
Each minute and unseen part;
For the Gods see everywhere.

Let us do our work as well,
Both the unseen and the seen;
Make the house, where Gods may dwell,
Beautiful, entire, and clean.

I shared my love of this with Wittgenstein; he had frequently quoted part of this poem as his motto when building a house for his sister in Vienna. He summarized the challenging complexity of building design, that I also found attractive, when he remarked: 'Philosophy is hard enough, but it is nothing to the difficulty of being a good architect.'

Despite having practised architecture somehow, I put books first in the order of importance in my creativity, although the excitement and elation felt after designing and constructing a building on a green meadow – out of nothing there grew an object, and then someone was able to occupy it, sleep in it and enjoy it – is hard to replace. However, early in the morning of the 1980 August bank holiday the fragility of buildings was brought home to me when I drove past Wallis Gilbert's Art Deco Firestone Building in West London. I saw with astonishment how this architectural masterpiece was being razed to the ground by a ball and chain, just before its preservation listing was due to take place the following week. I preferred books for their endurance; even if most could be burned or destroyed, one or two were always bound to survive on a dusty shelf somewhere.

When my children arrived it was a further joy, and I was so sorry that Rudolf was not there to enjoy them too. Daniel had complications when he was born and bravely bore the numerous and necessary operations. Susanna, when I took her for a trip to Hampton Court as a little girl, stood open-mouthed in front of a painting of a large naked woman, astonished at the new discovery she had made. I could not tear her away from it. As soon as he 'cracked out' Theo looked around the delivery room with wide eyes, wisely observing his surroundings, totally calm without uttering a cry, while Jan always behaved and talked as if he had been on this planet before, coming up with complicated words he could not have heard earlier.

'Mum, what is the last number before infinity?' was Theo's most memorable question when he was five years old. At the same age Jan wondered, standing in front of a map of the town, 'Dad, how does it know that I'm here?' and pointed at the map with which had an arrow and the legend 'You are here'. When Jan was older he often had nightmares and, on waking up, he mentioned while we looked at him, startled: 'I feel guilty even when I'm saying the truth.'

Children inherit looks, intelligence and behaviour from their parents, but more often from their grandparents, jumping one generation. I was hoping, rather foolishly, that I would be able to discover Rudolf in one of them. Each had one trait here or there which reminded me of my father. The one thing they all had in common were slightly crooked index fingers on both hands; Rudolf and I had the same fingers. Collectively, in all my children, I could see Rudolf live again.

Every time I remembered the city Prague left a bitter taste, but I was longing to get back and walk the old narrow streets and sleepy squares, green hills and parks dissected by the broad river, touch the faded façades and visit the shadows cast by the pavlače courtyard houses and the passageways. I had to forgive my native city and her setting for the awful crimes and her people, who by now must have repented their cowardly deeds.

The sudden 1989 Velvet Revolution, and the return to democracy in Czechoslovakia, was inspired by Gorbachev's perestroika and the fall of the Berlin Wall. It was instigated by the 50th anniversary memorial procession of Czech students in remembrance of Jan Opletal, a medical student from Charles

Student demonstration, Prague, November 1989 (Kaplan Productions Archive)

University shot by the Nazis during the Protectorate. The subsequent public demonstrations and strikes against the contemporary regime of President Gustav Husák completed the dramatic turnaround. This political reversal was unexpected; I never dreamt that I would see Prague again in my lifetime. I doubted that the stoic Czechs would have the stamina to rise against their eastern oppressors and the local old guard.

Coming back to Prague was like walking into Sleeping Beauty's castle that had woken up from a bad dream. We envisaged being welcomed on the border with a bunch of flowers and a big smile. We would drive east toward Prague with Smetana's *Vltava* trickling from the car speakers and tears streaming from our misty eyes. However, that sweet vision soured when we discovered that hordes of other people had the same idea; we had to wait over six hours to cross the frontier and have our paperwork cleared by the pedantic border guards. Finally we entered Prague exhausted, and rather than celebrate we crawled to bed to recuperate. To my surprise the same shop assistants that served me twenty-four years ago, in the same disinterested way, in the same stores, selling the same wares, were still there. People looked weary, but this time they had small smiles on their lips. More worries were coming, the new life would be more complicated and hard work, but opportunities, expectations and freedom of unimaginable proportions were opening in front of them. They wanted to look forward and not be reminded of the past and forget the Party doctrines dogmatically imposed on them for over forty years.

Heda and Pavel returned from the United States, both retired, and found a reasonable apartment in the centre of Prague. They still had a few friends there from the old days and, with their small pensions, life in Prague was quite comfortable. I travelled to see them on every occasion that I had time off work.

A Memorial to the Victims of Communism was erected in Prague in 2002. It took years to persuade the authorities to commemorate publicly the innocent people who suffered and died. This Monument is located at the bottom of Petřín Hill in Malá Strana and is designed with strange, disintegrating bronze figures set into unsuitable concrete steps. During my first visit, I was stunned to see a smoky Trabant car, the true symbol of the Communist era, driving along a path that was left halfway up, stretching perpendicularly across the Monument. This disrespect to the fallen and a convenient forgetfulness of the history of the recent past seems to permeate the current Czech attitude.

In the autumn of 2004 another blow awaited me. I was invited to the Czech Embassy reception organized in honour of President Václav Klaus's visit to Great Britain. He talked to and smiled at the people present and mingled with the crowd, earnestly chatting to the invited. His bodyguard was handing out Klaus's photographs for signature. I approached the President with a copy of his picture and introduced myself. 'Do you know my name?' I asked eagerly, in readiness to find out his opinion on the fate of my father.

'Yes, it is well known to me,' he replied quietly, clearly deeply shocked and embarrassed, without looking me in the eye or offering to shake my hand. With his head down he dedicated the picture, quickly signed it, passed it to me and before I had a chance to continue he had turned away.

In 1992 I had written to Klaus's predecessor President Václav Havel, who was himself imprisoned as a dissident for four and a half years, asking for a government commission to be set up to investigate the crimes of the 1950s. My letter was passed from Ministry to Ministry without any result. Someone else always had to deal with it. Nobody had the courage to take it on, including the President; it was not within his competence. In his first Presidential speech on 1 January 1990 Havel said that 'many of our citizens perished in the 1950s in prisons, many were executed, thousands of lives were destroyed ... No one who paid with his life for our current freedom should be forgotten. Independent courts should consider rightly the possible guilt of those who were responsible to seek the full truth about our recent past.' Havel's pledge made in the euphoric times of the Velvet Revolution has never been fulfilled.

To this day no proper offer of apology for Rudolf's murder, public or private, has ever been submitted to us from the Czech government, apart from the hesitant award from the uncomfortable

Dubček, and Klaus's ashamed reaction confirmed my suspicions that the government officials lacked the courage to face up to the past and that nothing would ever be done. While Heda was being invited for discussions, receptions and dinners by the American, Spanish and French Ambassadors in Prague, Czech government officials ignored her. Sadly, even long after the Velvet Revolution, the Czechs were not yet ready to reconcile themselves with the crimes their Soviet-inspired politicians committed over fifty years ago.

I aimed to fulfil Rudolf's wishes, expressed in his last letter, to the best of my abilities in order to honour his memory and do even more when I could. I appreciated that in his letter he could not say what he really felt and thought, knowing that it would be read by State Security before it came to me. I looked after Heda and kept in constant touch during our years of separation. For her enormous love and sacrifice, I must be forever grateful. Our lives were destined to be spent on different continents but modern communications and ways of travel have created a continuous unbreakable bond. I tried to succeed in my work and writing. Despite the fact that I live in a capitalist society my leanings are to the left of the political spectrum. In 1952, in Rudolf's circumstances, he could not have envisaged that one day I would become a tiny part of the oldest democracy in the world. I am sure he would have approved.

With all the work of designing, writing and having a family, I kept busy, but on many occasions I was conscious that there was a large piece of experience missing from of my life that could never be imagined or replaced. Had Rudolf remained, I suppose I would have no reason at times to be mistrustful of my native city and her people. I would have a deeper knowledge of my family history but, most of all, have a human being close by me in whom I could confide all my worries and joys, and express my love and support and get the same in return. There are thousands of cases where fathers disappear – they die, they leave the family or remain unknown to the child.

However, fathers are not often publicly hounded and liquidated, although completely innocent, by the country they served dutifully to the best of their abilities; nor, in these circumstances,

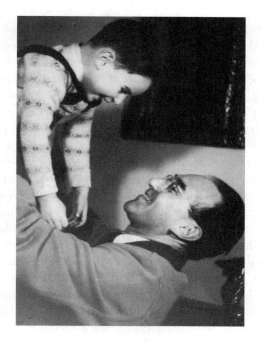

Rudolf and Ivan, 1951

is the sacrifice of their lives not visibly appreciated, vindicated or recognized by their leading countrymen even long after gaining democracy and freedom.

Apart from the man, something intangible and precious had been taken away from Heda, from me and my children that would have made our lives different and me another person. I have frequently speculated on how I would really have turned out had Rudolf lived on.

Excited, I try to inhale the odour of fresh pine needles, the wetness of bright green moss, the musty smell of mushrooms pushing their heads from under last year's rotten leaves, the peppery fragrance of yellow primroses turning their heads toward the sky, the powder of pollen from the fluffy catkins suspended from the willow branches. The dim shadows dance with the shafts of sun penetrating down to the forest floor. Deeper in the woods the carpets of bluebells mix with the young ferns endlessly stretching below the trees. Then the summer came and the vivid green colours changed to darker tones. Rudolf kept throwing me up toward the overhanging tree branches. Again and again, and higher and higher, and I kept falling into his outstretched arms and we both enjoyed it and I screeched. Heda observed this anxiously and pleaded: 'Rudlo, please don't drop him!'

My whole body's vertical flight through the air turned into a horizontal swing of locomotion. We were in Nouzov having a contest in sawing. Rudolf and I cut with a big two-man saw, slicing a log in half set in a wooden trestle, against Pavel Škeřík and a local boy who were tackling another piece, but we were winning; Rudolf made up for the strength I lacked. We pushed and pulled the saw, holding the handles, back and forward, smiling at each other over the swishing noise the saw made. The sawdust fell on the ground and smelled of freshly chopped wood, similar to the tree trunks stacked in the neat piles along the forest road behind us which exposed their painful cuts and oozed honey-like resin. Rudolf's forehead glistened with perspiration, we kept shoving and tugging at the saw that joined our movements together, we had grown to be inseparable by the rhythmic roll of our arms, becoming a united living being, working as one.

I had many such visions of our togetherness despite that Rudolf seemed to have disappeared from my life – he was with me again, looked after me, talked to me, patted my hair, took me for a drive in 'Ferda', made magic tricks, played the violin. He even pulled the trigger of the blue-steel pistol again and this time got the hare! Every now and then, he was so tangible and real I could almost touch him. As soon as I could detect a whiff of pipe tobacco in the air, I recalled Rudolf beside me . . .

●

I paused at Melantrich bookshop in Na Příkopě Street to look inside and check my reflection in the shop window. My hair was swept back, the receding hairline exposing my forehead. Rimless spectacles framed my brown eyes, glinting in the bright morning

light. I checked the time on my Omega watch and walked on through the crowds, turning into a dark passageway. At the far opening of a long tunnel-like arcade, I spotted my car parked at the kerb. She was a grey Tatraplan. Slowly I walked up to her and opened the door. A leather briefcase bulging with documents and a battered violin case rested on the back seat. I sat down behind the steering wheel, felt my fountain pen in my breast pocket and checked that the holster with the small semi-automatic pistol was snuggled deep inside the storage pocket. I waited patiently.

The passenger door opened and shut with a soft clank while the car seat springs creaked.

'All right, settle down and we'll be off,' I said looking straight ahead. I switched on the car radio and we departed in the direction of Benešov road to the sound of Dvořák's *Romance*, hoping to find the plastic butterfly charm dropped in the ditch.

Však voní-li dech dívek dosud vínem
a proč by nevoněl, ta vůně neprchá,
bloudí zas chlapec v háji pohostinném,
bláznivě šeptá dívce do ucha
opilé věty a pak jeho hlava
bezmocně klesne v překvapený klín.

Je jaro, léto, podzim! Poprchává.
Pak zase jaro s prsty od květin!
Básnířka mládí! Kolik cudné něhy
zůstalo v mechu po těch kročejích.
Čas rány sešívá milosrdnými stehy
a nové smutky jdou zas po jejich.

As long as the girls' breath tastes of wine,
and why shouldn't it, this scent never disappears,
a young man ambles again under the hospitable grove of trees,
madly whispering into the girl's ears
drunken words and then his head
drops powerlessly to her surprised bosom.

It drizzles. It's the spring, summer, autumn!
Then the spring came again with fingers coloured by the blossom!
The poetry of youth! How much chaste tenderness
remained in the moss after these steps.
Time stitched together the wounds in merciful mends
and again new sadness over them extends.

Jaroslav Seifert, *B. N.*, 1949

Dedicated to Heda Margoliusová by Seifert, Prague, June 1950

Appendices

Families and Friends

Bloch family:

Vilém Bloch, 1859–1935, father of Ervín
Kateřina Blochová, 1859–1942, mother of Ervín
Ervín Bloch, 1886–1944, father of Jiří and Heda
Marta Diamantová-Blochová, 1891–1944, mother of Jiří and Heda
Jiří Bloch, 1917–1942, son of Ervín and Marta
Heda Blochová-Margoliusová-Kovályová, 1919–, daughter of Marta
    and Ervín, mother of Ivan
Berta Blochová-Robitscheková, 1883–1942, sister of Ervín
Pavla Blochová-Friedová, 1884–1942, sister of Ervín
Julie Blochová-Löwyová, 1891–1942, sister of Ervín
Anna Blochová-Welleminská, 1901–1942, sister of Ervín
Evženie Blochová-Kohnová, 1901–1944, sister of Ervín
Pavel Kohn, 1929–, son of Evženie, cousin of Heda
Paula Robitscheková-Mattes, 1916–2005, daughter of Berta
Diana Mattes-Earle, 1945–, daughter of Paula
Stella Robitscheková-Shuttleworth, 1917–2006, daughter of Berta
Michael Shuttleworth, 1944–, son of Stella

Margolius family:

Josef Margolius, 1803–?, father of Šalomoun
Rosalia Polláková-Margoliusová, mother of Šalomoun
Šalomoun Margolius, 1846–1924, father of Vítězslav
Karolina Pražáková-Margoliusová, 1849–1922, mother of Vítězslav
Alois Margolius, 1875–1935, brother of Vítězslav
Gustav Margolius, 1877–1943, brother of Vítězslav
Emil Margolius, 1881–1944, brother of Vítězslav
Rudolf Margolius, 1887–1942, brother of Vítězslav

APPENDICES

Eduard Margolius, 1889–1944, brother of Vítězslav
Vítězslav Margolius, 1879–1942, father of Rudolf
Berta Löwyová-Margoliusová, 1884–1942, mother of Rudolf
JUDr Rudolf Margolius, 1913–1952, son of Vítězslav and Berta,
    husband of Heda, father of Ivan
Ivan Margolius, 1947–, son of Rudolf and Heda
Mandy Bates, 1962–, partner of Ivan
Olga Margolius, 1947–, first wife of Ivan
Daniel Margolius, 1973–, son of Ivan and Olga
Susanna Margolius, 1982–, daughter of Ivan and Olga
Theo Margolius, 1994–, son of Ivan and Mandy
Jan Margolius, 1998–, son of Ivan and Mandy
Elli Margolius, 2006–, daughter of Ivan and Mandy
Karel Margolius, 1917–1984, cousin of Rudolf
Josef Margolius, 1914–2003, cousin of Rudolf
Otto Margolius, 1907–1957, cousin of Rudolf
Dr Pavel Kovály, 1928–, second husband of Heda

Diamant family:

Emil Diamant, 1860–1930, father of Hedvika, Marta and Karel
Emilie Kohnová-Diamantová, 1865–1921, mother of Hedvika, Marta
    and Karel
Hedvika Diamantová-Kafková, 1890–1944, sister of Marta, mother
    of Máňa and Míša
Josef Kafka, 1885–1944, husband of Hedvika
Míša (Marie) Kafková-Blassová, 1914–1944, daughter of Hedvika
    and Josef
Máňa (Marta) Kafková, 1917–1944, daughter of Hedvika and Josef
Petr Blass, 1938–1944, son of Míša and Karel Blass
Karel Diamant, 1895–1944, brother of Marta
Eva Hayman, 1924–, daughter of Karel
Vera Gissing, 1928–, daughter of Karel

Löwy and Frieser family:

Jindřich Löwy, 1855–?, father of Berta Löwyová-Margoliusová
Emilie Nalosová-Löwyová, 1860–?, mother of Berta

Vilemína Löwyová-Frieserová, 1882–1957, sister of Berta
Josef Frieser, 1871–1945, husband of Vilemína
Franta Frieser, 1914–1936, son of Vilemína and Josef Frieser, cousin of Rudolf
Micula Frieserová-Bradová, 1912–1995, daughter of Vilemína and Josef Frieser, cousin of Rudolf
Rudolf Brada, 1909–1977, husband of Micula, friend of Heda and Rudolf
Eva Bradová-Ballová, 1939–, daughter of Micula and Rudolf Brada
Monika Bradová-Pavláková, 1945–, daughter of Micula and Rudolf Brada

Friends:

František Musil, 1897–1984, friend of Ervín, Marta, Heda and Rudolf
Kristina Musilová, 1901–1992, wife of František, *bába* to Ivan
Věra Musilová, 1928–, daughter of Kristina and František
Karel Poláček, 1901–1974, friend of Heda and Rudolf
Rudolf Syrovátka, friend of Heda and Rudolf Brada
Jiří Toman, friend of Rudolf
Ivan Wiesenberger, friend of Rudolf
František Mautner (Kennedy), friend of Heda and Rudolf
Hanuš Bonn, 1913–1941, friend of Heda and Rudolf
Jan Hanuš, 1915–2004, composer, friend of Heda, Rudolf and Ivan
Anna Hanušová, wife of Jan
Dr Rudolf Štursa, friend of Heda and Rudolf
Dr Rudolf Škeřík, friend of Heda and Rudolf
Dr Pavel Škeřík, friend of Heda and Rudolf
Jindřich Waldes, 1876–1941, Ervín's employer
Pavel Tigrid, 1917–2003, friend of Heda, Rudolf and Ivan
Josef Schwartz, friend of Heda and Rudolf
Pavel Eisler, 1919–1966, friend of Heda and Rudolf
Jean Layton-Eisler, 1916–, friend of Heda and Rudolf
Johnny Eisler, 1946–, friend of Ivan
Ivan Eisler, 1948–, friend of Ivan
Jan Kaplický, 1937–, friend of Ivan

Artists and writers

Antonín Balšánek, 1865–1921, architect
Max Brod, 1884–1968, writer, friend of Ervín
Josef Čapek, 1887–1945, painter and writer
Karel Čapek, 1890–1938, writer
Franz Kafka, 1884–1924, writer, friend of Brod
František Kupka, 1871–1957, painter, friend of Waldes and Ervín
Jiří Orten, 1919–1941, poet
Jiří Voskovec, 1905–1981, actor
Jan Werich, 1905–1980, actor and writer
Jaroslav Ježek, 1906–1942, composer

Defendants and other accused

Horáková Trial, May–June 1950:

Dr Milada Horáková, 1901–1950, Member of Parliament for the Czechoslovak National Socialist Party, executed 27 June 1950
Záviš Kalandra, 1902–1950, journalist, executed 27 June 1950
Jan Buchal, 1913–1950, Staff Sergeant of State Security, executed 27 June 1950
Oldřich Pecl, 1903–1950, former mine owner, executed 27 June 1950
Jiří Hejda, 1895–1985, economist, life imprisonment

Slánský Trial, November 1952:

Rudolf Slánský, 1901–1952, General Secretary of the Communist Party of Czechoslovakia, arrested 24 November 1951, executed 3 December 1952
Karel Šváb, 1904–1952, Deputy Minister of State Security, arrested 16 February 1951, executed 3 December 1952
Bedřich Reicin, 1911–1952, Deputy Minister of National Defence, arrested 8 February 1951, executed 3 December 1952
Vladimír Clementis, 1902–1952, Minister of Foreign Affairs, arrested 28 January 1951, executed 3 December 1952

Otto Fischl, 1902–1952, Deputy Minister of Finance, arrested 30 June 1951, executed 3 December 1952

Josef Frank, 1909–1952, Deputy General Secretary of the Communist Party of Czechoslovakia, arrested 25 May 1952, executed 3 December 1952

Ludvík Frejka, 1904–1952, Chief of the Economic Committee in the Chancellery of the President, arrested 31 January 1952, executed 3 December 1952

Bedřich Geminder, 1901–1952, Chief of the International Section of the Party Secretariat, arrested 24 November 1951, executed 3 December 1952

JUDr Rudolf Margolius, 1913–1952, Deputy Minister of Foreign Trade 1949–1952, arrested 10 January 1952, executed 3 December, 1952

André Simone, 1895–1952, editor of *Rudé právo*, arrested 9 June 1952, executed 3 December 1952

Otto Šling, 1912–1952, Regional Party Secretary, arrested 6 October 1950, executed 3 December 1952

Vavro Hajdů, 1913–1977, Deputy Minister of Foreign Affairs, arrested 2 April 1951, life imprisonment

Evžen Löbl, 1907–1987, Deputy Minister of Foreign Trade, arrested 24 November 1949, life imprisonment

Artur London, 1915–1986, Deputy Minister of Foreign Affairs, arrested 28 January 1951, life imprisonment

Politicians and interrogators

Tomáš Garrick Masaryk, 1850–1937, President of the Republic 1918–35

Edvard Beneš, 1884–1948, President of the Republic 1935–38, 1945–48

Emil Hácha, 1872–1945, President of the Republic 1938–39

Jan Masaryk, 1886–1948, Foreign Minister and diplomat

Klement Gottwald, 1896–1953, Chairman of the Communist Party of Czechoslovakia, President of the Republic 1948–53

Antonín Zápotocký, 1884–1957, Deputy Chairman of the Communist Party of Czechoslovakia, President of the Republic 1953–57

Antonín Novotný, 1904–1975, First Party Secretary, President of
  the Republic 1957–68
Alexander Dubček, 1921–1992, First Party Secretary 1968–69
Ludvík Svoboda, 1895–1979, President of the Republic 1968–75
Gustav Husák, 1913–1991, President of the Republic 1975–89
Václav Havel, 1936–, President of the Republic 1990–2003
Václav Klaus, 1941–, President of the Republic 2003–
Václav Nosek, 1892–1955, Minister of the Interior 1945–53
Ladislav Kopřiva, 1897–?, Minister of State Security 1950–52
Karol Bacílek, 1896–1974, Minister of State Security 1952–53
Alexej Čepička, 1910–1990, Minister of Defence 1950–56
Václav Kopecký, 1897–1961, Minister of Information 1945–53
Viliam Široký, 1902–1971, Minister of Foreign Affairs 1950–53
Rudolf Barák, 1915–1995, Minister of the Interior 1953–61,
  imprisoned 1962–68
Josef Urválek, 1910–1979, Chief Public Prosecutor

Miloslav Kukla, 1921–?, Rudolf's interrogator
Bohuslav Doubek, 1919–1975, chief interrogator
Vladimír Kohoutek, 1912–?, interrogator
Karel Košťál, 1921–?, interrogator, Deputy Minister of the Interior
Dr Josef Sommer, 1908–1968, prison doctor

Notes

The paragraphs in italics in the text are quotations from Rudolf's letters from prison.

Quotations, excerpts and research material are published with permission where appropriate and came from the following publications (translations from Czech by the author unless stated otherwise):

Hanuš Bonn, *Dozpěv*, Academia, Prague 1995

Albert Camus, *A Happy Death*, Penguin Books, London 2002

Karel Čapek, *Letters from England*, Geoffrey Bles, London 1938

Karel Čapek, *President Masaryk Tells His Story*, George Allen & Unwin, London 1934

František Cinger, *Smějící se slzy*, Formát, Prague 2004

Hermann Field, *Trapped in the Cold War*, Stanford University Press, Stanford 1999

František Halas, *Torso naděje*, Fr. Borový, Prague 1940

Jan Hanuš, *III. Sinfonia*, text by Jaroslav Šeda, SNKLHU, Prague 1960, translated by Jean Němcová

Václav Havel, *Projevy*, Vyšehrad, Prague 1990

Jiří Hejda, *Žil jsem zbytečně*, Melantrich, Prague 1991

György Hodos, *Show Trials*, Praeger, New York 1987

Josef Hora, *Máchovské variance*, Fr. Borový, Prague 1945

Gustav Janouch, *Conversations with Kafka*, Quartet Books, London 1985

Franz Kafka, *The Complete Short Stories*, Vintage, London 1999

Franz Kafka, *The Trial*, Penguin Books, London 1953

Karel Kaplan, *Report on the Murder of the General Secretary*, I. B. Tauris, London 1990

Rosemary Kavan, *Freedom at a Price*, Verso, London 1985

Arthur Koestler, *Darkness at Noon*, Penguin Books, London 1964

Jiří Kovtun, *Tajuplná vražda – Případ Leopolda Hilsnera*, Sefer, Prague 1994

Milan Kundera, *Testaments Betrayed*, Faber & Faber, London 1995

Jo Langer, *Convictions: Memories of a Life Shared with a Good Communist*, André Deutsch, London 1979

Evžen Löbl, *Sentenced & Tried*, Elek, London 1969

Artur London, *On Trial – L'Aveau*, Macdonald, London 1970

Arnošt Lustig, *Okamžiky*, A. Šťastný, Prague 2003

Heda Margolius Kovály, *Under A Cruel Star*, Plunkett Lake Press, Cambridge 1986

N. Richard Nash, *The Young and Fair*, Dramatists Play Service, New York 1949

Vítězslav Nezval, *Město v slzách*, Odeon, Prague 1929

Vítězslav Nezval, *Pražský chodec*, Československý spisovatel, Prague 1981

Jiří Orten, *Hrob nezavřel se*, Mladá fronta, Prague 1994

Jiří Orten, *Nech slova za dveřmi*, Dokořán, Prague 2003

Ota Pavel, *Povídky ze šuplíku*, 'Běh Prahou – A Race through Prague', Slávka Kopecká, Prague 2004, translated by Paul Wilson for Cross Currents Annual 1983

Ferdinand Peroutka, *Oblak a valčík*, Academia, Prague 1995

Josef Schwarz-Červinka, *Trpělivě obnošené tělo*, Torst, Prague 2003

Jaroslav Seifert, *Město v slzách*, Odeon, Prague 1929

Jaroslav Seifert, *The Poetry of Jaroslav Seifert*, Catbird Press, North Haven 1998, translated by Ewald Osers

Josefa Slánská, *Report on My Husband*, Atheneum, New York 1969

Miriam Šlingová, *Truth Will Prevail*, Merlin Press, London 1968

Bohuslav Šnajder, *Proces proti dvanácti miliónům*, Tvorba, Prague 1990

Béla Szász, *Volunteers for the Gallows*, Chatto & Windus, London 1971

Johannes Urzidil, *Here Comes Kafka*, Wayne State University Press, Detroit 1968

Erica Wallach, *Light at Midnight*, Doubleday, New York 1967

Alex Weissberg, *Conspiracy of Silence*, Hamish Hamilton, London 1952

Jan Zábrana, *Celý život*, Torst, Prague 2001

Koni Zilliacus, *A New Birth of Freedom?*, Secker & Warburg, London 1957

The Trial of the Leadership of the Anti-State Conspiratorial Centre led by Rudolf Slánský, Ministry of Justice, Prague 1953 (transcript)

Archives of Prague Castle, Czechoslovak Communist Party and Ministry of Interior and State Security, Prague

Images:

From the author's archive, and with permission from Jan Kaplan, Karel Kaplan, USHMM courtesy of Robert Abrams, Česká tisková kancelář Praha, Jiří Jírů: images from *Praha a Pražané* by Václav Jírů, Orbis, Prague 1962.

Attempts have been made to locate the sources of all quotations and illustrations and to obtain full reproduction rights, but in the very few cases where this process has failed to find the copyright holder, our apologies are offered.

Index

INDEX